# EARTH SCIENCE
# SUCCESS
## in 20 Minutes a Day

# EARTH SCIENCE
# SUCCESS
## in 20 Minutes
## a Day

Tyler Volk

LEARNING EXPRESS®

NEW YORK

Library of Congress Cataloging-in-Publication Data:
Volk, Tyler.
  Earth science success in 20 minutes a day / Tyler Volk.
      p. cm.
    ISBN 1-57685-496-5
  1. Earth sciences—Programmed instruction. I. Title. II. Title: Earth science success in twenty minutes a day.
QE26.3.V65 2005
550—dc22                                                                2005020316


Printed in the United States of America

9 8 7 6 5 4 3 2 1

ISBN 1-57685-496-5

For information on LearningExpress, other LearningExpress products, or bulk sales, please write to us at:
  LearningExpress
  55 Broadway
  8th Floor
  New York, NY 10006

Or visit us at:
  www.learnatest.com

# About the Author ▶

**Tyler Volk** is associate professor at New York University and codirects its program in earth and environmental science. He has published extensively on various aspects of the earth as a system and has written several books, including *Gaia's Body: Toward a Physiology of Earth*.

# Contents ▶

**Introduction**                                                              ix

**Pretest**                                                                    1

**Lesson 1**     Our Cosmic Home                                               9

**Lesson 2**     Exploring the Solar System                                   17

**Lesson 3**     Climate and the Seasons                                      27

**Lesson 4**     Earth's Deep Layers                                          35

**Lesson 5**     How Continents Move                                          43

**Lesson 6**     Earthquakes, Volcanoes, and Mountains                        51

**Lesson 7**     Types of Rocks                                               59

**Lesson 8**     Dating the Earth                                             67

**Lesson 9**     What Is Air?                                                 77

**Lesson 10**    The Dynamic Atmosphere                                       85

**Lesson 11**    Water Cycles                                                 93

**Lesson 12**    Water on the Land                                           101

**Lesson 13**    What's the Ocean?                                           109

**Lesson 14**    The Dynamic Ocean                                           117

**Lesson 15**    What Is Soil?                                               125

**Lesson 16**    Ice and Snow                                                133

**Lesson 17**    The Biosphere Puts It Together                              141

**Lesson 18**    Earth Science and Evolution                                 149

**Lesson 19**    Humans as a Geological Force                                157

**Lesson 20**    Frontiers in Earth Science                                  165

**Posttest**                                                                 171

**Answer Key**                                                               179

**Appendix A**   How to Prepare for a Test                                   185

**Appendix B**   Glossary                                                    191

# Introduction ▶

If you have never taken an earth science course and now find that you need to know the basics of earth science, this is the book for you. If you have already taken an earth science course, but feel like you never understood what the teacher was trying to tell you, this book can teach you what you need to know. If it has been a while since you have taken an earth science course, and you need to refresh your skills, this book will review the basics and reteach you the skills you may have forgotten. Whatever your reason for needing to know earth science, *Earth Science Success in 20 Minutes a Day* will teach you what you need to know. It gives you the earth science basics in clear and straightforward lessons that you can study at your own pace.

## ▶ How to Use This Book

*Earth Science Success* teaches basic concepts in 20 self-paced lessons. The book includes a pretest, a posttest, tips on how to prepare for a standardized test, and a glossary. Before you begin Lesson 1, take the pretest. The pretest will assess your current earth science knowledge. Each answer of the pretest and posttest includes the lesson number that the problem is testing. This will be helpful in determining your strengths and weaknesses. After taking the pretest, move on to Lesson 1.

Each lesson offers detailed explanations of a new concept. Numerous examples are given, each with step-by-step solutions. As you proceed through a lesson, you will find tips and shortcuts that will help you learn a concept. Each new concept is followed by a practice set of problems. The answers to the practice problems are found at the end of the book.

When you have completed all 20 lessons, take the posttest. It has the same format as the pretest, but the questions are different. Compare the results of the posttest with the results of the pretest you took before you began Lesson 1. What are your strengths? Do you have weak areas? Do you need to spend more time on some concepts, or are you ready to go to the next level?

## ► Make a Commitment

Success does not come without effort. If you truly want to be successful, make a commitment to spend the time you need to improve your skills. When you achieve earth science success, you have laid the foundation for future challenges and opportunities.

So sharpen your pencil and get ready to begin the pretest!

# EARTH SCIENCE
## SUCCESS
### in 20 Minutes a Day

# Pretest

Before you begin Lesson 1, you may want to get an idea of what you know and what you need to learn. The pretest will answer some of these questions for you. The pretest is 40 multiple-choice questions covering the topics in this book. While 40 questions can't cover every concept, skill, or shortcut taught in this book, your performance on the pretest will give you a good indication of your strengths and weaknesses. Keep in mind the pretest does not test all the skills taught in this book.

If you score high on the pretest, you have a good foundation and should be able to work your way through the book quickly. If you score low on the pretest, don't despair. This book will take you through the earth science concepts, step by step. If you get a low score, you may need to take more than 20 minutes a day to work through a lesson. However, this is a self-paced program, so you can spend as much time on a lesson as you need. You decide when you fully comprehend the lesson and are ready to go on to the next one.

Take as much time as you need to do the pretest. When you are finished, check your answers with the answer key at the end of this section. Along with each answer is a number that tells you which lesson of this book teaches you about the earth science skills needed for that question. You will find the level of difficulty increases as you work your way through the pretest.

## ANSWER SHEET

| | | | |
|---|---|---|---|
| 1. | ⓐ | ⓑ | ⓒ | ⓓ |
| 2. | ⓐ | ⓑ | ⓒ | ⓓ |
| 3. | ⓐ | ⓑ | ⓒ | ⓓ |
| 4. | ⓐ | ⓑ | ⓒ | ⓓ |
| 5. | ⓐ | ⓑ | ⓒ | ⓓ |
| 6. | ⓐ | ⓑ | ⓒ | ⓓ |
| 7. | ⓐ | ⓑ | ⓒ | ⓓ |
| 8. | ⓐ | ⓑ | ⓒ | ⓓ |
| 9. | ⓐ | ⓑ | ⓒ | ⓓ |
| 10. | ⓐ | ⓑ | ⓒ | ⓓ |
| 11. | ⓐ | ⓑ | ⓒ | ⓓ |
| 12. | ⓐ | ⓑ | ⓒ | ⓓ |
| 13. | ⓐ | ⓑ | ⓒ | ⓓ |
| 14. | ⓐ | ⓑ | ⓒ | ⓓ |
| 15. | ⓐ | ⓑ | ⓒ | ⓓ |

| | | | |
|---|---|---|---|
| 16. | ⓐ | ⓑ | ⓒ | ⓓ |
| 17. | ⓐ | ⓑ | ⓒ | ⓓ |
| 18. | ⓐ | ⓑ | ⓒ | ⓓ |
| 19. | ⓐ | ⓑ | ⓒ | ⓓ |
| 20. | ⓐ | ⓑ | ⓒ | ⓓ |
| 21. | ⓐ | ⓑ | ⓒ | ⓓ |
| 22. | ⓐ | ⓑ | ⓒ | ⓓ |
| 23. | ⓐ | ⓑ | ⓒ | ⓓ |
| 24. | ⓐ | ⓑ | ⓒ | ⓓ |
| 25. | ⓐ | ⓑ | ⓒ | ⓓ |
| 26. | ⓐ | ⓑ | ⓒ | ⓓ |
| 27. | ⓐ | ⓑ | ⓒ | ⓓ |
| 28. | ⓐ | ⓑ | ⓒ | ⓓ |
| 29. | ⓐ | ⓑ | ⓒ | ⓓ |
| 30. | ⓐ | ⓑ | ⓒ | ⓓ |

| | | | |
|---|---|---|---|
| 31. | ⓐ | ⓑ | ⓒ | ⓓ |
| 32. | ⓐ | ⓑ | ⓒ | ⓓ |
| 33. | ⓐ | ⓑ | ⓒ | ⓓ |
| 34. | ⓐ | ⓑ | ⓒ | ⓓ |
| 35. | ⓐ | ⓑ | ⓒ | ⓓ |
| 36. | ⓐ | ⓑ | ⓒ | ⓓ |
| 37. | ⓐ | ⓑ | ⓒ | ⓓ |
| 38. | ⓐ | ⓑ | ⓒ | ⓓ |
| 39. | ⓐ | ⓑ | ⓒ | ⓓ |
| 40. | ⓐ | ⓑ | ⓒ | ⓓ |

1. Which event occurred 300,000 years after our universe began in the Big Bang?
   a. First protons and neutrons formed.
   b. First atoms formed.
   c. First stars formed.
   d. First electrons formed.

2. What does the term *red shift* refer to?
   a. Light from close galaxies is shifted to brighter wavelengths.
   b. Light from nearby galaxies is shifted to dimmer wavelengths.
   c. Light from distant galaxies is shifted to longer wavelengths.
   d. Light from distant galaxies is shifted to shorter wavelengths.

3. Compared to the age of the earth, the age of the sun is about
   a. a billion years older.
   b. ten billion years older.
   c. the same.
   d. a billion years younger.

4. Consider the force of gravity between two masses. If the distance between them is halved, the force of gravity between them is now
   a. $\frac{1}{4}$.
   b. $\frac{1}{2}$.
   c. 2 times.
   d. 4 times.

5. The distance from the center of the earth to the equator is about 4,000 miles. What is the distance from the center of the earth to the South Pole?
   a. 2,000 miles
   b. 8,000 miles
   c. 12,000 miles
   d. 4,000 miles

6. You are floating above the equator with your head facing the direction in which the sun will rise at dawn. Your arms are stretched out to your right and left, perpendicular to the line of your body, as if you are flying like an airplane. Your left arm is facing which direction?
   a. north
   b. south
   c. east
   d. west

7. The earth's north magnetic pole is located closest to
   a. 0° north latitude.
   b. 90° north latitude.
   c. 90° south latitude.
   d. 0° south latitude.

8. Compressing a liquid causes it to become solid even if the temperature is kept the same. This fact is relevant to which fact about the earth's inner and outer portions of the core?
   a. The inner core is liquid even though it's at a higher temperature.
   b. The inner core is liquid even though it's at a lower temperature.
   c. The inner core is solid even though it's at a higher temperature.
   d. The outer core is solid even though it's at a lower temperature.

**9.** A key piece of evidence in the modern theory of how continents move came from
   **a.** Earth's magnetic field recorded in continental rocks.
   **b.** Earth's magnetic field recorded in oceanic rocks.
   **c.** Earth's seismic field recorded in continental rocks.
   **d.** Earth's seismic field recorded in oceanic rocks.

**10.** Which is true?
   **a.** The lithosphere gets thicker as it moves away from a mid-ocean ridge.
   **b.** The mantle gets thinner as it is subducted beneath a plate.
   **c.** The mid-ocean ridge is a collision boundary between two plates.
   **d.** The oceanic crust is thicker than the continental crust.

**11.** Compared to magma, lava is
   **a.** deeper and cooler.
   **b.** shallower and cooler.
   **c.** deeper and hotter.
   **d.** shallower and hotter.

**12.** A pyroclastic flow can come from
   **a.** an explosive hot spot.
   **b.** an explosive volcano.
   **c.** a mid-ocean ridge eruption.
   **d.** a subduction eruption.

**13.** The most abundant element in Earth's crust is
   **a.** oxygen.
   **b.** calcium.
   **c.** iron.
   **d.** silicon.

**14.** The two kinds of rock that will be least likely to have fossil evidence of the earliest life on Earth are
   **a.** igneous and sedimentary.
   **b.** igneous and metamorphic.
   **c.** sedimentary and metamorphic.
   **d.** shale and igneous.

**15.** Stratigraphers study
   **a.** the upper layer of the atmosphere.
   **b.** ocean density layers.
   **c.** geological layers.
   **d.** soil layers.

**16.** A nonconformity is the zone between
   **a.** an igneous layer below and a sedimentary layer above.
   **b.** one igneous layer below and a different igneous layer above.
   **c.** a sedimentary layer below and a metamorphic layer above.
   **d.** two sedimentary layers that were separated by an interval of time.

**17.** Compare the (1) absolute change in air pressure from sea level to 10 kilometers in altitude with the (2) absolute change in air pressure from 5 kilometers in altitude to 15 kilometers. Which is the larger change?
   **a.** 1
   **b.** 2
   **c.** They are the same.
   **d.** It depends on latitude.

**18.** What does the moist adiabatic lapse rate describe?
  **a.** the change in temperature with altitude as water evaporates
  **b.** the change in pressure with altitude as water evaporates
  **c.** the change in temperature with altitude as water condenses
  **d.** the change in pressure with altitude as water condenses

**19.** The Hadley cell circulates approximately between
  **a.** 30° N and 60° N.
  **b.** 90° N and 60° N.
  **c.** 30° S and 30° N.
  **d.** 0° and 30° N.

**20.** Compared to a planet with a stagnant atmosphere, the earth's atmospheric circulation causes
  **a.** the poles to be cooler and the topics warmer.
  **b.** the poles to be warmer and the tropics cooler.
  **c.** the poles to be cooler and the tropics cooler.
  **d.** the poles to be warmer and the tropics warmer.

**21.** The third largest reservoir of water on Earth is
  **a.** the ocean.
  **b.** glaciers and ice caps.
  **c.** groundwater.
  **d.** lakes.

**22.** Which of the following is NOT true for water?
  **a.** The latent heat of melting is less than the latent heat of vaporization.
  **b.** The latent heat of vaporization is less than the latent heat of freezing.
  **c.** The latent heat of melting is less than the latent heat of freezing.
  **d.** The latent heat of condensation is less than the latent heat of vaporization.

**23.** Deserts are usually defined by the criterion that the rainfall is less than
  **a.** 2 inches per year.
  **b.** 5 inches per year.
  **c.** 10 inches per year.
  **d.** 20 inches per year.

**24.** The Mississippi River, in terms of discharge, carries 350 million metric tons of sediment per year. How many kilograms per person living in the United States is that per year? Assume that the U.S. population is 280 million people. Also, assume 1,000 kilograms per metric ton.
  **a.** 1,250
  **b.** 800
  **c.** 0.8
  **d.** 1.25

**25.** The geographical region of the ocean that meets the deep ocean floor is the
  **a.** continental alluvium.
  **b.** continental abyss.
  **c.** continental shelf.
  **d.** continental slope.

**26.** The three most abundant ions in seawater are
  **a.** sodium, chloride, sulfate.
  **b.** sulfate, magnesium, calcium.
  **c.** chloride, magnesium, calcium.
  **d.** chloride, calcium, sodium.

**27.** The thermohaline circulation of the ocean is driven by
  **a.** winds and temperature.
  **b.** salinity and pressure.
  **c.** pressure and temperature.
  **d.** salinity and temperature.

**28.** The two places on Earth where the densest surface seawater is formed are
  **a.** Antarctica and Greenland.
  **b.** the North Pacific and Antarctica.
  **c.** Greenland and the Mediterranean.
  **d.** the Mediterranean and Antarctica.

**29.** The organic content of tropical soil is
  **a.** low because the large amount of rain washes the material downward.
  **b.** high because of the large amount of plant debris.
  **c.** high because the sun stimulates photosynthesis.
  **d.** low because the hot climate stimulates bacteria activity.

**30.** *"No-till"* refers to
  **a.** the natural soil without human activity.
  **b.** an advance in agriculture that directly minimizes erosion.
  **c.** growing crops directly in water-nutrient solutions.
  **d.** applying seeds broadly over the fields.

**31.** Ice floats because of the unusual behavior of the
  **a.** oxygen-hydrogen bond.
  **b.** hydrogen bond.
  **c.** oxygen bond.
  **d.** ice-water bond.

**32.** Ice sheets today exist in
  **a.** Greenland and Antarctica.
  **b.** Antarctica and Alaska.
  **c.** Canada and New Zealand.
  **d.** Russia and Canada.

**33.** Compared to the carbon in the form of carbon dioxide in the atmosphere, the amount of carbon in the form of organic carbon in Earth's soils is about
  **a.** 3 times.
  **b.** 5 times.
  **c.** 7 times.
  **d.** 9 times.

**34.** A flux of about 60 billion tons of carbon per year takes place
  **a.** between ocean and atmosphere.
  **b.** in marine photosynthesis.
  **c.** in terrestrial photosynthesis.
  **d.** marine respiration.

**35.** The first great rise in atmospheric oxygen in Earth's atmosphere occurred
  **a.** 1 billion years ago.
  **b.** 2 billion years ago.
  **c.** 3 billion years ago.
  **d.** 4 billion years ago.

**36.** Because the sun was about 30% weaker in its energy output 4 billion years ago and would have frozen an Earth with today's atmosphere, we surmise the greenhouse gases in Earth's early atmosphere must have been stronger than they are today, because
   **a.** a weaker sun creates more volcanic release of greenhouse gases.
   **b.** continents were smaller.
   **c.** low oxygen levels led to more greenhouse effect.
   **d.** sedimentary rocks show liquid water was on the planet.

**37.** The chemical that endangers the protective ozone shield is
   **a.** $HNO_3$.
   **b.** $CO_2$.
   **c.** CFCs.
   **d.** $H_2SO_4$.

**38.** How many square meters are in one hectare?
   **a.** 100 meters
   **b.** 1,000 meters
   **c.** 10,000 meters
   **d.** 100,000 meters

**39.** A new science that can help us figure out how to live in balance with nature is called
   **a.** bioastronomy.
   **b.** sustainability.
   **c.** econology.
   **d.** genetics.

**40.** Planets around stars other than our sun have been found by
   **a.** observing wobbles in those stars.
   **b.** measuring the gravity of the planets upon space telescopes.
   **c.** weighing the absorption of light by gas clouds around those stars.
   **d.** calculating the probabilities of planet formation from theory.

▶ **Answers**

**1.** b. Lesson 1
**2.** c. Lesson 1
**3.** c. Lesson 2
**4.** d. Lesson 2
**5.** d. Lesson 3
**6.** a. Lesson 3
**7.** b. Lesson 4
**8.** c. Lesson 4
**9.** b. Lesson 5
**10.** a. Lesson 5
**11.** b. Lesson 6
**12.** b. Lesson 6
**13.** a. Lesson 7
**14.** b. Lesson 7
**15.** c. Lesson 8
**16.** a. Lesson 8
**17.** a. Lesson 9
**18.** c. Lesson 9
**19.** d. Lesson 10
**20.** b. Lesson 10

**21.** c. Lesson 11
**22.** b. Lesson 11
**23.** c. Lesson 12
**24.** a. Lesson 12
**25.** d. Lesson 13
**26.** a. Lesson 13
**27.** d. Lesson 14
**28.** a. Lesson 14
**29.** d. Lesson 15
**30.** b. Lesson 15
**31.** b. Lesson 16
**32.** a. Lesson 16
**33.** a. Lesson 17
**34.** c. Lesson 17
**35.** b. Lesson 18
**36.** d. Lesson 18
**37.** c. Lesson 19
**38.** c. Lesson 19
**39.** b. Lesson 19
**40.** a. Lesson 20

# Our Cosmic Home

## LESSON SUMMARY

Look out into the sky at night. That's right—look out, not just up. Because when you look at the sparkling stars, you are gazing out across vast distances of space and time. You see light from stars that has taken tens, hundreds, even tens of thousands of years to reach your eyes. That's how vast space is. And one of the major, remarkable findings of astronomy is that the universe is expanding and has been expanding ever since it began with what is called the *Big Bang*.

## ▶ Expanding Universe

Here is the outline of the events that occurred in the birth of our universe (see Figure 1.1). (We will review the main piece of evidence—the red shift—in more detail in the next section.)

- The Big Bang occurred about 13.7 billion years ago (with an uncertainty of a few hundred million years).
- **Time:** Between the Big Bang and the one second mark. **Temperature:** Many billions of degrees above absolute zero. **Event:** Matter and antimatter nearly annihilated each other, leaving a small amount of residual matter.

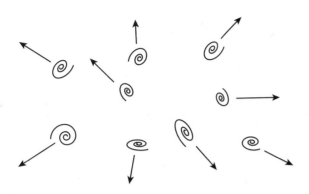

Figure 1.1 The expanding universe

- **Time:** One second after the Big Bang. **Temperature:** About 1 billion degrees above absolute zero. **Event:** Protons, neutrons, and electrons exist as *stable particles*, or what physicists call *subatomic* particles, because they are basic constituents of atoms.
- **Time:** 300,000 years after the Big Bang. **Temperature:** 3,000° above absolute zero (close to the surface temperature of our sun). **Event:** Atoms are born. This happened because the universe cooled enough for electrons to remain bound to nuclei of protons and neutrons. At this point, matter consisted of 76% hydrogen and 24% helium (with a trace of lithium). No other elements existed.
- **Time:** Millions of years to a billion years after the Big Bang. **Temperature:** Much cooler. **Event:** First stars and galaxies are born. Other elements are created in the nuclear furnaces of stars.
- **Time:** Today. **Temperature:** About 3 degrees above *absolute zero* (2.7 *degrees Kelvin*, in which a unit of temperature on the Kelvin scale is the same as a °C, a degree Centigrade or Celsius, except rather than the zero point references to the freezing temperature of water, zero Kelvin is absolute zero, about −476 degrees Fahrenheit).

Note this is only the average temperature. **Event:** We are here to discover this story.

## ▶ Practice

1. How many years ago was the Big Bang?
   a. 13.7 trillion years ago
   b. 13.7 quadrillion years ago
   c. 13.7 million years ago
   d. 13.7 billion years ago

2. Put in order the following events, from the earliest (closest in time of the Big Bang) to the latest (closest in time today): Electrons become stable around atomic nuclei (E); stable combinations of protons and neutrons (S); near annihilation of matter and antimatter (N); protogalaxies start to form (P).
   a. N, S, E, P
   b. E, S, N, P
   c. P, E, S, N
   d. S, E, P, N

3. What of the following did not occur at about 300,000 years after the Big Bang?
   a. Matter was left over from matter–antimatter annihilation.
   b. The universe became transparent.
   c. The first atoms formed.
   d. Electrons started orbits around atomic nuclei.

4. What is the current temperature of the universe?
   a. 2.7° C
   b. −2.7 K
   c. −2.7° C
   d. 2.7 K

**5.** When atoms first formed, the matter in the universe consisted almost entirely of which two elements?

    **a.** helium and carbon

    **b.** oxygen and carbon

    **c.** hydrogen and oxygen

    **d.** hydrogen and helium

## ▶ Red Shifts

*Visible light* consists of a mix of *wavelengths*. Wavelength determines the color of light. Red light has longer wavelengths than green light has, for example. Green light has longer wavelengths than blue light. Study the diagram in Figure 1.2, which shows the spectrum of different wavelengths.

What we call visible light is only a small part of the *electromagnetic spectrum*, which consists of all waves that are both electric and magnetic. Note the relative sizes of the wavelengths and the fact that some wavelengths are too long for our eyes to see (*infrared*), whereas other wavelengths are too short (*ultraviolet*).

All elements glow at particular wavelengths. Light that we normally see is a mixture of thousands and thousands of specific wavelengths. Scientists can examine light in great detail and see specific patterns of wavelengths, revealing specific elements that emitted the wavelengths. Thus, elements in space can be measured by the wavelengths that they emit. Furthermore, as light passes through gases that contain particular

elements, the elements in the gases also absorb wavelengths in specific patterns. Thus, patterns of both emissions and absorptions can provide astronomers with information about the elements in outer space. When light from galaxies is examined, an interesting pattern is discovered. Study the diagrams in Figure 1.3.

The top figure shows some of the locations of wavelengths of light given off by calcium on Earth. Note that they occur in a particular location and pattern on the spectrum. The bottom figure shows that in light from a distant galaxy, the characteristic pattern of calcium occurs at longer wavelengths. The calcium pattern has been shifted toward the red. This is the famous *red shift*.

The shift toward the red in the patterns of wavelengths that are characteristic of specific elements could occur only if the galaxies are moving away from the earth. As the galaxies move away, the light from them is stretched by the motion. (If the galaxies were moving toward us, the shift in the wavelengths of the patterns would have been toward the blue, which is not observed.)

The red shift is the primary evidence for the expanding universe. By extrapolating the expansion back in time, astronomers have concluded that the expansion started with all matter concentrated in a very small point and a single explosive event known as the Big Bang. Many other kinds of evidence have confirmed this theory.

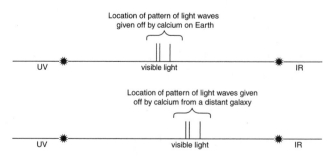

Figure 1.3 The red shift

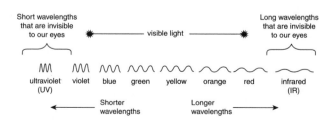

Figure 1.2 The electromagnetic spectrum

**Question:** If all galaxies are moving away from us, does that imply that we are at the center?

**Answer:** No, because inhabitants of any galaxy would also observe that they appear to be at the center. It's like raisins in an expanding raisin cake. To each raisin, all the others are moving away.

## ▶ Practice

**6.** Which of the following is not true?
  **a.** Blue light has a shorter wavelength than red light has.
  **b.** Red light has a shorter wavelength than ultraviolet light has.
  **c.** Ultraviolet has a shorter wavelength than infrared light has.
  **d.** Green has a shorter wavelength than blue light has.

**7.** Consider a pattern of wavelengths of light from a calcium atom here on Earth. Assume that these wavelengths are in the green portion of the spectrum light that we can see. Looking at the same pattern of calcium in the spectrum from a distant galaxy, you will find that the pattern is shifted toward which set of wavelengths?
  **a.** It shifted to ultraviolet.
  **b.** It shifted to blue.
  **c.** It shifted to red.
  **d.** It isn't shifted.

**8.** What feature of our universe is demonstrated by the *red shift*?
  **a.** an increase in supernovas
  **b.** the contraction of black holes
  **c.** the expansion of the universe
  **d.** the decrease in gravity

**9.** The best evidence that the universe began with a Big Bang is which one of the following?
  **a.** the formation of stars
  **b.** the expanding universe
  **c.** the existence of black holes
  **d.** red light

**10.** The raisins in a loaf of raisin bread, which is rising in the oven, are like what in comparison to the universe?
  **a.** galaxies
  **b.** planets
  **c.** Big Bangs
  **d.** people

## ▶ Galaxies and Stars

It is important to know that as we look out in space, we look back in time. That's because the speed of light, though fast, is finite. Light travels at 186 thousand miles per second (300,000 kilometers per second). The light from stars in our own galaxy, generated hundred of thousands of years ago, or from stars in other galaxies, generated billions of years ago, is just now reaching us. Study the diagrams in Figure 1.4 and see how the term *light-year* is an astronomical unit of distance.

The figure shows that light from the sun needs to travel 93 million miles to reach Earth, and this takes the light 8.3 minutes. Thus, we see the sun as it was 8.3 minutes ago. We simply cannot see the sun as it is right

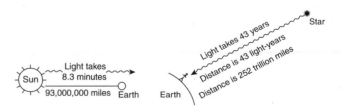

Figure 1.4 The light-year

now, because it takes time for the light to travel. This has important implications when we look at stars and galaxies. The other portion of the figure shows light reaching the eye of an observer from a star that is 252 trillion miles away. (Many stars that you see are this far, and many are much farther.) Light take 43 years to make the journey from star to eye. Thus, the star is 43 light-years away. If the star were to explode today, we would not know it for 43 years!

A light-year is nearly 6 trillion miles of distance (5.86 trillion miles, which is 9.4 trillion kilometers). When we start to look at galaxies, this "looking back in time" gets really serious. For example, the nearest large galaxy that is similar to our own *Milky Way* galaxy is *Andromeda*, and it is 2 million light-years away. Today, we see the light that it emitted 2 million years ago, during a time when the ancestors of humans were just making the first crude stone tools in Africa.

Many galaxies were formed in the first billion years or so after the Big Bang, as clumps of matter floating in space condensed under the attractive power of gravity. *Galaxies* are cities of stars. Just as gravity made the galaxies, gravity also made the stars within the galaxies. *Stars* are created when gas clouds in space condense, pulled together by gravity. During the condensation, the gas becomes hotter and hotter. If the density and temperature are high enough, the *protostar* ignites and is sustained as a glowing star by nuclear fusion. New stars are being formed all the time. Astronomers today have found regions of star births. Stars also die (see the next section). Our own galaxy is called the *Milky Way* (see Figure 1.5).

Our Milky Way galaxy contains about 400 billion stars, an incredible number. It is shaped somewhat like two dinner plates put together face to face, with a bulge in the middle, and within the bulge, a zone exists that is extremely rich with stars. From above, these appear as giant spiral arms. Astronomers have also found evidence for a massive black hole in the center. *Black holes*

occur when matter has contracted to such a high density that even light cannot escape. We know black holes by certain effects they have on radiation in the space around them. Note that our sun is located about three-fifths away from the center of the galaxy.

## ▶ Practice

11. A supernova (an exploding star) is observed to occur at a distance of 500 light-years from Earth. That means we now see the supernova as which of the following?
    a. as it was 500 years in the past
    b. as it was 500 years after the Big Bang
    c. as it will be 500 years in the future
    d. as it is, basically, today

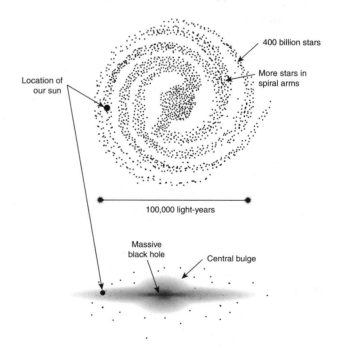

Figure 1.5 The Milky Way galaxy

**12.** Assume that you are far out in space, looking at the Milky Way galaxy as a circular disk. Pretend this disk is a dart board, with an inner circle of 100 points, the next ring of 50 points, the next ring of 20 points, and the outermost ring of 10 points. The widths of the center circle and the rings are about the same. In which ring would you see our sun?

    **a.** ring 100

    **b.** ring 50

    **c.** ring 20

    **d.** ring 10

**13.** San Francisco, California, and Detroit, Michigan, are about 2,000 miles apart. Consider a beam of light traveling that distance. In one second, how many times could the beam of light go back and forth, making a round trip betgeen Detroit and San Francisco?

    **a.** 2,300 times

    **b.** 23,000 times

    **c.** 4,600 times

    **d.** 46,000 times

**14.** Stars form when which of the following happen?

    **a.** galaxies contract them

    **b.** gravity contracts gas clouds

    **c.** black holes ignite them

    **d.** Big Bangs release them

**15.** Which of the following is not true?

    **a.** Galaxies can hold hundreds of billions of stars.

    **b.** The speed of light is infinite.

    **c.** Our galaxy has a central, massive black hole.

    **d.** Light is an electromagnetic wave.

## ▶ How Elements Are Born

You, me, the other animals, all the trees, even the atmosphere and rocky Earth itself are made of chemical elements that were born (manufactured) in the nuclear furnaces of stars. Elements can be characterized by their atomic numbers, which is the number of protons in their nuclei. As we have seen, the elements that existed at 300,000 years after the Big Bang were only the ones with the lowest atomic numbers, the light elements of hydrogen, helium, and a trace of lithium. The key concept to the formation of all other elements is nuclear fusion.

Figure 1.6 shows a general diagram for how *nuclear fusion* works. Atomic nuclei from two or more elements are squeezed by hot temperatures and pressures in the center of a star to create a new *fused nucleus*. For atoms from hydrogen up to the atomic number of iron, energy is released when atoms are fused to make larger atoms. This is because the protons and neutrons inside the nuclei of the larger atoms (again, up to iron) contain less mass per subatomic particle and therefore less energy according to *Einstein's equation* $E = Mc^2$ (where $E$ is energy, $M$ is mass, and $c$ is the speed of light). The excess energy of fusion is released as heat and radiation. To us, this released energy is the warm sunlight we feel and all the light we see from stars.

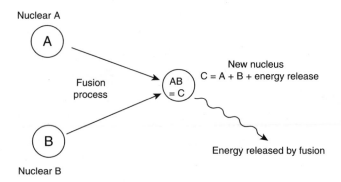

Figure 1.6 Nuclear fusion

Stars are hot and are able to emit vast quantities of radiation into space because of fusion reactions deep within their cores. Inside stars, the first element to be fused is hydrogen, the most abundant primordial element. Under intense temperature and pressure, two hydrogen atoms are fused into one atom of helium, releasing energy and making stars hot, thus sustaining further fusion reactions. When the hydrogen is used up, helium is fused into carbon, and then the carbon and some helium are fused into oxygen. All the elements up to iron can be made in this way. Note the sequence of how elements are made: Hydrogen (H) → Helium (He) → Carbon (C) → Oxygen (O). All these fusion reactions release energy.

Stars can run out of matter to fuel fusion, they can "die." Some stars die by throwing off gases then withering into small, smoldering white dwarfs. Don't worry; we still have billions of years to go before that!

Very massive stars, on the order of ten times the mass of our sun, can create *supernova* explosions at their deaths. One supernova, for example, occurred in our galaxy in A.D. 1066, which is now the *Crab Nebula*. Ancient people then observed this bright new star in the sky before it faded.

Supernovas are important parts of how our universe works. They do two special things. First, all elements heavier than iron (such as gold and uranium) are made in the intense heat and pressure of the supernova. Second, the supernovas disperse all the elements inside the former star out into space. We can see these elements in the emission and absorption spectra in the regions surrounding former sites of supernovas. Note that in the dispersal of elements by supernovas, two categories of elements can be found: those that were made earlier in fusion reactions during the long, ordinary lifetime of the star, as well as those that are new (that is made only in the supernova itself).

The elements dispersed into space can eventually gather into gas clouds and possibly contract, after mixing with remnants of other supernovas, into totally new stars and their planets. We are, literally, stardust!

## ▶ Practice

16. In the stages of nuclear fusion inside stars, which element in the list, compared to the others, is formed last?
    a. hydrogen
    b. helium
    c. carbon
    d. oxygen

17. Which is the correct name for the events or processes that disperse elements born in the internal nuclear fires of stars, making those elements available for subsequent formations of new stars and planets?
    a. supernovas
    b. expanding universe
    c. fusion reactions
    d. red shift

18. Which element is not made in stars?
    a. aluminum
    b. boron
    c. carbon
    d. hydrogen

19. Which element out there in various places in the universe (including inside our sun) is both primordial (meaning some of it was made shortly after the Big Bang, before any stars formed) and made inside stars during fusion reactions?
    a. carbon
    b. hydrogen
    c. helium
    d. iron

**20.** In the stages of nuclear fusion inside stars, which
element in the list, compared to the others, is the
ultimate building block for all the others?
  **a.** hydrogen
  **b.** helium
  **c.** carbon
  **d.** oxygen

LESSON

# 2 ▶ Exploring the Solar System

## LESSON SUMMARY

From the dawn of time, humans have looked up at the stars. Planets were once thought to be stars, but planets were special because they wandered across the sky, against the other fixed stars. The word *planet,* in fact, comes from the ancient Greek for *wanderer.* We now know that planets look like stars because they reflect light from the sun, and that they and the earth orbit around the sun in a *solar system.* How do the planets stay in orbit? How does the solar system work? What makes our moon, the subject of so much poetry and romance, wax and wane in the sky?

## ▶ Our Sun

About 5 billion years ago, a cosmic gas cloud began to condense into the star that is now our sun, which has been burning since that birth. Around the sun, the cosmic gas cloud also condensed into smaller bodies (picture small whirlpools of contraction around a large central one). What started as dust grains coalesced into rocks, then boulders, then objects the size of mountains. By collisions and gravitational attraction, which held the bodies together, the objects grew. Sometimes, the collisions created smaller bodies but, on the whole, growth in size ruled. The sun, the earth, and all the other planets and their moons were formed by about 4.5 billion years ago.

The sun is a star, just like the others we see as points of light in the night sky. Because it's so relatively close to Earth, the sun looms large. In fact, the nearest other star is about 250,000 times farther away than our sun. Wow!

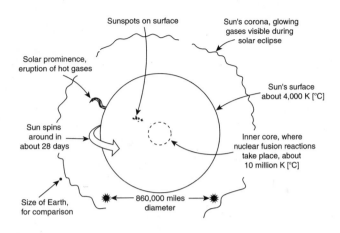

**Figure 2.1 The sun**

Figure 2.1 shows the sun, its size, surface temperature, inner core, sunspots, prominences, and the outer corona. The earth is shown to the same scale of size, but not distance! To draw it to scale, the correct location of the earth's orbit would be about 110 times the diameter of the sun. See if you can figure out where the Earth (to the scale as the sun in the figure) would go in the room where you are reading this book.

The sun is 860,000 miles in diameter (1.4 million kilometers). Because the earth is a little less than 8,000 miles in diameter, that means that the sun's diameter is more than 100 times that of Earth's. In volume, more than one million Earths could fit inside the sun.

The secret of the sun is its very hot inner core of 10 million degrees Kelvin (essentially the same as °C for temperatures this high). In the core, nuclear fusion reactions take place. Hydrogen is fused into helium, with the release of energy. We care a lot about this release of energy, for without this energy, life as we know it would not and could not exist. Not only would the earth be cold, near absolute zero, but photosynthesis by plants and algae, which requires sunlight, would be nonexistent, meaning no food for animals such as people.

The sun's surface that we see (but don't look directly at it!) is about 4,000 degrees Kelvin (7,000° F,

or about 4,000° C). But the sun extends even farther out as a *corona* of glowing gases visible only during a solar eclipse (discussed later in this lesson). Note that the sun spins on its axis, like the earth does, taking about a month to turn. We can see the turning by observing *sunspots*, which are dark regions of storms on the sun's surface. Sunspots are darker because they are a bit cooler, but still extremely hot. The number of sunspots rises and falls in a cycle that is approximately 11 Earth years in length, as do the number of *solar storms*, seen in the previous figure as a prominence erupting from the surface.

## ▶ Practice

**1.** The sun spins around on its own axis once in approximately the length of time that we call
   **a.** a day.
   **b.** a week.
   **c.** a month.
   **d.** a year.

**2.** If the diameter of a clay model Earth were about the same diameter as a U.S. quarter (about an inch), how big would the diameter of a model sun have to be to maintain the same scale?
   **a.** 10 inches
   **b.** 8 feet
   **c.** 80 feet
   **d.** $\frac{1}{15}$ of a mile

**3.** How old is the sun?
   **a.** 450 million years
   **b.** 4.5 billion years
   **c.** 1,400 million years
   **d.** 14 billion years

**4.** Which of the following is true?

    **a.** The sun's core, which is where nuclear fusion reactions take place, is hotter than its surface.

    **b.** The sun's surface, which is where nuclear fusion reactions take place, is cooler than its core.

    **c.** The sun's core, which is where nuclear fission reactions take place, is hotter than its surface.

    **d.** The sun's surface, which is where nuclear fission reactions take place, is cooler than its core.

**5.** Which of the following pairs both occur as storm events on the sun's surface?

    **a.** coronas and prominences

    **b.** sunspots and glowing gases

    **c.** prominences and glowing gases

    **d.** sunspots and prominences

## ▶ Gravity and Orbits

*Gravity* is the physical force that makes the objects of the universe. Gravity unites the stars, gas clouds, and other forms of matter into galaxies. Gravity condenses gas clouds into stars and planets.

In the late 1600s, Englishman Isaac Newton defined the *law of gravity*, or *Newton's law*, which he used to mathematically describe both the orbit of the moon and the fall of an apple to Earth. Newton's law was modified by *Einstein's theory of relativity*, but these modifications come into play in scales of space-time and levels of detail that need not concern us here. Here we look at our own solar system.

Newton described the force of gravity in one of the most important equations ever written in the history of physics. If *F* is the force of gravity, *G* is a constant needed to equalize the units of the equation, $M_1$

is the mass of one object, $M_2$ is the mass of a second object, and *D* is the distance between the objects, then:

$$F = \frac{G \times M_1 \times M_2}{D^2}$$

It is crucial that you understand the general meaning of this equation. The force of gravity between two objects is proportional to the mass of each of them (because the two masses are multiplied in the equation). So if either $M_1$ or $M_2$ doubles, then the force of gravity doubles. What happens to the force of gravity if both $M_1$ and $M_2$ double (see the practice questions)? Which object in the solar system contributes most to the force of gravity in all the other objects in the solar system?

The answer is the sun, because it has the biggest mass. Note also that the force of gravity gets weaker as the square of distance between two masses increases (because distance is in the denominator of the right-hand side of the equation). This is the famous *inverse square* aspect of the Law of Gravity. In other words, if the distance between two objects is increased by a factor of 3, the force of gravity decreases to $\frac{1}{9}$ (compute: $\frac{1^2}{3}$ ) of its original value.

Newton was able to use the law of gravity to compute the shapes of the orbits of the planets. He found that the shapes were ellipses. Decades before Newton, Johannes Kepler had discovered by analyzing data on how the planets moved in the sky that the planets travel in ellipses. But not until Newton's law of gravity was it understood why the planets orbit in ellipses.

A planet and the sun are linked to each other by the gravitation force *F* (see Figure 2.2). Note that the shape of the planet's orbit is an ellipse. An ellipse has a *major axis* that is longer than its *minor axis*. That means that the planet is not exactly the same distance away from the sun at each point during the year, as it

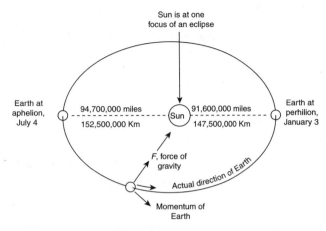

Figure 2.2 Earth's orbit around sun. (The slope of the ellipse is exaggerated.)

would be if the orbit were a perfect circle. In the case of our planet, Earth is about 3% closer to the sun in the time of year we call January than it is during July. That's because Earth's orbit is an ellipse. Also note in this diagram how the force of gravity works on the planet to keep the planet in orbit, countering the planet's inertia, its tendency to remain in its forward line of motion (roughly, its momentum, its velocity times its mass), which tends to shoot the planet off into space. This concept is described next in the text.

If you attach a rock to a string and then spin the rock around your head, the rock stays in orbit around you. Now what if you were to cut the string during this motion? The rock would fly away. With the string intact, the rock stays in orbit because two forces are in balance: The tendency for the rock to fly away is balanced (controlled) by the force of tension in the string.

The rock on a string can be used as an analogy to the situation in the solar system between a planet and the sun. Gravity is like the string. Earth is moving at close to 20 miles per second in a direction tangent to its orbit (see Figure 2.2, a tangent to a circle is a line perpendicular to a radius). For an object as massive as the earth, that is a lot of momentum. But gravity also pulls the earth toward the sun. What is the result of the

momentum and gravity? Earth is made to travel in a closed loop, in a balance between its linear momentum and the gravitational pull toward the sun. One final important fact: As they move in their elliptical orbits, planets travel faster when they are closer to the sun than when they are farther away.

## ▶ Practice

**6.** Who first formulated a working law of gravity?
   **a.** Newton
   **b.** Einstein
   **c.** Kepler
   **d.** Galileo

**7.** Consider the force of gravity between two masses. If the masses of both of them double, the force of gravity between them does which of the following?
   **a.** increases by 2 times
   **b.** increases by 4 times
   **c.** decreases to $\frac{1}{2}$
   **d.** decreases to $\frac{1}{4}$

**8.** The mass of the planet Venus is about 80% that of Earth's mass. The distance from Venus to the sun is about 70% that of the Earth to the sun. Therefore, the force of gravity between Venus and the sun, compared to the force of gravity between Earth and sun, is which one of the following?
   **a.** between 5 and 6 times greater
   **b.** between 1 and 2 times greater
   **c.** smaller, between $\frac{1}{5}$ and $\frac{1}{6}$
   **d.** smaller, between $\frac{1}{2}$ to 1

**9.** What is the shape of the orbit of a planet around the sun?

 **a.** a circle

 **b.** a hyperbola

 **c.** an ellipse

 **d.** a parabola

**10.** The speed of the earth as it orbits around the sun is slightly greatest during which month?

 **a.** January

 **b.** March

 **c.** July

 **d.** September

## ▶ Rocky and Gaseous Planets

When the gas cloud condensed to become our sun between 5 and 4.5 billion years ago, the planets also condensed. The solar system has nine planets, plus the belt of asteroids between Mars and Jupiter. In the first few million years after the sun ignited, it gave off intense flares in the vast distances of space, which stripped the planets closest to the sun of their gases hydrogen and helium. The solar system was left with its most significant pattern: the difference between the inner and outer planets. Thus, although the planets probably began with roughly the same chemical compositions, the violent activity of the newborn sun left the inner planets as mostly rock.

The planets closest to the sun (the inner, or *terrestrial planets*) are rocky (Mercury, Venus, Earth, and Mars). Note that this doesn't mean that they don't have some gases; Venus and Earth, for example, have substantial atmospheres. One property of planets is their average density, which is their mass per unit volume. The density of the rocky planets is between 4 and 5.5 grams per cubic centimeter. (For comparison, the density of water is 1 gram per cubic centimeter.)

The planets farthest from the sun are sometimes called the *Jovian planets*, or just outer planets, or gaseous planets. They are Jupiter, Saturn, Uranus, Neptune, and Pluto. Their density varies from about 0.7 to 2 grams per cubic centimeter. Jupiter, for example, at 1.3 grams per cubic centimeter, is 98% hydrogen and helium and only 2% of the heavy elements that are most of Earth's mass. The density of Saturn, as another example, is less than that of water, which means that if you could find an ocean big enough to fit it, Saturn would float.

What follows is a list of the planets, in order, starting with the planet closest to the sun—Mercury. Data is given on each planet's diameter relative to that of the earth (we'll call the earth's diameter = 1, which is 12,756 kilometers). Data is also given on each planet's distance from the sun, relative to the earth's distance (Earth distance = 1, which is 150 million kilometers, or 93 million miles from the sun). Note also that each planet's period of revolution around the sun is given in Earth years. A few additional observations about each planet will also be made at the end of each section.

**Mercury.** Diameter = 0.38. Distance = 0.39. Period of revolution = 0.24 years. Mercury is heavily cratered, with virtually no atmosphere, like our moon.

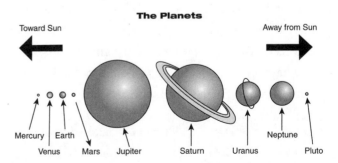

**The Planets**

Toward Sun — Away from Sun

Mercury   Earth   Neptune   Pluto
Venus   Mars   Jupiter   Saturn   Uranus

Figure 2.3 The names and relative sizes of the planets, from closest to the sun on the left to farthest from the sun on the right

**Venus.** Diameter = 0.95 (almost the same size as Earth!). Distance = 0.72. Period of revolution = 0.62 years. Venus has thick clouds and is extremely hot, partly because it is closer to the sun but mostly because the atmosphere is about 600 times more massive than that of Earth and is mostly carbon dioxide. This amount of $CO_2$ produces an intense greenhouse effect, which is a property of a planet's atmosphere that keeps, in the case of Venus, the planet hot. No water vapor or oxygen exists in the atmosphere.

**Earth.** Diameter = 1 (by definition). Distance = 1 (by definition). Period of revolution = 1 year (by definition, our year equals the time for the earth to go once around the sun). We'll be talking a lot about Earth in the rest of this book, so for now, let's just note it's the third planet from the sun, and because it's rocky, it's sometimes called *the third stone from the sun.*

**Mars.** Diameter = 0.53. Distance = 1.52. Period of revolution = 1.88 years. In 2004, the United States (NASA) successfully deployed two new rovers on the surface of Mars. The rovers have analyzed minerals and have concluded, through multiple lines of evidence, that Mars was once wet. Rivers flowed, and there was possibly a shallow ocean. The atmosphere is very thin and the average temperature at the equator is about the same as that of Antarctica on Earth. Burr!

**Asteroid belt.** Asteroids are chunks of rock of various sizes, between the orbits of Mars and Jupiter. There are millions of asteroids. Some have irregular orbits, and a few have almost certainly smashed into the Earth at several times in Earth's long history.

**Jupiter.** Diameter = 11.2. Distance = 5.2. Period of revolution = 11.9 years. Jupiter is famous for its large moons and the bands across its surface, which are weather patterns.

**Saturn.** Diameter = 9.4. Distance = 9.5. Period of revolution = 29.5 years. Saturn is famous for its rings, a spectacle that can be seen even through a home telescope.

**Uranus.** Diameter = 4.06. Distance = 19.1. Period of revolution = 84 years. It has recently been discovered that Uranus also has rings, much fainter than those of Saturn.

**Neptune.** Diameter = 3.9. Distance = 30.0. Period of revolution = 165 years. Neptune was named after the Roman god of the sea.

**Pluto.** Diameter = 0.47. Distance = 39.4. Period of revolution = 248 years. This most distant planet (so far) is smaller than Earth, and its diminutive size among the giants of the Jovian outer planets have led some to question whether it should even be called a planet.

**Comets.** These balls of ice and rock occur in great numbers in several zones out beyond the planets. Occasionally, a comet is perturbed into an irregular orbit that is so highly elliptical that it can be brought closer to Earth at its closet point than it normally would. It is certain that comets, like asteroids, have smashed into Earth at times in its history.

Here's a key fact regarding the time it takes each planet to cycle in its orbit once around the sun: The farther the planet is from the sun, the longer its year. The "year" of each planet has nothing to do with its size; it has only to do with its distance from the sun. Also, note that because the gaseous planets retained much of their original gases from the cosmic gas cloud that condensed to form the solar system, the gaseous planets are larger than the four inner, rocky planets. (Pluto is the exception, as was already discussed.)

## ► Practice

**11.** The four rocky planets are which of the
following?
   **a.** Uranus, Venus, Neptune, Earth
   **b.** Earth, Uranus, Mercury, Mars
   **c.** Neptune, Venus, Earth, Uranus
   **d.** Earth, Mars, Venus, Mercury

**12.** Which planet is farther away from the sun than
Saturn?
   **a.** Jupiter
   **b.** Uranus
   **c.** Mars
   **d.** Venus

**13.** Which is the correct statement?
   **a.** The closer a planet is to the sun, the greater
   its number of moons.
   **b.** The farther a planet is from the sun, the
   longer its "year."
   **c.** The farther a planet is from the sun, the
   greater its mass.
   **d.** The closer a planet is to the sun, the smaller
   its diameter.

**14.** In which pair of planets is the density of the first
definitely greater than the density of the second?
Use your overall knowledge about the solar system to figure out the answer.
   **a.** Uranus compared to Mercury
   **b.** Earth compared to Jupiter
   **c.** Saturn compared to Venus
   **d.** Neptune compared to Mars

**15.** This planet is currently being explored by
robotic rovers, searching for the possibility that
water, and therefore the possibility of life, once
existed.
   **a.** Venus
   **b.** Earth
   **c.** Mercury
   **d.** Mars

## ► Phases of the Moon

Though it was once thought that the moon might have
condensed separately around the earth, the following
scenario is now known to be true (from multiple lines
of evidence). A few hundred million years after the formation of the earth, a rogue body about the size of
Mars and having an odd orbit around the sun,
smashed into the earth. Material from both the colliding body and the earth flew off and condensed
around the earth to form the moon. The moon was
much closer at that time and has been slowly moving
away from the earth ever since.

The moon revolves around the earth in 29.5 days,
from which we derive the calendar division called our
*month.* The moon keeps its same face to the earth during this revolution. The side of the moon facing away
from the earth, often referred to as the "dark" side of
the moon, is not really dark. It's just that we never see
it from Earth. Both "our" side of the moon and its
"dark" side are lit by the sun and then go into shadow,
as the moon goes through its phases.

Figure 2.4 shows the phases of the moon. It's
great fun (I promise) to look at the moon in the sky
and from its phase be able to sense where the moon is
along its orbit, in relation to Earth and sun.

The moon's gravity is largely responsible for the
oceans' tides—the rise and fall of sea level that we

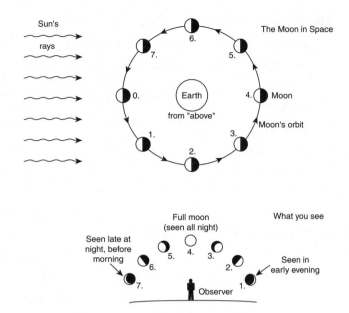

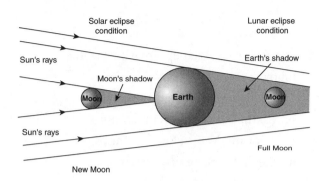

Figure 2.5 On the left, a solar eclipse. On the right, a lunar eclipse. This diagram cannot be made to scale because of the great distances involved compared to the relatively small sizes of the objects.

Figure 2.4 Phases of the moon

notice when we visit a beach for several hours or kayak in a marine bay. (To a lesser degree, the sun contributes to the tides as well.) The sun is less important because even though it's huge compared to the moon, it's also very far away. Tides are high at places on the earth that are either closest to the moon or on the opposite side of the earth from the moon. Therefore, two high tides and two low tides happen each day, with the low tides coming between each of the two high tides. The time interval from high tide to low tide, or from low tide to high tide, is about 6 hours.

The shapes of the coastlines and the local topography of the ocean's depths affect the exact timing of the tides locally. That is why we need tide tables that are specific to each locality. Furthermore, tides are particularly high and low when the moon and sun are in alignment with the earth, which occurs during either new or full moon.

The moon is also responsible for the exciting astronomical events we call eclipses. Two kinds of eclipses happen (see Figure 2.5). In the solar eclipse, the moon blocks out either a portion of the sun (a partial solar eclipse) or all the sun (a total solar eclipse).

That can occur only during new moon and, for any particular city on Earth, only once in a great while.

The second kind of eclipse is the lunar eclipse, which occurs only at full moon, when the earth's shadow is cast upon the moon. Lunar eclipses can also be full or partial. The moon doesn't disappear completely during a full lunar eclipse but turns a deep reddish-brown in the night sky. Because the earth's shadow is so large, lunar eclipses can be seen more often from any place on Earth, but they are still special astronomical events worth watching.

## ▶ Practice

**16.** The moon was born when which of the following happened?
   **a.** A large body smashed into the early earth.
   **b.** It condensed from the cosmic gas cloud that formed the solar system.
   **c.** It was captured by the sun's gravity in the same orbit as the early earth.
   **d.** The early earth split up from internal instability.

**17.** For a solar eclipse to occur, the moon must be which in one of the following positions?
  a. new, between the earth and sun
  b. new, opposite the sun
  c. full, between the earth and sun
  d. full, opposite the earth and sun

**18.** You are told that a lunar eclipse will occur tomorrow night. That tells you that the moon will then be in which phase?
  a. right half
  b. full
  c. left half
  d. new

**19.** This is a tough one. You see the moon in the sky as the left half (like looking at the left side of half a coin). The moon will next be full in about how many days?
  a. 29 to 30 days
  b. 7 to 8 days
  c. 21 to 22 days
  d. 14 to 15 days

**20.** You are enjoying yourself on a beach and remark that the ocean level on the sand was highest about 3 hours ago. That means that the low tide will be in how many hours?
  a. 18 hours
  b. 12 hours
  c. 9 hours
  d. 3 hours

# LESSON

# 3 ▶ Climate and the Seasons

## LESSON SUMMARY

The earth is a giant spherical ball whose shape is called an *oblate spheroid,* in space, lit by the sun. This fundamental, grand fact sets the environmental context for much of our lives, including the length of the day, the length and diversity of the seasons, and climate.

## ▶ Latitude and Longitude

Human beings have wrapped the earth in a coordinate system that is partly based on the sphere of the planet and is partly arbitrary. Why does latitude go from 0° at the equator to 90° at the poles? That is obviously rooted in the geometry of the circle, because ever since the Babylonians, the circle has been divided into 360 degrees. To go around the earth from the equator, up past the north pole (from 0° to 90° N), then back down to the equator on the other side of the planet (from 90° N to 0°), then south to the south pole (from 0° to 90° S), and then back up to your starting point on the equator (from 90° S to 0°), you will go through 360 total degrees of *latitude.*

It's the same with *longitude*: 360° total. The 0° line of longitude passes through Greenwich, England. (Guess what country established the system of longitude?) Rather than north and south, like latitude, longitude is measured east and west, with the numbers going to 180° at the line on the opposite side of the earth from the 0° line through England. Thus, longitude is measured from 0° to 180° W and from 0° to 180° E.

Subdivisions of the degrees of latitude and longitude are the *minutes* and the *seconds*. (These are not minutes and seconds of time, but obviously, the names in our geographical system of degrees are related to

**Latitude and Longitude**

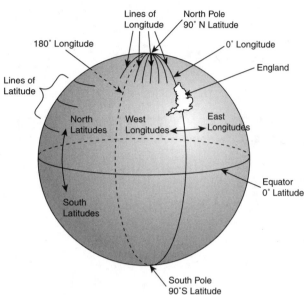

Figure 3.1 The earth's coordinate system of latitude and longitude. Note that the distance between degrees of latitude stays the same everywhere. But the distances between degrees of longitude become smaller as one moves from the equator to either pole.

the names for time.) There are 60 minutes of latitude and longitude in each degree. The symbol for minute is a single straight quote, or single prime ('). There are 60 seconds of latitude or longitude in each minute. The symbol for second is the double straight quote, or primes (").

Here's another difference between latitude and longitude. Lines of latitude are all parallel to each other. Lines of longitude all intersect through the north and south poles. Please study Figure 3.1.

The fact that the earth is a giant ball set in the bath of sunlight, which comes in as nearly parallel rays of light, has tremendous effects on the amount of solar energy received at different latitudes. A unit parcel of ground, say a square meter, becomes tipped more and

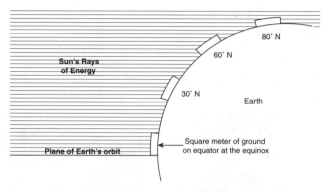

Figure 3.2 Solar energy and the curvature of the earth. Note how the parcel of ground (or a solar collector put on the ground) intercepts fewer and fewer of the sun's rays as the latitude becomes higher.

more, relative to the direction of the rays of the sun, as one moves into higher and higher latitudes. You can think of it as fewer and fewer rays of sun striking the parcel of ground as the latitude becomes higher. See Figure 3.2 for an illustration of how this works.

Assume that the time of year is when the sun is overhead at the equator and that one knows the amount of solar energy falling at the equator ($S_{eq}$) per square meter (also assume no clouds). Then, with the following equation, one can calculate the amount of solar energy falling at any latitude ($S_{lat}$) on a square meter of ground, by knowing the latitude ($\Pi$) and computing its cosine of that latitude $\cos(\Pi)$ (in a right triangle, the cosine of either of the other two angles is their respective adjacent sides divided by the hypotenuse):

$$S_{lat} = \cos \phi \, S_{eq}$$

If the latitude is 60° N, then cos (60) = 0.5. That means that the amount of sunlight falling on a square meter of ground at 60° N is, on average over the year, only half of the amount of solar energy that falls at the equator on a square meter of ground.

Finally, here's the equation for the circumference $C$ of Earth at the equator in terms of the diameter and the constant $\pi$ (which is approximately 3.14):

$$C = \pi D$$

Because the diameter $D$ is twice the radius $R$ of a circle, we also have the equation for Earth's circumference in terms of $R$:

$$C = 2\pi R$$

## ▶ Practice

**1.** If Earth's diameter is 8,000 miles, how far is it from the center of the earth to the surface?
- **a.** 4,000 miles
- **b.** 16,000 miles
- **c.** 25,120 miles
- **d.** 12,560 miles

**2.** In the United States, we are at which longitude and latitude?
- **a.** east longitude and north latitude
- **b.** east longitude and south latitude
- **c.** west longitude and north latitude
- **d.** west longitude and south latitude

**3.** Boston and Seattle are close to 45° N latitude. If a square meter of land at the equator receives about 1,000 watts per square meter, then a square meter of land at the latitude of 45° receives how many watts per square meter?
- **a.** about 500
- **b.** about 2,000
- **c.** about 1,400
- **d.** about 700

**4.** Assume you travel south from the equator along a line of longitude that is 30° E. When you cross past the South Pole along the same circle of longitude, you are now on a different number for the line of longitude. Traveling on the other side of the earth, back toward a point on the equator exactly opposite the point you started from, you are now on what line of longitude?
- **a.** 150° E
- **b.** 60° E
- **c.** 150° W
- **d.** 60° W

**5.** The line of 0° longitude passes through which country?
- **a.** United States
- **b.** Japan
- **c.** Russia
- **d.** England

## ▶ Earth's Spin and Tilt

People long ago did not know that Earth spun around once a day. They thought that the stars turned around, as a great sphere far above the atmosphere, and that the sun, moon, and planets traveled around the earth on their own sphere or path, with different periods. It was not known that Earth was also a planet. Dawn came each day when the sun literally rose; the earth, obviously because it was so huge, stood still, or so people thought.

With the discoveries of Copernicus and Galileo, the true nature of the solar system was recognized. The stars move at night and the sun rises and sets because Earth spins. We say it spins once a day. But don't forget that the day is in fact defined by the earth's spin.

If the earth spun only half as fast, then the day would be 48 hours. Or would it still be 24 hours, with each hour being 120 minutes long? I'll leave you to ponder these issues as we move on to the direction of the earth's spin.

Which way does the earth spin? Imagine yourself looking at a globe, or in space looking down at the real Earth of clouds and continents, the way astronauts do. Suppose you face the United States the way it is normally shown on maps with Central and South America below it, in the direction of your feet. Which way is the earth spinning? Left to right or right to left? Think of the answer before reading on.

The spin is from left to right. How did you figure this out? One way is to realize that dawn comes to the east coast before the west coast (that is, to New York before Los Angeles). Sunset is the same. The only way this can happen is if the spin is from left to right. Now what if you were turned upside down, so your head is toward South America and your feet are toward Canada?

Earth spins around an *axis* that stays constant. The spin axis is an imaginary line that goes through the diameter of the earth, from what we call the South Pole to the center of the earth and then up through the North Pole. Furthermore, and crucially for our lives, the spin axis is not perpendicular to the plane of Earth's orbit around the sun. Earth's spin axis is tilted at 23.5° away from that perpendicular direction to the plane of Earth's orbit.

The other important fact about Earth's spin axis, which will prove consequential for understanding the seasons and climate in the next section of this lesson, is that it keeps pointing to the same direction in space. Today, the axis always points to the North Star (which is really, really far away).

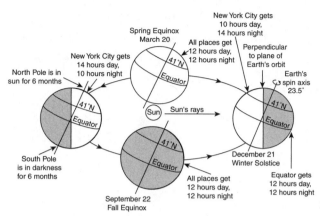

**Figure 3.3** The earth's tilt and day length during the course of the year. The earth's spin axis and the line of day and night are shown for four crucial points along the earth's orbit. Also shown are the paths taken by a point on the equator and at New York City (about 41° N) during one spin cycle at these times of the year. Note that the length of the daylight hours is always 12 at the equator, and that the length of daylight changes with the seasons for New York. Also note that during the equinoxes (a word that means equal nights in Latin), daylight and night are 12 hours long each everywhere on Earth. Earth and sun are not to scale, of course.

The facts, (1) that the spin axis is tilted and (2) that it always points to the same direction in space, together create the same changes that those who live in the high latitudes see in the length of the daylight hours. (Note that we speak of the daylight hours as the *day*, but *day* also means the total 24 hours for the earth to spin once around. Yes, it's a bit confusing, but that's our English language.) In Figure 3.3, you can see how day length changes with time of year. Please study it closely before moving on to the practice questions.

## ► Practice

**6.** You are floating in the sky (horizontally, in a flying position) in the southern hemisphere, with your head toward the equator and your feet toward the south pole. You have a friend who is in the northern hemisphere, also floating (in a "flying" position) with her head toward the north pole and feet toward the equator. Which one is true about the turning of the earth, given the positions of you and your "distant" friend?

   **a.** Earth turns from right to left for you, from left to right for your friend.

   **b.** Earth turns from right to left for you, from right to left for your friend.

   **c.** Earth turns from left to right for you, from right to left for your friend.

   **d.** Earth turns from left to right for you, from left to right for your friend.

**7.** If the earth's axis were perpendicular to the plane of the earth's orbit around the sun, which of these statements would be true?

   **a.** Half the planet would have 24 hours of daylight and half would have 24 hours of night, all year long.

   **b.** Daylight and night would be the same everywhere on Earth all year long.

   **c.** Daylight and night would vary from 24 hours and 0 hours, respectively, and then reverse during the course of the year.

   **d.** Changes in daylight and night would be opposite to the way they are now during the course of the year.

**8.** The tilt of Earth's axis is how much off perpendicular (vertical) to the plane of Earth's orbit around the sun?

   **a.** 23.5°

   **b.** 31.5°

   **c.** 42.5°

   **d.** 12.5°

**9.** What is unique about a point along the equator?

   **a.** They have the longest length of daylight of any place on Earth.

   **b.** The length of time for the complete cycle of day to night is longer than anywhere else.

   **c.** The sun at noon is always directly overhead.

   **d.** They have 12 hours daylight and 12 hours night all year long.

**10.** On June 21, the North Pole has 24 hours of daylight. True or false? And why?

   **a.** false, because it's tilted into Earth's shadow

   **b.** false, because nowhere gets that much daylight

   **c.** true, because it's tilted toward the sun

   **d.** true, because the spin axis points to the North Star

## ► Seasons and Climate

We now have the pieces we need to understand the seasons and climate. These pieces include: latitude and longitude, how the amount of sun energy varies with latitude (because the earth is nearly a sphere, an oblate spheroid), and how the earth's spin axis is tilted and remains pointed in the same direction in space during the course of the year.

The easiest way to grasp the essentials of the situation is to ask: At what latitude is the sun overhead at noon on June 21 and December 21? Recall that these

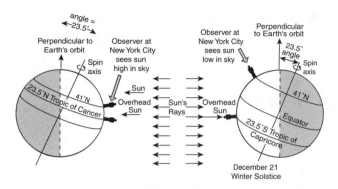

Figure 3.4 The sun and the seasons

dates are the two dates with extreme points in the earth's tilt relative to the plane of the earth's orbit. On June 21, the *summer solstice*, the sun is overhead at noon for an observer at latitude 23.5° N. Study this fact in Figure 3.4, and then we'll discuss the situation at the time of the *winter solstice*.

On June 21, the summer solstice, the sun is overhead at noon at the latitude 23.5° N. At the same time, you can see that for a place in the northern hemisphere, say New York City at 41° N, the sun is very high in the sky and the ground receives a large amount of solar energy per square meter (if necessary, review Figure 3.2). This time of year, of course, is summer in the northern hemisphere. On December 21, the winter solstice, the situation is quite different. Now the southern hemisphere is maximally tilted toward the sun and the latitude of 23.5° S has been "lifted" to the place where the sun at noon is directly overhead. During the winter solstice, the northern hemisphere is tilted away from the sun; in fact, all sites above 67.5° N are in complete darkness all that day. If we consider an observer in New York City during the winter solstice, you can see from the figure that the observer sees the sun very low in the sky. That site receives relatively little solar energy per square meter because the sun's rays are spread out along the ground (if necessary, review Figure 3.2).

On the winter solstice, December 21, it is latitude the 23.5° S that sees the sun overhead at noon, as explained in the previous paragraph. The southern hemisphere is in summer and the northern hemisphere is in winter. The fact that the tilt of the earth remains pointing to the same position in space (always at the north star) makes the noon sun's angle change everywhere on Earth during the course of the year. At the latitudes of sites in the United States, for example, the sun at noon is high during summer and low during winter. This changes the amount of solar energy received per square meter of ground, which causes the seasons' changing amount of solar energy per square meter over the course of the year is the cause of the seasons.

On the equinoxes, September 22 and March 20, the sun is overhead at noon for places exactly on the equator. In fact, at the equator, the sun is almost always overhead, varying from 23.5° from vertical in one direction at one solstice, to exactly vertical at the equinox, then to 23.5° from vertical in the other direction at the other solstice, to vertical at the other equinox, and then back to the first solstice. The large amount of solar energy per square meter received by the equator and places near the equator is the reason that the temperature is warm all year round. In fact, the temperature is tropical. We call these low latitudes the *tropics*. Basically, this includes all the latitudes between 23.5° N and 23.5° S. These 23.5° latitude lines are known, respectively, as the *Tropic of Cancer* and the *Tropic of Capricorn*.

The way the sun changes during the course of the year provides Earth with three main climate bands. The climate actually varies continuously with latitude, but humans tend to classify nature into regions. The first we've already seen—the *tropics*. The second is called the *midlatitudes*, which includes the United States, Europe, and China in the northern hemisphere.

Climate in this belt is also called *temperate*. The midlatitudes have a high amount of seasonality, with definite summers and winters. The annual average temperatures in the midlatitudes are lower than the annual average temperatures of the tropics. Of course, the specific average temperature and how much the seasons vary depend on the latitude within the midlatitudes. Contrast Florida, for example, with Vermont, both of which are in the midlatitudes.

The third major climate belt is in the *high latitudes*, which includes the types of climates called *subarctic* and *polar*. Where the high latitudes begin is arbitrary. Some would say around 50° N and 50° S, then stretching to the poles in both hemispheres. Others would say at the Arctic and Antarctic Circles (67.5° N and 67.5° S, respectively), the places that have at least one full day each year in which the sun doesn't rise and one full day each year in which the sun doesn't set. In the high latitudes, the seasons are extreme, and the annual temperatures are lower than those of the midlatitudes.

The changes in daylight hours in the high latitudes are amazing. The most dramatic examples come from the poles themselves. From March 20 to September 22, the sun is continuously above the horizon at the north pole and continuously below the horizon at the south pole. From September 22 to March 20, the sun is continuously above the horizon at the south pole and continuously below the horizon at the north pole. The south pole and north pole only have one sunrise and one sunset per year. In fact, sunsets and sunrises last almost a week at the poles. That's a nice, leisurely time to enjoy the colors in the sky, if you happen to be there and are dressed warmly enough.

We can now see how so much about our lives is determined by the simple geometric relationships among the spinning sphere of the earth, its orbit around the sun, and the rays of energy from the sun that warm our planet.

## ▶ Practice

**11.** What are the three main factors that cause the midlatitudes to have seasons?
   **a.** The distance from Earth to the sun changes, Earth's spin axis is tilted, and the sun's energy varies with latitude.
   **b.** Earth's spin axis is tilted, Earth's spin axis remains pointed in the same direction in space, and the distance from Earth to the sun changes.
   **c.** The sun's energy varies with latitude, Earth's spin axis remains pointed in the same direction in space, and the distance from Earth to the sun changes.
   **d.** Earth's spin axis remains pointed in the same direction in space, the sun's energy varies with latitude, and the earth's spin axis is tilted.

**12.** What are the two times of year in which the sun is exactly overhead at noon within the tropics?
   **a.** June 21 and December 21
   **b.** June 21 and September 22
   **c.** March 20 and September 22
   **d.** March 20 and June 21

**13.** You are in a ship that crosses the Tropic of Cancer from north to south. In terms of climate zones, you have crossed from which zone into which other zone?
   **a.** midlatitudes to tropics
   **b.** high latitudes to midlatitudes
   **c.** tropics to midlatitudes
   **d.** midlatitudes to high latitudes

**14.** Between the winter solstice and the spring equinox, an observer in Australia watching the angle of the sun at noon each day would see which of the following?

   **a.** the sun get lower and lower

   **b.** the sun get lower and then higher

   **c.** the sun get higher and higher

   **d.** the sun get higher and then lower

**15.** You fly in an airplane from New York City to Buenos Aires, Argentina (35° S). What series of climate zones describes your path?

   **a.** temperate to tropical to subarctic

   **b.** subarctic to temperate to tropical

   **c.** temperate to midlatitudes to tropical

   **d.** temperate to tropical to temperate

# Earth's Deep Layers

## LESSON SUMMARY

The soil we step on when we take a stroll in the woods is only a thin layer, sitting on top of rock that goes down mile after mile after mile—indeed thousands of miles. What is inside the earth? At the earth's core, temperatures are estimated to be those at the surface of the sun. Earth's interior is like an onion: layers all the way down. But the earth is more complex.

## ▶ Earth's Core and Magnetic Field

When the earth formed approximately 4.5 billion years ago, the heat generated from all the impacts that formed it and heat from the high levels of radioactive elements in rock put the earth into a molten state. Being molten, elements and minerals could separate according to their density. The heavier materials sank toward Earth's center. The lighter materials floated, so to speak, nearer the surface.

As the earth cooled over geological time, layers were permanently created based on the original separation of types of materials. Plus the properties of the rock layers changed with temperature and pressure. The innermost layer is called the *core*.

The core begins at 2,880 kilometers (1,800 miles) beneath Earth's surface. Because the radius of the earth is 6,370 kilometers (3,960 miles), we can calculate that the radius of the core is about 3,490 kilometers (2,160 miles). We cannot drill down deep enough to know about the core directly. But we know a great deal about the core indirectly (this will be discussed in greater detail in the final section of this lesson). For example, the core is made primarily of the element iron. There are smaller amounts of nickel and other elements.

Furthermore, although the composition of the core is about the same throughout, its properties change dramatically at a depth of about 5,140 kilometers (3,190 miles) below Earth's surface. This depth separates the innermost core, which is solid rock, from the outer core, which is molten. In other words, the outer layer of the core is liquid.

Estimates of the temperatures of the core show that the core is about 5,000° C (about 9,000° F). These temperatures are in the range of those at the surface of the sun. Thus, the core would glow, if only you could see it. Such temperatures cause the iron to be in a molten state, which accounts for the liquid outer layer of the core. But why is the inner core solid? The answer has to do with the great pressures at those unimaginable subterranean depths.

As noted in the description of the core, the temperature at which a certain material makes a change of state—from solid to liquid during melting or from liquid to gas during boiling—depends upon the pressure. An example occurs to anyone who attempts to cook high on top of a mountain. Water boils at lower temperatures with higher altitudes. That is because the pressure of the surrounding air is less. Reversing this logic, we can say it takes a higher temperature to boil water at a lower altitude, say at sea level (as the surrounding air pressure goes up).

The situation is the same for the melting or freezing of water (going from solid to liquid or from liquid to solid). The temperature at which that transition occurs goes up as the surrounding pressure goes up. Finally, the same is true for the transition of iron between liquid and solid in the earth's core. The extreme pressure from all the overlying rock keeps the earth's centermost region as solid iron, even though the temperature is high. Surrounding the solid layer of the core, the pressure is less (because there is less overlying rock weighing down)—enough less that the iron is molten.

The molten layer of the core provides an important property of our planet: its *magnetic field.* The molten iron in the core flows. The flows are complicated and not well understood (many scientists are working on this problem, which is highly mathematical). But the flows are related to the loops of rising and falling currents similar to those that you might see in a pan of hot water. The flows are also structured by the earth's spin, which is why the north and south poles of Earth's magnetic field are close to the poles of Earth's spin axis.

The magnetic field is caused by the circulating flows in the molten core, which create electrical currents. These in turn create the magnetic field. Like the field from any magnet, the earth's magnetic field has an axis; the two ends of this axis are called the north and south poles of the magnetism. The presence of Earth's magnetic field allows us to use compasses to find our location, because the compass aligns itself to Earth's magnetic field. It is important to note, however, that the earth's magnetic poles are close to, but do not exactly coincide with, the poles of Earth's spin axis (the North and South Poles geographically).

To complicate matters even more, the magnetic poles do not stay in the same place. They wander. In fact, we can measure this wandering over a period of time as short as decades. And at times in Earth's history, the direction of the north and south magnetic poles switch (they reverse). If this switch were to happen today, tomorrow your compass (which had pointed north) would now point south. But don't worry—the reversals occur only every one hundred thousand to a million years or so and take thousands of years to complete the switch.

The magnetic reversals play a crucial role in understanding events in Earth's history. When molten rock reaches Earth's surface and cools, it locks into its mineral structure the earth's magnetic field. In other words, the rock becomes slightly magnetized.

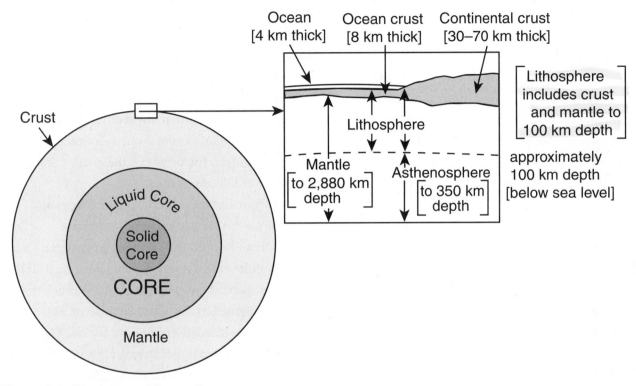

Figure 4.1 · The layers of the earth

Depending on the age of the rock, it can be magnetized by a *normal magnetic field* (like today's) or by a *reversed magnetic field*. As we will see in the next lesson, this record of magnetization was instrumental in the discovery of *plate tectonics*, the governing theory of how the earth's continents and oceans change over time.

Figure 4.1 shows the earth's layers that are discussed in this lesson. Study it for its information about the core, then move on to the practice questions. Later, you will need to refer back to this figure as we describe the upper layers of the earth.

### ▶ Practice

1. If the core is 2,880 kilometers below Earth's surface, and Earth's radius is 6,370 kilometers, then what is the diameter of the core?
   a. about 3,500 kilometers
   b. about 600 kilometers
   c. about 7,000 kilometers
   d. about 1,200 kilometers

2. Which of the following is important in establishing the direction of Earth's magnetic field?
   a. the earth's rotation
   b. the sun
   c. the earth's elliptical orbit
   d. the orbit of the moon

**3.** What is true about the core?

   **a.** The inner layer is solid, and the outer layer is liquid.

   **b.** The outer layer is solid, and the inner layer is liquid.

   **c.** The outer layer is gaseous, the middle layer is liquid, and the inner layer is solid.

   **d.** The outer layer is solid, the middle layer is liquid, and the inner layer is gaseous.

**4.** Where do the lines of force of the magnetic field of the earth emerge from the surface?

   **a.** at a point on the equator

   **b.** at a point near 0° latitude

   **c.** at a point on 0° longitude

   **d.** at a point near the North Pole

**5.** The different properties of the layers of Earth's core are related to what general fact?

   **a.** Releasing pressure from a solid raises its solidifying temperature.

   **b.** Compressing a liquid raises its solidifying temperature.

   **c.** Climbing a mountain requires energy.

   **d.** Hard-boiling eggs on a mountain requires less time than at sea level.

## ▶ Earth's Mantle and Crust

Look at Figure 4.1 and find the layer of the earth called the mantle. The *mantle* lies outside the core and is made of material less dense than the core. Unlike the core, the mantle is not primarily iron. Scientists don't know exactly what the mantle is made of, but it's probably similar to material at Earth's surface but contains slightly larger amounts of some of the denser elements.

The lower boundary of the mantle is at the upper boundary of the core, 2,880 kilometers below Earth's average surface. The upper boundary of the mantle reaches up to a point only about 8 to 70 kilometers (about 5 to 40 miles) below the surface of the earth.

At the upper boundary of the mantle, we find the beginning of the outermost layer of Earth, the *crust*. The crust is less dense than the mantle and is primarily made of rock that comes from volcanoes and then solidifies. In fact, the origin of the crust is from volcanism over billions of years.

Two main types of crust exist: *continental crust* (basically, what we live on) and *ocean crust* (the floor of the ocean beyond the continental shelves). Ocean crust is quite thin (about 8 kilometers, or 5 miles). Continental crust, on the other hand, is much thicker (30 to 70 kilometers, or about 20 to 40 miles).

Now the discussion gets a bit trickier. Geologists also distinguish two upper layers of the earth called the *lithosphere* and the *asthenosphere*. The translation of these terms means, respectively, *rock sphere* and *weak sphere*. What is tricky is that the lithosphere includes all the crust and the uppermost portion of the mantle. The asthenosphere begins at about 100 kilometers (60 miles) down from the surface and is completely within the mantle. While the crust and mantle are distinguished primarily by their compositions, the lithosphere and asthenosphere are distinguished by their physical properties.

Once again, the issue of how pressure affects the properties of rock is crucial to the explanation. The lithosphere, as the top 100 kilometers of Earth, has relatively little pressure on it, and therefore, lithosphere rock is like rock we know: completely solid and brittle. But at the border between lithosphere and the underlying asthenosphere, a change in the behavior of rock occurs, from brittle to plastic. The word *plastic* here does not refer to the plastic packaging materials, but rather to "plastic" as a physical property, meaning pliable or capable of being molded.

As we go down into the earth, the rock experiences more and more pressure, because more material is on top of it, which presses down because of gravity. At the depth of about 100 kilometers (the upper boundary of the asthenosphere), the high pressures make the rock plastic. This is not rock that we are familiar with. The temperature is about 1,300° C (about 2,300° F). The term *plastic* means that the rock of the asthenosphere can deform over long time periods, but not like liquid moves. It is somewhat like silly putty. If you tried to snap it, it could crack apart like ordinary brittle rock. But if you applied a constant push to it, say from above, the plastic rock of the asthenosphere would very slowly flow outward. The plastic rock is like a substance that behaves differently from liquid or solid.

Because of its property of being plastic, the asthenosphere can circulate, driven by Earth's tremendous interior heat. This circulation, primarily its downward sinking over long, geological time periods, is the main driving factor in *plate tectonics*. (More details will be discussed about plate tectonics in the next lesson.) Because the earth is hot and circulates at its great depths, continents shift positions over long time periods, and mountains are built to replace old mountains that have eroded away. Because the earth is hot and circulates at its great depths, we have volcanoes and earthquakes. And earthquakes, as we will see in the next section, are crucial in the discovery of all these layers of the planet.

## ▶ Practice

6. Which is true as we go from Earth's surface downward toward the center?
   a. Temperature increases, and pressure decreases.
   b. Density increases, and pressure increases.
   c. Temperature increases, and density decreases.
   d. Pressure increases, and temperature decreases.

7. Which crust is usually thickest?
   a. asthenosphere crust
   b. continental crust
   c. mantle crust
   d. oceanic crust

8. Which layer of Earth is "plastic," meaning it behaves like silly putty over long time periods?
   a. mantle
   b. lithosphere
   c. asthenosphere
   d. crust

9. Which layer is about 100 kilometers (60 miles) thick?
   a. lithosphere
   b. oceanic crust
   c. mantle
   d. upper core

**10.** Rock reaches a temperature of about 1,300° C at a depth of 100 kilometers below the surface. We can therefore compute a heat gradient, which is the average change in temperature per kilometer of depth. What is the heat gradient in the upper 100 kilometers of Earth?

    **a.** 130,000° C

    **b.** 1.3° C per kilometer

    **c.** 13° C per kilometer

    **d.** 1,200° C

## ► How Do We Know about the inside of the Earth?

How do scientists know about these layers of the earth? It's been obvious to some people for thousands of years that the earth gets hot down below the surface. Volcanoes are evidence of this. So is the heat experienced by miners when they dig down, searching for coal or gold. But how do we know about Earth's iron core? Our deepest mines only scratch the surface of the planet. How do we know, for example, about the asthenosphere or the depth of the oceanic crust?

The key piece of evidence is provided by the waves in the earth created by *earthquakes.* Earthquakes can be disastrous for people in the vicinity. But each year, many thousands of small earthquakes happen. By using *seismographs* to monitor the *seismic waves* generated by both large and small earthquakes, geologists have been able to study the interior of the earth that cannot be directly seen.

Seismic waves travel through rock, and their speed and direction are altered by the properties of the rock they travel through.

*Seismologists*—scientists who study seismic waves and earthquakes—have established a network of seismographs all over the earth, because it is vital to monitor small earthquakes in a greater attempt to predict potentially large, future earthquakes and volcanic activity. In their simplest form, seismographs are needles attached to springs that respond to and record the various shakings of the earth, most of which are far too small to be felt directly by humans.

For our purposes, the most important two types of seismic waves are the *P* and *S* waves. *P* stands for *primary*, because these waves travel fastest and reach the recording stations first. *P* waves travel at about 6 km/s (3.7 miles/s). The *S* stands for *secondary*. The *S* waves reach the observing stations after the *P* waves. The *S* waves travel at about 3.5 km/s (2.2 miles/s).

A further distinction exists between *P* and *S* waves. *P* waves are like sound waves in air. *Sound waves travel by compressing and expanding zones in the air* as the waves travel outward. You can think of sound waves as traveling layers of compressions between layers of expansions. *P* waves, in a sense, are sound waves in rock. And like sound waves in air, the speed of the waves depends on the rigidity of the medium. The more rigid the rock is, the faster the *P* waves travel.

As already noted, the speed of *S* waves is slower than the speed of *P* waves. But like the *P* waves, the speed of the *S* waves are greater in rocks of greater rigidity. The key difference is in how the *S* waves travel. *S* waves stretch the rock back and forth. The situation is like a string that is jiggled up and down to make trains of waves ungulate along the length. Unlike *P* waves, which can travel in rock that is either solid or liquid, *S* waves do not travel in liquid. This property is important, as we will see.

Both *P* waves and *S* waves are altered by the rock in which they travel, and not altered only in wave speed. Their direction can be changed, in the same way that light waves are bent by a change in the medium (for example, when a spoon in a glass half full of water appears bent). In addition to being bent, both *P* and *S* waves can be reflected, in the way that sound reflects off a wall or light off a mirror.

When earthquakes occur, the waves given off travel through the rock in all directions. Locations with seismographs near the point of quake generation (the *epicenter*) receive the *P* and *S* waves. In fact, the times of arrival of the waves to these recording stations are used to calculate the exact latitude and longitude of the epicenter. About one hundred years ago, timings of waves revealed a discontinuity in the composition of the rock some miles down. This was the discovery of the earth's crust and therefore the boundary between the crust and mantle.

By studying the seismic waves recorded on the side of the earth opposite to the epicenter of large earthquakes (those powerful enough to send waves through the entire earth), an *S-wave shadow* was discovered. An *S*-wave shadow is a large zone where no *S* waves are recorded. Because *S* waves do not travel through liquids, this *S*-wave shadow shows us that there is a deep liquid layer within the earth. This is evidence for the liquid layer of Earth's core.

Furthermore, by studying the *P* waves all around the earth following a large earthquake, seismologists discovered that Earth's core has a solid inner layer. Other layers have also been discovered and are constantly being studied in more and more detail.

Geologists have even been able to compute the *density* of the core. The average density of the earth is known from the strength of gravity at the surface, and the average density of rock at the surface is known. Furthermore, by studying the arrival times of the *P* waves and *S* waves, a reliable estimate for how the density of the mantle changes with depth can be known. Given the size of the core, it is then relatively simple to calculate the density of the core that is needed to make the density of the entire planet come out to be what it is, given the known density of the crust and mantle.

The density of the core is nearly four times the density of rock at Earth's surface! The only reasonable substance that we know that would have been around in large enough quantities at the formation of Earth to create a core of that density is iron. This is how we know that the earth has a core that is primarily iron. Finally, the facts that iron has magnetic properties and that the earth has a magnetic field are additional indications that it is indeed iron that forms the bulk of the large spherical core of the earth.

## ▶ Practice

11. The waves from earthquakes that travel through rock are called what?
    a. lithosphere waves
    b. seismic waves
    c. subterranean waves
    d. shear waves

12. The knowledge that the earth's core has a liquid layer comes from analyzing earthquake waves on the side of the earth opposite to the point that generated the earthquake. What is the key piece of evidence?
    a. the absence of *S* waves
    b. the absence of *P* waves
    c. the presence of *S* waves
    d. the presence of *P* waves

13. At a recording station some distance from the epicenter of an earthquake, which are the first waves to arrive?
    a. *S* waves
    b. seismic waves
    c. asthenosphere waves
    d. *P* waves

**14.** We know that Earth's core is iron because of the density required to balance the other layers of known density and the known density of the entire earth. Compared to the rocks at Earth's surface, the density of the rock of the core is approximately how much larger?

   **a.** 2 times

   **b.** 1.3 times

   **c.** 4 times

   **d.** 2.5 times

**15.** Sound waves in air are most similar to what kind of waves in the earth?

   **a.** *S* waves

   **b.** seismic waves

   **c.** velocity waves

   **d.** *P* waves

# How Continents Move

## LESSON SUMMARY

One of the most important discoveries of science in the last fifty years is that the Earth's continents move. Not only the continents, but the oceans move, too. In fact, oceans grow and shrink over tens to hundreds of millions of years. How this all works is described by the grand theory of *plate tectonics*.

## ▶ Seafloor Spreading

In 1912, German scientist Alfred Wegener proposed that continents could move around—that they could "drift." One of Wegener's clues to the movement was the fact that the east coast of South America could fit into the lower half of the west coast of Africa, almost as if they were two pieces of a puzzle that once were joined together.

Wegener also pointed to evidence in South America, Africa, India, and Australia of the previous existence of ice sheets at about the same time, 300 million years ago. This made no sense with the continents in their present positions, because some of these sites are at today's equator. In Wegener's day, his theory was dismissed because no one could think of any mechanism for how objects as gigantic as continents could move across the earth's surface.

In the 1960s, new lines of evidence bore fruit for the idea that continents and oceans can radically shift. The key measurements came from geological research ships that drilled into the floor of the Atlantic Ocean. Scientists who participated in this *Ocean Drilling Project* hoisted back up to the ship cylindrical cores of the ocean's rocky floor, part of the oceanic crust. Then they analyzed each core for the direction of magnetism in the rock.

In Lesson 4, we saw that Earth's magnetic field, in the geological past, periodically underwent reversals, in which the south magnetic pole became the north magnetic pole, and the north magnetic pole became the south magnetic pole. When magma comes up from deep in the earth—for example, when a volcano erupts—the liquid lava is not magnetized. Then, as the lava cools into rocky minerals, the rock takes on a slight magnetization. This magnetization records the direction of the earth's magnetic field at the time of cooling when the rock was created.

In a line approximately running down the middle of the Atlantic Ocean, from north to south, is a great underwater mountain chain of volcanoes, the Mid-Atlantic Ridge. The ships measured the magnetism of the volcanic rocks that form on the sea floor on either side of this Mid-Atlantic Ridge. Some rocks showed a magnetic field similar to that of today's Earth. Other rocks showed a reversed field. You can see a diagram of what was found in Figure 5.1.

This diagram of a cross-section of the Mid-Atlantic Ridge shows how the patterns of the magnetic field directions (normal or reversed) are symmetrical on both sides of the ocean floor, which has been spreading away from the ridge for nearly 200 million years. Note how *magma* (molten rock) comes up from the asthenosphere to create new ocean crust and lithosphere, and how the lithosphere gets thicker as it moves away from the hot ridge.

When maps were drawn of the ancient magnetic field directions in the ocean floor, the maps showed symmetrical stripes on the two sides of the Mid-Atlantic Ridge. Back in deep time, when molten magma emerged from the volcanic ridge, the rock that formed as part of the new ocean crust recorded the direction of the magnetic field. This rock then moved away from the ridge in both directions as new magma erupted from the ridge. That new magma, as it in turn emerged a few million years later and cooled, experienced a reversed magnetic field and so it recorded that direction of Earth's magnetism.

The process continued for many tens of millions of years as Earth's magnetic field was continuously recorded in the stripes in the rocks of the Atlantic Ocean's floor. The resulting pattern has been compared to a tape recorder whose tape has symmetrical patterns on both sides of the Mid-Atlantic Ridge.

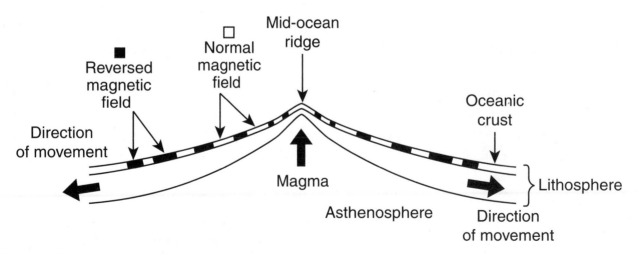

Figure 5.1  Seafloor spreading

Obviously, material had been emerging from and spreading away from the ridge. This was the great discovery of seafloor spreading. The ocean's floor was growing, which meant that the Atlantic Ocean was widening. Earthquakes along the mid-ocean ridges confirmed that the ridges were spreading.

The molten material that flows upward at an ocean ridge to form new ocean crust (which is part of the lithosphere) comes from the hotter, deeper asthenosphere. When ductile asthenosphere cools enough to behave like an elastic solid, it becomes lithosphere. The new lithosphere on both sides of the ridge spreads away from the ridge. In fact, the hot ridge cools and contracts as it spreads the emerging material outward to the sides. As it cools, it becomes denser and floats deeper than the younger, less dense lithosphere at the ridge. The depth of this slab of lithosphere increases as it cools during its move away from the continuously forming ridge.

Other examples of spreading ridges across Earth's oceans include a zone between Antarctica and Australia, Africa and India, and a faster spreading rise in the eastern Pacific Ocean. How fast do the oceans spread? That depends on the location of the spreading zones.

The spreading rate of the Atlantic Ocean is 2 to 4 centimeters per year (about 1 to 2 inches per year). That won't affect the cost of an airplane ticket to Europe. The spreading rate in the eastern Pacific Ocean is much faster, on the average about 10 centimeters per year (or 4 inches per year). These rates are far less than snail paces. But consider the rates as operating over tens of millions of years. South America, Africa, and Antarctica were all joined as recently as about 200 million years ago.

▶ **Practice**

**1.** The discovery of how continents move came from geological studies of what area?
   **a.** of the Rocky Mountains
   **b.** of the Himalayan Mountains
   **c.** of the Atlantic Ocean
   **d.** of the Indian Ocean

**2.** Seafloor spreading is the term used for what process?
   **a.** the creation of new sea floor at mid-ocean ridges
   **b.** the creation of new sea floor as continental edges erode
   **c.** the lifting up of the sea floor from the underlying mantle
   **d.** the lifting up of the sea floor near the continents

**3.** Earth's magnetic field plays an important role in the theory of how continents move, because of which of the following facts?
   **a.** Molten magma comes up magnetized from the asthenosphere.
   **b.** Earth's field switches from normal to reversed and back again.
   **c.** The direction for the spreading of the sea floor follows the magnetic field.
   **d.** Continents act to create a magnetic tape in the mountains.

**4.** If the coasts of Africa and North Carolina, United States, are about 5,000 kilometers apart and have been spreading apart at a constant rate of 2.8 centimeters per year, how long ago were they joined as part of the same continent?

    **a.** 14 million years ago

    **b.** 18 million years ago

    **c.** 140 million years ago

    **d.** 180 million years ago

**5.** Which is NOT true?

    **a.** The lithosphere gets thicker as it moves away from a mid-ocean ridge.

    **b.** As magma turns to rock, it records Earth's magnetic field.

    **c.** The mid-ocean ridge is a bulge made by the two sides of the ocean moving together.

    **d.** Alfred Wegener developed the theory of drifting continents from looking at the shapes of South America and Africa.

## ▶ Subduction Zones

If the Pacific Ocean has an ocean ridge with spreading sea floor and so does the Atlantic, then something major is amiss. All the oceans cannot be growing and also moving the continents around. North America cannot be moving westward and eastward at the same time.

It turns out that the Pacific Ocean is not growing. In fact, the Pacific Ocean is shrinking as the Atlantic Ocean grows. This shrinking occurs despite the fact that the Pacific Ocean has a spreading ridge in its eastern portion. The key is that the Pacific Ocean, unlike the Atlantic Ocean, has what are called *subduction zones* at its far eastern and western sides.

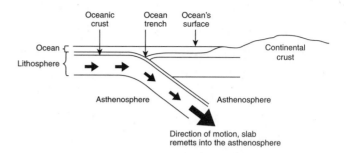

Figure 5.2 A typical subduction zone, where the lithosphere sinks back down into the asthenosphere of the mantle

Subduction zones are places where the ocean's floor dives downward and disappears back into Earth's deep mantle, remelting in the asthenosphere. In the Pacific Ocean, subduction zones occur both along the coast of South America and across Japan. Such places of downward diving of the ocean's floor are another important feature in the grand theory of plate tectonics. Study Figure 5.2 to see how a subduction zone works.

Because the earth is a constant size, it must be true overall that the net creation of ocean floor must balance its destruction in the subduction zones. What happens to the ocean's crust and lithosphere in the subduction zone? Recall from Lesson 4 that the boundary between the lithosphere and asthenosphere is usually about 100 kilometers. That's the depth at which the rock grows hot enough to become plastic, or able to flow like silly putty over very long time periods. The subducting lithosphere—called a *subducting slab*—goes downward and gets hotter and hotter. Eventually, it rejoins the material of the asthenosphere in the deep mantle.

What drives the subducting ocean slabs downward? As noted, the moving slabs of lithosphere cool and thicken as they spread away from the hot mid-ocean ridges. Cooler rock is more dense. Eventually, it can become dense enough to start sinking downward. It's like when you are floating on your back on the surface of a pool or lake and you let out the air from your lungs. Your body becomes more dense, and you start to sink.

In the subduction zones, we find the deepest parts of the ocean. For example, at the *Mariana Trench* in the western Pacific Ocean near the island of Guam, the ocean is more than 11 kilometers deep, almost three times the average depth of the world's oceans. Such depths are created by the subducting slabs, because the ocean's floor is literally going down.

Because new ocean floor is continually being formed and then subducted, the ocean's floor has a limited lifetime. In fact, the average age of the oldest ocean floor is about 100 million years. The Atlantic Ocean, as we said earlier, is almost twice that age, but the Mid-Atlantic Ridge is a particularly slow spreading center.

## ▶ Practice

6. Ocean floor dives downward and disappears into the mantle at what points?
   a. subduction zones
   b. mid-ocean ridges
   c. continental coasts
   d. tectonic rifts

7. Because the Pacific Ocean is shrinking in size, which of the following can we say about the Pacific's geology that is relevant to the shrinking?
   a. Its mid-ocean ridges are stronger than its subduction zones.
   b. Its subduction zones are further away from its ridges than in the Atlantic Ocean.
   c. Its subduction zones are closer to its ridges than in the Atlantic Ocean.
   d. Its subduction zones are stronger than its mid-ocean ridges.

8. In a subduction zone, which is NOT true?
   a. The slab heads toward the mantle.
   b. The subducting slab is very dense.
   c. Asthenosphere becomes lithosphere.
   d. The slab is thicker than it was at the mid-ocean ridge.

9. The deep ocean trenches are found where?
   a. mid-ocean ridges
   b. volcanic vents
   c. subduction zones
   d. sites of warmest waters

10. The subducting slab essentially ends its journey at what depth?
    a. 10 meters
    b. 10 kilometers
    c. 100 meters
    d. 100 kilometers

## ▶ Continental Plates

We can now put the entire story together in the theory of plate tectonics. By the way, the word *tectonics* comes from the ancient Greek word *tekton*, for *builder* or *carpenter*. Thus, the theory of plate tectonics is how the plates build the earth's surface.

What are these plates? The plates are the slabs of lithosphere that float on top of the asthenosphere, like

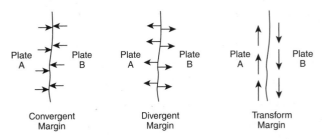

Figure 5.3 There are three main types of edges between Earth's plates.

rafts of plywood that completely cover a pool of water. Imagine now that the rafts of plywood have some blocks of foam in their middles or at the edges—those are the continents. Now also imagine that in some places, new wood is being added to the edges of the plywood rafts—those places are the mid-ocean ridges. Now imagine that at some edges, one sheet of plywood is curved downward and is diving underneath another—those are the subduction zones.

The plywood rafts are Earth's tectonic plates. About a half dozen or so are large ones, and quite a few are smaller ones. Note that sometimes, the plates are called *continental plates*, even though they include the portions of the plates that have huge portions of ocean as well.

The situation of the earth's plates has been likened to the shell of an egg, all cracked into zones. But you never actually see the egg inside. Similarly, with all the motions of the earth's plates described in the section on seafloor spreading and subduction zones, we never see directly into the earth. In the way that the eggshell covers the egg, the plates completely cover the earth's inside. But unlike the static, unmoving pieces of eggshell, the earth's plates, as we have seen, are dynamic. They grow and shrink, like the rafts of plywood imagined in the previous paragraph.

In the theory of plate tectonics, the key parts are the plates themselves. The ocean basin and continents (as parts of the plates) are along for the rides as portions of the motions of the plates. As the Atlantic Ocean grows because the sea floor is spreading at the Mid-Atlantic Ridge, North America moves westward because North America is on the same plate as the western half of the Atlantic Ocean.

Indeed, in the theory of plate tectonics, the edge of two of the plates runs down the north–south mid-dle of the Atlantic Ocean. Thus, you can see that the edges of plates do not necessarily coincide with the edges of oceans *or* continents. Of course, in some places, there is coincidence between the edge of a plate and the edge of a continent. One example is the western coast of South America. But such a match is not always the case because the eastern edge of the United States is not the plate boundary, which is found in the middle of the Atlantic Ocean, as we have seen.

In the theory of plate tectonics, three different types of edges are possible where one plate meets another. The edges are called *margins*. We have already seen two different types of margins. The third type will be briefly noted to end this lesson. Here are the three types of margins:

1. **Divergent margins**. These are spreading centers, such as the Mid-Atlantic Ridge, which result in seafloor spreading. Though spreading centers occur in oceans when they are mature, they begin under continents. The material under continents can become so hot that the continents rupture and start to split. An ocean can be born. Some believe that the Red Sea might eventually become a new ocean, because it split about 30 million years ago. Or this divergent margin could just fizzle out as an ocean starts at some other divergent margin on Earth.

2. **Convergent margins**. Two basic types of convergent margins exist. We have already seen one type: subduction zones. The second type will be described more in the next lesson. This second type is called the *collision margin* and results in the uplifting of great mountain ranges.

**3. Transform margins.** In transform margins, plate edges are neither moving apart as in divergent margins nor moving together as in convergent margins. Instead, in transform margins, the two plates are sliding past each other. As they slide, they grind one against the other, causing earthquakes. The most famous transform margin is the San Andreas fault in California, which runs approximately north–south. The city of Los Angles lies on the west side of the transform margin and is moving north. The city of San Francisco lies on the east side of the margin and is moving south. In about ten million years, the two cities will be next to each other.

## ▶ Practice

**11.** In the theory of plate tectonics, the net amount of subduction equals the net amount of seafloor spreading, because of which of the following facts?
   **a.** The 5,000 K temperature of Earth's core makes this fact so.
   **b.** Earth's surface must remain the same size and thus in balance.
   **c.** Heat comes up, not down, from the deeper mantle.
   **d.** Transform margins are available to make up any difference.

**12.** Which type of margin initially begins under a continent?
   **a.** convergent margin
   **b.** transform margin
   **c.** subduction margin
   **d.** divergent margin

**13.** Which is NOT true about the Earth's plates?
   **a.** Interactions occur at the edges.
   **b.** Some plates have both subduction zones and seafloor spreading.
   **c.** The edge of South America cannot be the edge of a plate.
   **d.** The edge of the plate that includes North America is in the middle of the Atlantic Ocean.

**14.** Which type of margin causes earthquakes in California?
   **a.** convergent margin
   **b.** transform margin
   **c.** subduction margin
   **d.** divergent margin

**15.** In the analogy between plate tectonics and either the eggshell of an egg or the rafts of plywood on water, which is true?
   **a.** The rafts are like the plates.
   **b.** The plate edges are the meetings of eggshell and egg.
   **c.** The cracked eggshell is more dynamic than Earth's plates.
   **d.** The eggshell is like the continents.

LESSON

# 6 ▶ Earthquakes, Volcanoes, and Mountains

## LESSON SUMMARY

The key to the workings of earthquakes, volcanoes, and mountains is the theory of plate tectonics. Most of the action occurs at the edges of plates, the margins at which they slide, bump, and collide. What causes earthquakes and volcanoes? How are mountains made?

## ▶ Earthquakes

Almost a million people died in China during an earthquake in 1556. An earthquake in Iran in 1990 killed 50,000. As the entire world recently witnessed in helpless dismay, more than 100,000 died in Indonesia and India from a tsunami started by the huge earthquake of December 2004. All told, about a million people have been killed just in the last 100 years from sudden shifts in the earth's plates.

With earthquakes, it's not a matter of *if* but *when*, because Earth's geological plates are in motion. In fact, hundreds of small earthquakes occur every day, but most are measurable only by seismographs. Less frequently occur medium-size ones; and very infrequently, the big ones strike.

Why do earthquakes take place where they do? The key to the answer lies along the margins of geologic plates. In Lesson 4, we discussed the San Andreas Fault, a crack along the transform margin between two plates that happen to meet in California. These plates slide past each other, causing earthquakes. In 1906, a large earthquake along the San Andreas Fault destroyed most of San Francisco.

Earthquakes occur along the other types of margins, too. We don't worry too much about earthquakes from a diverging margin of a mid-ocean ridge, because they occur deep under water and too far away and they are smaller. But dangerous earthquakes can occur along convergent margins, when plates are colliding or one is subducting under the other.

Long ago, before the theory of plate tectonics presented a global explanation for earthquakes, geologists recognized a Pacific *Ring of Fire*. Roughly, a ring of fire exists around the outer edge of the Pacific Ocean, a ring where huge numbers of earthquakes and volcanoes occur. Why? The Pacific Ring of Fire occurs because the Pacific Ocean is ringed by many plate edges, and because earthquakes and volcanoes tend to occur at the boundaries between two plates. Japan, for example, sits on the Ring of Fire and has a boundary between two plates passing right through the country. Plate boundaries around the Pacific Ocean occur at the edge of North America, the Kamchatka Peninsula of Russia, Japan, Indonesia, and New Zealand.

The main concept behind the dynamics of earthquakes is the following. As plates move against each other (either along a transform margin or along a convergent margin), the friction between them often locks the edges together, even though the main bulk of the plate has shifted its position ever so slightly.

For example, press down with your fingers on the table with enough friction so that as you also try and slide them across the table, the friction holds your fingers in place. But as you apply more and more horizontal force, eventually your fingers jump ahead, often in little leaping steps.

Earthquakes are caused when plates that have been locked together suddenly overcome the tension (or compression) that has built up between them and they jerk ahead in whatever direction was being forced by plate tectonics. If the jerking steps are small, the earthquakes are small. If the steps are large, the earth-

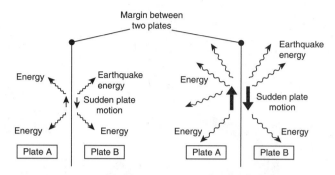

Figure 6.1 Earthquakes and plate movements. Small, sudden steps in the motion along a plate boundary result in small earthquakes. Large steps create large earthquakes. This diagram shows steps along a transform margin (or edge), but earthquakes also occur along the other kinds of plate margins, too.

quakes are, too. Earthquakes are thus releases of stored energy (like a spring) from the rocks at the edges of continental plates. On Earth's surface, these plate boundaries form faults, or fractures, in the rock. That is why the line along which earthquakes occur in California is called the San Andreas Fault.

The standard scale to measure the strength of earthquakes is the *Richter scale*. The Richter scale converts the readings that seismographs make of seismic waves into a number representing a measure of the amount of energy released by the earthquake. Each number grade in the Richter scale, from 1 to 10, represents an earthquake that is 30 times larger in terms of energy than the preceding number represented.

Rock has limits in how much energy can be stored in the locked plate edges before the friction gives way and the energy is released in the movement that creates an earthquake. These limits might be the reason why the largest earthquakes measured are about 8.6 on the Richter scale. This is the energy of 10,000 Hiroshima-size nuclear bombs and is about the magnitude of the Indonesian earthquake of December 2004.

When earthquakes occur in the shallow ocean or near the coast, the heaving of the crust can create a *tsunami* in the ocean, a giant wave. This giant wave is really a wall of water, very unlike a regular ocean wave, that travels across the ocean and can devastate coastlines when it breaks on shore.

Much of the danger that earthquakes pose come from tsunamis and from buildings that collapse on people, who usually have no warning. It is obviously necessary to have strong but flexible architecture. For example, earthquake-prone Japan has strict laws for designing buildings, to make them resistant to earthquakes. The need to predict earthquakes is the main reason for the global network of seismographs and seismologists, as an increase in activity of small earthquakes often precedes a large earthquake. This, however, is not always the case.

## ▶ Practice

**1.** Of the different kinds of margins (edges) between plates, which kind is usually of least concern for humans?
   **a.** collision margin
   **b.** subduction zone
   **c.** mid-ocean ridge
   **d.** transform margin

**2.** If one earthquake measures 3 on the Richter scale and another earthquake is Richter 5, how much larger is the second earthquake, compared to the first?
   **a.** 900 times
   **b.** 30 times
   **c.** 100 times
   **d.** 2 times

**3.** What country or state was devastated by an earthquake in December 2004?
   **a.** Kenya
   **b.** Iran
   **c.** Alaska
   **d.** Indonesia

**4.** What type of motion between plates best describes what is happening to rocks on two sides of a plate boundary during earthquakes?
   **a.** cycles
   **b.** flows
   **c.** jerks
   **d.** rises

**5.** People are killed by earthquakes primarily because of what?
   **a.** poisonous gases are released
   **b.** the ground shakes violently
   **c.** buildings collapse
   **d.** roads are tossed and twisted

## ▶ Volcanoes

Most of the world's volcanoes are found at the margins of geologic plates. An enormous amount of heat is created by the friction that is generated when the subducting slabs of the lithosphere descend into the mantle. Plumes of magma rise up toward the surface in these subduction zones, forming volcanoes at the edges of continents and arcs of volcanic islands in the ocean.

Important to the study of volcanoes are the terms *magma* and *lava*. Magma is molten rock under the earth's surface, and it is magma that rises up to form the mid-ocean ridges of seafloor spreading centers. Indeed, the mid-ocean ridges are underwater chains of volcanoes.

Magma also exists in chambers under the continents, in places where pressure from the hot, deep Earth's astheosphere below pushes up rock toward the surface. Even before it gets to the surface, the reduced pressure (from the reduced amount of overlying rock) allows the rock to melt. This often forms chambers of magma, awaiting release through volcanoes. When the magma reaches the surface and flows out, it becomes what is known as lava.

One of the most famous places for lava, because the public can view it in action, is the big island of Hawaii in the Hawaiian chain of islands (Maui, Kauai, and others). On the big island of Hawaii, in Volcanoes National Park, vents open up and release lava, which flows down, sometimes destroying property but also literally creating new land when the lava solidifies into rock. Two giant mountains on the island (Moana Loa and Moana Kea) have been built over many thousands of years of nearly continuous volcanic activity.

The Hawaiian Islands, of course, extend below the surface of the water all the way down to the bottom of the ocean. They have been formed by a conduit within the earth that brings magma up from the deep mantle. Remarkably, as the tectonic plate that covers a large portion of the Pacific Ocean has moved westward in its course over many millions of years, this conduit (called a *hotspot*) has remained essentially in the same place relative to the mantle below. That is why the youngest of the Hawaiian Islands, the big island of Hawaii, is in the eastern part of the chain. Further west about 50 miles, the island Maui grew and was volcanically active about a million years ago. Another 100 miles or so west, lies the even older island of Kauai, which was volcanically active five million years ago.

The Hawaiian Islands support the theory of plate tectonics. As the Pacific Plate slid from east to west over what geologists now call the Hawaiian hotspot, the Hawaiian Islands have been formed, one by one. Millions of years from now, new islands will have emerged even further to the east. Many hotspots exist all around the world, often forming chains of islands. These hotspots provide important clues to the directions and speeds of the tectonic plates.

The volcanoes of the Hawaiian Islands are called *shield volcanoes*. These do not explode in the way, for instance, that Mount Saint Helens did in its massive eruption of 1980. Instead, shield volcanoes are built gradually, as lava flows out, sometimes at the top, often at the sides, but through various vents. The slopes of the sides of shield volcanoes are relatively gentle, usually about 5° near the top and 10° on the lower sides, somewhat like an inverted kitchen saucer.

In contrast, *stratovolcanoes* are gently sloped on the lower sides, perhaps 8°, and become steeper and steeper toward the summit, which sometimes has a slope as steep as 30 to 40°. One famous stratovolcano is Mount Fuji in Japan, probably the world's most photogenic volcano. The United States has many stratovolcanoes, primarily located in the active range of volcanic mountains near the Pacific Northwest coast. Examples include Mount Rainer, Mount Baker, and the famous Mount Saint Helens.

The shield volcanoes of Hawaii tend to be nonexplosive, even though individual eruptions can be quite violent to our human eyes. But compare the slow outflow of lava in Hawaii to the 1980 blast from Mount Saint Helens, which within a minute, took off 500 meters of the mountain's top, sent a column of hot ash into the stratosphere, killed trees within a radius of 20 miles, and killed 63 people who were simply in the wrong place at the wrong time.

An even larger eruption of a stratovolcano occurred in 1883, on the island of Krakatau, killing 36,000 people, primarily from the tsunami that resulted. So much material (dust and sulfuric gases) was put into the atmosphere that the earth's climate was globally cooler by about 1° F for the next year, and sunsets became more intense for months all over the world.

At the tops of volcanoes, in particular stratovolcanoes, are depressions called *calderas*. Calderas form when material that has built up slowly over time plugs the volcano. Pressure builds up inside and the volcano explodes and forms a depression, like a cup, at the summit. Calderas can sometimes be huge. For example, the famous, picturesque Crater Lake in Oregon is a caldera that is now filled with water. That caldera resulted from a giant explosion more than 6,000 years ago.

If lava comes from a shield volcano, what is the material that explodes from a stratovolcano? In a stratovolcano, gases burst out, as do hot pieces of magma in various sizes that have been suddenly shot up into the atmosphere. The large ones can fall like bombs close to the volcano; the smallest ones become ash high in the atmosphere. These fragments of magma are called *pyroclasts*. When tremendous amounts of pyroclasts explode out and form a giant wall of material that rumbles down the sides of the volcano, we witness what is known as a *pyroclastic flow*. One famous disaster of volcanic poisonous gases and a pyroclastic flow buried the Italian coastal city of Pompeii and in the year A.D. 79 from an eruption of Mount Vesuvius.

Volcanologists study the chemistry of the material that comes from volcanoes and have discovered that significant variability exists in the key component called *silica* (a combination of the elements silicon and oxygen). Silica affects the viscosity, which is the fluidity. Lower amounts of silica are one factor that creates magmas with a lower viscosity. High temperatures, too, create magmas of lower viscosity. *Viscosity* can be thought of as the liquidity of a liquid. For example, water has a relatively low viscosity, compared to the high viscosity of molasses.

Magma with lower viscosity tends to result in eruptions of lava that are nonexplosive, creating volcanoes that are shield volcanoes, like the Hawaiian Islands. In contrast, higher viscosity magma, which

also usually has slightly lower temperatures, tends to build up and then explode in eruptions of pyroclasts from stratovolcanoes.

## ▶ Practice

**6.** The Hawaiian Islands are NOT an example of which one of the following?
   **a.** shield volcanoes
   **b.** a plate moving over a hotspot
   **c.** stratovolcanoes
   **d.** lava flows

**7.** The difference between lava and magma is which one of the following?
   **a.** Lava comes from stratovolcanoes.
   **b.** Lava is hotter.
   **c.** Magma creates pyroclastic flows.
   **d.** Magma is deeper.

**8.** Crater Lake in Oregon is an example of which one of the following?
   **a.** shield volcano
   **b.** stratovolcano
   **c.** caldera
   **d.** pyroclast cup

**9.** Lava will flow more if it has what characteristics?
   **a.** low temperature and high silica
   **b.** low temperature and low silica
   **c.** high temperature and high silica
   **d.** high temperature and low silica

**10.** When Mount Saint Helens exploded, you would best guess that the eruption resulted in which of the following?

    **a.** a new hotspot

    **b.** a pyroclastic flow

    **c.** global warming

    **d.** a tsunami

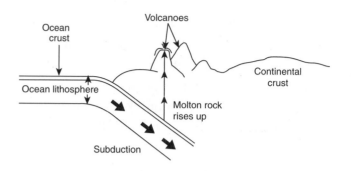

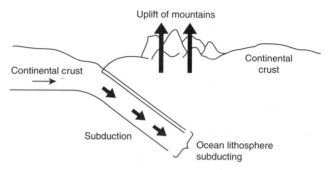

Figure 6.2 Collision margins and mountain building. On the top, a subduction collision margin, when ocean crust subducts under a continent at the edge of a plate. Mountains are born from the resulting volcanism. On the bottom, a continental collision margin raises mountains when two pieces of continental crust collide.

## ► Mountains

As we have seen in Lessons 4 and 5, continents are part of the crust but are much thicker than the crust of the ocean floor. Furthermore, the crustal material that makes continents is much lighter than the oceanic crust. Continental material forms when relatively light magma bursts from below to the surface, solidifying as rock. Later, this is sometimes reworked into sedimentary and metamorphic rocks (see Lesson 7).

Plate movements that rub bits of crust together can cause continents to grow as the lightest, most buoyant material ends up staying on the surface. Thus, continents have generally been growing throughout time because once the light rock reaches the surface, it tends to stay there. Unlike the oceanic crust, which is about 200 million years old at most (because it continues to go back down into subduction zones), continents can contain rocks that are billions of years old. Rocks in parts of Canada, for example, are more than three billion years old.

Wind and water *erode* the continents, attacking the highest lands and carrying sediments into the ocean. These sediments tend to stay on the parts of the continental crust that are underwater, the *continental shelves* (see Lesson 14). So erosion takes from the highlands and gives to the lowlands. Without other forces that lift the land up, the continents would be extremely flat.

The forces of continental uplift are the forces that make mountains. What are they? Volcanoes are one answer, because some volcanoes are mountains. Many mountain systems of the world have formed when volcanism proceeded over great areas and over long periods of time.

When ocean crust of one plate subducts under a continent that sits at the edge of another plate, it is called a *subduction collision margin*. Mountains are born from the resulting volcanism; they appear in giant arcs on the continent above the subducting ocean crust, which becomes intensely hot and melts as it descends into the mantle. The molten rock, as pressurized liquid, pushes up into the volcanic range of mountains.

An example of an impressive mountain range formed by this subduction collision margin is the

Andes Range, along the western coast of South America. Another example is the Cascade Range of the northwest U.S. coast.

But other kinds of mountains are not volcanic—the Himalayas, for example. How did the Himalayas form? What about other nonvolcanic systems of mountains? The answer, again, mostly involves the margins of the geological plates.

The Himalayas have formed as a result of the type of a convergent plate margin called a *continental collision margin*, or *continental collision zone*. In this type of collision, one plate with ocean crust subducts under another. But continental crust is also carried on the same plate as the one with the ocean crust that is subducting. The continental crust, being lighter than the ocean crust that is going down, cannot also go down. It smashes into the continental crust of the other plate. Thus, two masses of continental crust smash into each other. The result is a huge uplift, a massive system of mountains.

In the case of the Himalayas, they began when the plate that carried the land that is now most of India collided with the plate that had the continental crust that is today's Tibet. That was about 40 million years ago. By 20 million years ago, serious uplift of Tibet had begun, resulting in the tallest mountain range on Earth.

Another example of a mountain range formed by a continental collision zone is the mighty Alps in Europe. Yes, another example is the Appalachians, in the eastern United States. The Appalachians? The mountains of Smoky Mountain National Park in North Carolina, a part of the Appalachian chain, are very pretty mountains, but they are no towering Alps or Himalayas. What is their story?

A very long time ago, the Appalachians, it turns out, were like the Himalayas. They were lifted by collision activities around 400 million years ago. That occurred during a closure of a prior "Atlantic" Ocean, which created a gigantic supercontinent called *Pangaea*

by geologists. Then, when Pangaea split about 200 million years ago, today's Atlantic Ocean started to form (which is widening year by year, as we have seen). Erosion by wind and water has taken the Appalachians down to a height that is perhaps a third of their former glory 400 million years ago. The Urals in eastern Europe are another example of a relatively humble mountain range that had been formed in a very ancient continental collision margin.

## ▶ Practice

**11.** Which pair of mountain ranges was formed from subduction collision margins, and are therefore partially volcanic?
   **a.** Himalayas and Andes
   **b.** Cascades and Alps
   **c.** Alps and Himalayas
   **d.** Cascades and Andes

**12.** Which of the following is NOT true?
   **a.** All oceanic crust rock is younger than the oldest continental rocks.
   **b.** Some oceanic crust rock is older than the oldest continental rocks.
   **c.** Oceanic crust rock is more dense than continental rocks.
   **d.** Some oceanic crust rock is more dense than continental rocks.

**13.** The Appalachian Mountains are lower than the Himalayan Mountains because of which of the following?
   **a.** They are younger.
   **b.** Their uplift was not as great.
   **c.** They are older.
   **d.** They have had more subduction.

**14.** Which of the following mountains resulted from a continental collision zone about 400 million years ago?

a. Alps

b. Appalachians

c. Himalayas

d. Cascades

**15.** Mount Everest is about 29,000 feet high. If it has been uplifting as part of the Himalayan mountain range for about 20 million years, calculate how many inches per year of uplift has occurred.

a. 12

b. 1.4

c. 20

d. $\frac{2}{100}$

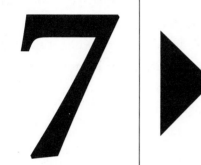

# Types of Rocks

## LESSON SUMMARY

The dynamic earth churns new matter up to its surface and returns other matter back down to the mantle. Through all this activity, including through the actions of water and wind as well as deposition of sediments to form new types of rock, continents are created and changed. Continents are, in essence, made of rock, spanning a scale of sizes from dust particles to mountains and the underlying bedrock of the continental masses themselves. Here we look into the science of rock.

## ▶ Elements, Minerals, and Rocks

Different elements exist because of the different kinds of atoms that can be made from the same basic three atomic building blocks. *Atoms* are the most finely divisible parts of matter that possess the characteristics of a particular element—elements such as copper, gold, carbon, or hydrogen. Atoms *alone* (not in molecules or ions) are electrically neutral and contain equal amounts of positive and negative electrical charges. The positive charge is concentrated in a tiny central massive region called the *nucleus*. The negative charge is in one or more tiny *electrons* (the first of the atomic building blocks). Electrons whirr around the nucleus, bound to it by electrical attraction.

The nucleus of atoms contains *protons* and *neutrons*, which are the other two atomic building blocks. Protons are the carriers of the positive charge. Neutrons, as their name suggests, are neutral. Now, all the atoms of a particular element have the same number of protons in their nuclei (which determine the charge of the nucleus, thus the number of electrons around the nucleus, and thus the chemistry of the element). But atoms of the same element can vary in the number of neutrons in their nuclei. These variants are called *isotopes* and will be discussed more in other lessons in this book. In summary, the atoms of elements are made from the atomic building blocks of protons, neutrons, and electrons.

Table 7.1 outlines the amounts of different kinds of elements in Earth's continental crust.

Table 7.1 Elements in the continental crust

| ELEMENT | PERCENT OF THE CONTINENTAL CRUST |
|---------|----------------------------------|
| Oxygen | 45.2% |
| Silicon | 27.2% |
| Aluminum | 8% |
| Iron | 5.8% |
| Calcium | 5.06% |
| Magnesium | 2.77% |
| Sodium | 2.32% |
| Potassium | 1.68% |
| Titanium | 0.86% |
| Hydrogen | 0.14% |
| Manganese | 0.10% |
| Phosphorus | 0.10% |
| All the others | 0.77% |

*98% of all rock* (handwritten annotation bracketing Oxygen through Potassium)

Note that nearly $\frac{3}{4}$ of Earth's rock is oxygen and silicon. Furthermore, the top eight elements (down to and including potassium) make up 98% of all rock. What is element number 3? Number 4? From the table, we know that rocks will be mostly oxygen and silicon, and we can surmise that differences between kinds of rock will be found in how the oxygen and silicon are arranged and what kinds of small amounts of other elements are in the rock. Is calcium and manganese there? Is iron and phosphorus there?

This discussion already assumes that rocks are made of several elements. Note that it is rare to find elements by themselves, such as a vein of pure gold. We don't dig up elements as pure veins of calcium or aluminum, for example. So to understand more about the structure of rocks, we have to review a bit of chemistry.

The *science of chemistry* studies the interactions of atoms, how they form molecules, and the interactions of those molecules. *Molecules* range from simple ions, such as sodium dissolved in seawater, to complex organic molecules of life, such as proteins and lipids. The key concept in how atoms form molecules is the *atomic bond*, that is, the connection that joins atoms into molecules.

The atomic bond occurs between electrons of atoms. For example, electrons can be shared in what is called a *covalent bond*. In another type of bond, called the *ionic bond*, electrons are taken from one atom and are joined to another. The bonds between metals, say in copper or gold, are unique and are named the *metallic bond*. Whatever it is that allows certain types of bonds to form between particular kinds of atoms has to do with the number of electrons the atoms of an element possess. And, as we have seen, the number of electrons depends on the number of protons in the nucleus of an atom of an element. So the bonds among atoms in molecules depend directly on the atomic structure of the atoms.

Now, even though we have been discussing the fact that rocks are made of elements, an intermediate level of organization is crucial to the study of rock. In that level, we find what are called *minerals*. Geology is mainly concerned with the broad type of molecular organization of minerals. Minerals are always larger than a single molecule. Indeed, crucial to the existence of minerals is that they have crystalline structure. Having a crystalline structure means that the atoms create a network of repeating units, a crystal.

Common table salt is an excellent example of a crystal. The salt crystal is a network (or lattice) of sodium and chlorine atoms. Many types of crystals exist, and the terminology and geometry can get quite complex. These topics won't concern us here. Just be aware that rocks are made of minerals, and that minerals are solids made of certain elements drawn from the list of elements in Earth's crust. Minerals have specific chemical compositions and have crystal structures.

Now let's return to the fact that the two most abundant elements are oxygen and silicon. Silicon and oxygen alone can form the mineral called quartz. The chemical formula of quartz is $SiO_2$. It has one atom of silicon (Si) and two atoms of oxygen (O). Of course, this basic unit of $SiO_2$ is linked with others of the same formula to create the gorgeous crystals of quartz we have all seen.

Many other minerals are combinations of silicon and oxygen along with other elements. In general, these minerals are *silicon oxides*, also known as *silicates*. Other elements join in to create different kinds of silicates, such as magnesium–iron silicates, magnesium–aluminum silicates, and so forth. Geologists have given the most common minerals names. Perhaps you have heard, for instance, of *feldspar*. The chemical formula for the abundant mineral called feldspar is $KAlSi_3O_8$. It has one atom of potassium (K), one atom of aluminum (Al), three atoms of silicon (Si), and eight atoms of oxygen (O). If you are shown the chemical formula for a mineral and know the symbols for the different elements in the formula, you should be able to say how many atoms of each element are in the basic molecular unit of the mineral. (As an example of a symbol, the chemical symbol for magnesium is Mg.) We just went through an example for feldspar.

Geologists have developed ways to tell minerals apart by classifying them according to a number of basic properties. Here is the classic list of the basic properties of minerals used in geology.

## Properties of Minerals

- **Cleavage**. In what preferred direction does the mineral break?
- **Luster**. Is the surface of the mineral polished, glassy, or oily?
- **Color and streak**. When the mineral is rubbed on an unglazed porcelain plate, what is its color? (This can be quite different from the color of the mineral itself.)
- **Density and specific gravity**. How heavy is the mineral, compared to water of the same volume?
- **Hardness**. What is the mineral's number on the Mohs scale of hardness? Diamond, of course, is the most hard, with number 10. Talc is the softest, with number 1 on the scale. Here are other examples: Calcite has hardness 3, and quartz has hardness 7. Hardness is found by finding out what the mineral can and cannot scratch. Can it scratch glass (between 5 and 6)? Can it scratch a copper penny (between 3 and 4)? A fingernail (between 2 and 3)?

Mineralogists know of about 3,600 different minerals. Are minerals the same as rocks? We are almost at the end of our story that has gone from atomic building blocks, to atoms of elements, to bonds between atoms, to molecules, and to minerals. Yes, rocks can be pure minerals, but that is rare. It is always a treat for geologists in the field to find a rock that is a pure mineral, say a large chunk of quartz. But more often, rocks are made of many minerals. A rock will generally be a mixture of small particles of different minerals (which can be seen by the eye or better with a magnifying glass). Thus, a rock can contain quartz as one of its minerals. Rocks are assemblages of minerals. After the practice questions, we will take up the question of different types of rocks.

## ▶ Practice

1. Which of the following are the two most abundant elements in Earth's crust?
   a. silicon and iron
   b. oxygen and calcium
   c. calcium and iron
   d. oxygen and silicon

2. Here is the chemical formula for the basic molecular unit of the mineral called olivine: $Mg_2SiO_4$. How many atoms are in the mineral's basic molecular unit?
   a. 7
   b. 5
   c. 2
   d. 1

3. The technique of rubbing a mineral on an unglazed porcelain plate is used to tell about what property of a mineral?
   a. streak
   b. luster
   c. hardness
   d. cleavage

4. An example of a network made of exactly repeating basic parts is called which of the following?
   a. atom
   b. molecule
   c. crystal
   d. rock

5. Which is true about the numbers of parts in an atom?
   a. Electrons equal neutrons.
   b. Protons equal neutrons.
   c. Protons equal electrons.
   d. Nuclei equal electrons.

## ▶ Igneous, Sedimentary, and Metamorphic Rocks

Three main types of rocks are recognized by geologists: igneous, sedimentary, and metamorphic. We will begin with igneous, because all rock is born, so to speak, as igneous rock.

*Igneous rock* is rock that was once very hot and molten (think "ignition"). Molten magma from under the earth's surface, when it cools and solidifies, becomes igneous rock (intrusive igneous rock). So does lava that flows or erupts from volcanoes (extrusive igneous rock). As we have seen, the ocean's crust emerges from volcanism at the mid-ocean ridges, so the ocean's floor is mostly igneous rock (the exception is the sediments that fall on to the ocean's floor). Importantly, most (95%) of Earth's continental crust is igneous rock although very little of it is exposed at the surface.

Types of igneous rock include granite, rhyolite, gabbro, and basalt. These and others are all different kinds of silicates and can be classified into types by how much silica are in them (as well as other properties). The discussion of these types and how they are formed can get complex (and are still debated by geologists!), so we will pass that issue by. But you will recall from the previous lesson that the less silica a magma or lava has in it, the less viscous the molten rock is.

Like all rocks, igneous rocks have crystals of minerals. However, in the case of igneous rocks, the crystals form when the magma cools to become rock. One important concept regarding crystal sizes in the igneous rocks should be noted: The slower the cooling, the larger the crystals. Therefore, crystals are larger in intrusive igneous rocks.

Logically, the next type of rock to discuss is *sedimentary rock*, because sedimentary rocks form when other rocks have been physically or chemically broken down and deposited as sediments. The sediments, usually in the shallow waters of continental shelves, get piled up more and more over time. The sediment load can get heavy, even pushing the edge of the continent crust downward, allowing the buildup of more sediments on top. Eventually, the pressure can get so great that the sediments are fused into solid rock. Sedimentary rock is basically recycled rock, and is formed at temperatures and pressures near those at the surface of the earth.

If sedimentary rocks form primarily underwater, why is it that substantial portions of the land area of the United States are made of sedimentary rock? Also, consider the fact that sedimentary rock is found 5 miles high in the Himalayan mountains. Indeed, if we consider the surface of the earth, it turns out that 75% of all rock at the surface is sedimentary and only 25% is igneous. In these numbers, geologists include the third type of rock, *metamorphic rock*, depending on whether the metamorphic rock was derived from sedimentary or igneous rock. (There will be more about that in a couple paragraphs.) Compare these numbers to the percentages for all rock in the crust: 95% igneous and 5% sedimentary. At the surface, the numbers are turned around. Thus, more of the rock exposed at the surface is sedimentary, even though most of crustal rock is igneous.

The secret to the abundance of sedimentary rock at the surface is, once again, plate tectonics. Tens of millions of years ago, plate tectonics smashed the once separate continent of India into what is now Tibet and lifted the Himalayas. Plate tectonics brings parts of continents that were formed underwater (sedimentary rock, in other words) to the surface. Finding a piece of shale (a common type of sedimentary rock) when you are hiking inland in the hills shows you that vast changes have taken place over hundred of millions of years.

Let us return to the part of the story in which pieces of sediment are moved from the continents to the oceans, to be deposited and eventually become sedimentary rock. Elements in these pieces are shifted from rock to the ocean by two different processes: physical weathering and chemical weathering. In *physical weathering*, particles of rock are sloughed off and transported by rivers to the ocean. Deposited in the ocean and eventually cemented together into rock, the particles create different kinds of rock, depending on the size of the particles. You can see this in Table 7.2.

The second way that matter is transported from continent to ocean is by *chemical weathering*. In chemical weathering, minerals are actually dissolved in water and transported as ions that are invisible to our eyes. Dissolved salt, for example, cannot be seen, even though sodium and chloride ions are dissolved in the water.

Very often, the dissolved ions are precipitated out from the water, creating deposits in the sediments on the ocean floor. Salt, for example, can come out from the seawater when the water in a lagoon evaporates away and leaves the salt. If this happens time after time, sedimentary rocks of the types called *halite* (salt) and *gypsum* (calcium sulfate) are formed.

Table 7.2   Particle size

Note: Some types of sedimentary rock are made from physical particles cemented together. This sequence progresses from course to fine particles.

| | |
|---|---|
| Conglomerate (from sedimented gravel) | Most course particles |
| Sandstone (from sedimented sand) | Course particles |
| Siltstone (from sedimented silt) | Fine particles |
| Shale (from sedimented mud) | Finest particles |

Life is a powerful force in precipitating dissolved elements from water and creating deposits of sediments. The most important of these sediments come from shells of creatures such as coral and certain single-cell organisms. Two types of sedimentary rock are made primarily from this biological precipitation: *limestone* (from the mineral calcite) and *dolostone* (from the mineral dolomite). Calcite and dolomite are calcium carbonate and calcium-magnesium carbonate, respectively. Thus, the shells were fused into rock. Examples of limestone are the white cliffs of Dover in England and much of Indiana, Illinois, and Florida.

Sedimentary rock is the kind of rock in which we find fossils, from ancient cells to dinosaurs. Sedimentary rock that contains fossils is called *fossilferous*. Our best current evidence for the origin of life comes from sedimentary rocks, formed 3.5 to 3.9 billion years ago. It must be so, because life began in the water; life needs water.

The third main type of rock is called *metamorphic*. Metamorphic rock, in a sense, is a recycled rock, too, but not in the direct way that sedimentary rock is. Metamorphic rock is created when either igneous, sedimentary, or other metamorphic rock is subjected to great heat and pressure and transformed (metamorphosed). How does this happen?

The simplest way is called *contact metamorphism*. Contact metamorphism occurs when magma intrudes into another rock, say a sedimentary rock. The places where the sedimentary rock touches the magma, which is itself now cooling into igneous rock, become so hot that they turn into metamorphic rock.

Another way to create metamorphic rock is by deep burial. Older rock can be covered by new rock and get deeper and deeper. The heat and pressure turns the deepest rock into metamorphic rock. One final way to create metamorphic rock takes place in mountain building during continental plate collisions. Sedimentary rock, for example, can be squeezed, twisted, and folded during the collision. So much heat and pressure occurs that the rock can be turned into metamorphic rock.

Table 7.3 offers a few examples of some of the most well-known kinds of metamorphic rock and the kind of rock from which the metamorphic rock was derived. Note that some kinds of metamorphic rocks are made from other metamorphic rocks!

Table 7.3  Metamorphic rocks

| ROCK FROM WHICH THE METAMORPHIC ROCK WAS DERIVED | | METAMORPHIC ROCK |
| --- | --- | --- |
| Shale (sedimentary) | → | Slate (metamorphic) |
| Slate (metamorphic) | → | Phyllite (metamorphic) |
| Phyllite (metamorphic) | → | Schist (metamorphic) |
| Sandstone (sedimentary) | → | Quartzite (metamorphic) |
| Limestone (sedimentary) | → | Marble (metamorphic) |
| Basalt (sedimentary) | → | Greenshist (metamorphic) |

## ▶ Practice

**6.** The sedimentary rock called conglomerate is made from cemented what?

   **a.** shells

   **b.** sand

   **c.** mud

   **d.** gravel

**7.** What is the secret to why so much sedimentary rock is found at Earth's surface?

   **a.** It formed underwater.

   **b.** It formed through extrusion.

   **c.** It formed during plate tectonics.

   **d.** It was fast cooling.

**8.** Which of the following is igneous rock?

   **a.** marble

   **b.** dolostone

   **c.** shale

   **d.** basalt

**9.** Geologists who seek evidence for origin of life on Earth will search in what kind of rock?

   **a.** igneous

   **b.** sedimentary

   **c.** basaltic

   **d.** metamorphic

**10.** The type of rock that forms at the point of contact where magma wells up and intrudes into another previous kind of rock is called what?

   **a.** sedimentary

   **b.** metamorphic

   **c.** fossiliferous

   **d.** igneous

LESSON

# 8 ▶ Dating the Earth

## LESSON SUMMARY

The earth, as we've seen, is about four and a half billion years old. Some rocks exist for all ages, except for the very oldest times. The geological cycles have created and destroyed mountains and even continents during the saga of plate tectonics, changing igneous rocks into sedimentary rocks, and both of those into metamorphic rocks, which in turn can again become sedimentary rocks. But how do we know about the ages of the continents, the mountains, and indeed the earth itself?

## ▶ Sedimentary Layers

The striking thing about sedimentary rock is that it often occurs in layers, which are called *beds* or strata by geologists. Sometimes, you see beds when a hill has been sliced through using dynamite so a road can pass. You can also see beds on a massive scale in the Grand Canyon where rock 2,000 meters thick was deposited, on and off, during an interval of 300 million years. Beds are the distinct layers of rock on a small scale. Often, in places such as the Grand Canyon, beds of a similar color and type of rock are built into even larger layers called *formations*. If beds are the layers of a layer cake, a formation is the cake itself.

Thus, beds are thinner than the formations as they make up the actual formations. Both beds and formations are types of *strata*, which is the general term used by geologists for the layers of rock. Igneous and metamorphic rock can occur in strata as well, such as when lava overflows a layer of sedimentary rock, adding a stratum (the singular of strata) of igneous rock to the sedimentary strata. The geological study of strata is called *stratigraphy*, and the scientists are called *stratigraphers*.

The first principle used by stratigraphers is what they call the *law of original horizontality*. This law applies to sedimentary rock layers, which for the most part, were formed when sediments were laid down under water. The seabed where the sediments are deposited is usually the shallow offshore area called the *continental shelf*, which is under water but actually part of the geology of continents. The continental shelf is nearly horizontal. In other cases, sedimentary rock was laid down when sea level was higher and there were large expanses of regions that are now land but which long ago were covered with a shallow sea. In the United States, for example, much of what is now Texas and Oklahoma was under water. Sediments deposited there were laid down horizontally as well.

Thus, according to the law of original horizontality, sedimentary rock began as horizontally deposited layers. That means that wherever we see sedimentary rock whose strata are tilted, we know that tremendous geological forces have been at work that raised up and tilted massive volumes of rock. Plate tectonics is such a force.

Another guiding scientific rule that is important to stratigraphers is the *principle of superposition*. This rule states that more recent (younger) sedimentary layers of rock were laid down on top of older layers. As you hike, for example, down into the Grand Canyon (whose layers are still fairly horizontal), you descend back in time as you go downward into the strata.

Of course, because of the mighty forces of plate tectonics, one must apply the principle of superposition with care. What if the strata are vertical? That means the layers have been tilted by 90°. Then which is the oldest? To the right or to the left? You cannot tell just from looking. Furthermore, because complete folding sometimes occurs in the layers, it is even possible for an older layer to now sit on top of a younger one. Imagine, for example, folding a sandwich in half. Assume you had originally layered the lettuce on top of the ham. In a portion of a folded sandwich, the lettuce is now under the ham.

To find younger layers completely under older ones is relatively rare. For the most part, the principle of superposition works fine, because rocks are tilted only slightly, or at least not up to 90° or completely over.

Another concern for stratigraphers is the concept of *conformity*. Conformity involves the following question: If you see strata, how continuous was their formation? In other words, do they represent an unbroken interval of deposition? If so, over how many thousands, millions, or hundreds of millions of years? Stratigraphers are excited to find a region of rock with a high degree of conformity, because then they can study an unbroken record of geological history.

However, numerous breaks can be found in the rock record of various regions of the world's strata. Such breaks in sedimentation are called *unconformities*, which are classified into three basic types. Study Figure 8.1 and then read the more detailed descriptions when you return to the text.

An *angular unconformity* occurs when a relatively horizontal stratum sits on top of a number of tilted strata, which seem to have been sliced off horizontally. What happened? At some point back in time, a formation of horizontal strata was tilted at angle. Then it was subjected to erosion, which wore it down across the layers. Next, it perhaps ended up again under water, at which time new layers of sediment were deposited. This situation results in what is known as an angular unconformity. A large interval of time passed between the deposition of the tilted layers and the deposition of the horizontal layer.

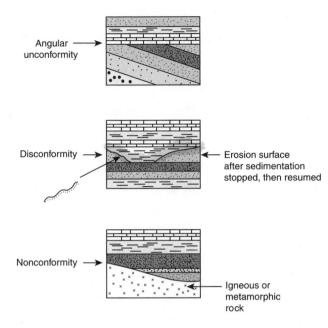

Figure 8.1 Three types of unconformities: angular unconformity, disconformity, and nonconformity

The second type of unconformity is called a *disconformity*. Nothing is very difficult about this type; sedimentation simply stopped for a long time interval and then resumed. For example, if the sea level falls (which happens, because of plate tectonics), the layers of sediment that had been under water will now be above water and will no longer be receiving what would have been their next bed of sediment. Then if the sea rises again, sedimentation resumes. The disconformity makes life tough for geologists, because they have no information about the missing interval of time.

A *nonconformity* is the third type of unconformity. A nonconformity has igneous or metamorphic rock underneath sedimentary strata. For example, as you go down deeper into the continents, what you tend to find is more and more igneous rock. The place where sedimentary rock ends and igneous rock begins is a nonconformity. You cannot tell exactly what happened at that spot and what the time interval was step by step like you can when the sediments have been laid down in conforming layers.

For another example of how nature creates a nonconformity, imagine underwater sedimentary strata that are then lifted up to become continental land. Next, volcanism spreads lava over the surface to form a thick layer of igneous rock. Eventually, the surface is again under water and new sedimentation begins on top of the igneous bed. That's a nonconformity. The sedimentation was not continuous.

Stratigraphers search across large geographical regions for what they call *correlations*. Correlations occur when a stratum of rock is clearly the same over hugely separated regions. If the geologists can figure out something about the stratum in one region—its age, for example—then they know the age of the stratum in other places. For example, over the last two million years, there have been widespread ash layers from tremendous volcanic explosions, which covered large regions of the western United States. Because the same ash layer is found in different places, and we know that the ash layer was deposited at the same time in all these places, we can use the ash layer to start unraveling the stratigraphic story at all the places just before and just after the eruption.

Another way to find correlations is to seek the same fossils in similar-looking beds of sedimentary rock. Particularly important to geologists are what is known as *index fossils*. A extinct ancient species can be an index fossil if the species was highly biologically distinctive (unique) and it existed on Earth for only a relatively brief and confined period of time. For example, assume it can be determined that a particular ancient species of trilobite (a crab-type creature) existed for only ten million years, say, from 500 to 490 million years ago. Then wherever you find rock with that species of trilobite, you know the rock's approximate age.

## ▶ Practice

**1.** Geologists whose specialty is to study the layers of rock are called
   **a.** tectonicists.
   **b.** metamorphologers.
   **c.** stratigraphers.
   **d.** volcanologists.

**2.** An extinct kind of ancient tree whose fossils are so well defined in time that they can be used to date rocks is called which of the following?
   **a.** keystone fossil
   **b.** index fossil
   **c.** bedded fossil
   **d.** specific fossil

**3.** What is the name of the kind of unconformity between a lower, thick layer of igneous rock and the sedimentary beds above (assume no folding)?
   **a.** nonconformity
   **b.** disconformity
   **c.** horizontality
   **d.** angular unconformity

**4.** Which of the following is true?
   **a.** Formations are parts of strata; both are types of beds.
   **b.** Strata are parts of formations; both are types of beds.
   **c.** Beds are parts of formations; both are types of strata.
   **d.** Formation are parts of beds; both are types of strata.

**5.** The sediments that form the Grand Canyon were deposited over approximately what time interval?
   **a.** 3 billion years
   **b.** 300 million years
   **c.** 30 million years
   **d.** 3,000 thousand years

## ▶ Atomic Clocks

How old is the earth and its various rocks? How can geologists be so sure when they say that a given igneous layer of rock is 200 million years old, or 1.5 billion years old?

One early attempt to date geological time used the ocean's salinity. We know how much salt goes into the ocean by the world's rivers. We also know the total amount of salt in the ocean. Assuming that the flows of rivers have stayed approximately constant over long periods of time, and assuming that the ocean started off as fresh water, one might compute how long the rivers have been carrying salt to the ocean. In 1889, the answer was first calculated as 90 million years. That's a long time but still way too low, compared to our modern values for the scale of geological time. (Some of the assumptions were not good.)

Modern accurate methods use atomic clocks. The key concept to understanding these clocks is the fact that the radioactive breakdown of certain isotopes occurs at a known rate. First, we will review isotopes and radioactive decay. Then we will discuss how these facts are used in geological dating.

Recall that atoms of a particular element all have the same number of protons in their nuclei. Furthermore, the number of protons determine the charge of each nucleus, thus the number of electrons around each nucleus, and thus the chemistry of the element. But atoms of elements can vary in the number of neutrons in their nuclei. These variants are called *isotopes.*

Here's an example. The element carbon comes in three isotopes: carbon-12, carbon-13, and carbon-14. Most of the carbon in your body is carbon-12, a stable isotope with six protons and six neutrons in the atomic nucleus. Carbon-13 is also a stable isotope with six protons and seven neutrons in its nucleus. Finally, we come to carbon-14, a radioactive isotope (sometimes called a radioisotope). The atomic nucleus of carbon-14 has six protons and eight neutrons.

A stable isotope is an atom whose nucleus stays the same, basically forever. A radioactive isotope is different in that the energy balance in the nucleus between protons and neutrons is not right and the nucleus will undergo radioactive decay. At some point in time, that is randomly determined. The nucleus spontaneously shifts to a new form during radioactive decay, in the direction of more stability. Five different kinds of radioactive decay exist, but the details of all five do not concern us here. It is enough to know that in the case of carbon-14, one neutron in the nucleus will spontaneously transform into a proton, with the emission of an electron.

Note that in the case of the radioactive decay of carbon-14, when the neutron changes into the proton, the resulting new nucleus, instead of the six protons and eight neutrons of carbon-14, now has seven protons and seven neutrons. The atomic element itself has changed, from carbon with six protons, into nitrogen with seven protons. The electron that is shot out of the decaying atom's nucleus is energy given off by the nuclear transformation, and the electron can be recorded by human instruments.

A remarkable fact has been discovered from measuring the number of decay events from a mass of radioactive isotopes (for example, measuring the rate of electrons given off by a mass of carbon-14). The number of decay events is proportional to the mass. In other words, doubling the mass doubles the number of decay events. Cutting the mass to one-quarter cuts the

decay events to one-quarter. This fact seems simple, but as we will see, it has profound implications for measuring the ages of rocks.

Let us consider, then, a particular mass $M$ of some radioisotope, say, of carbon-14. It decays at a rate $R$ (measured as $R$ number of events per second). Because the carbon-14 turns into nitrogen as it decays, the mass of the carbon-14 decreases over time. As some point, it reaches a mass $0.5\,M$, or half its original mass $M$. At that time, the decay rate will also be half and equal to $0.5\,R$. Now more time passes, and as atoms of carbon-14 one by one turn into nitrogen, eventually the mass $0.25\,M$ is reached. At that time, the decay rate is $0.25\,R$.

Theory shows this fact to be true and measurements have verified it: The time it takes for $M$ to change to $0.5\,M$ is the same time it takes for $0.5\,M$ to change to $0.25\,M$. In other words, the amount of time it takes for any given amount of mass to decay to half that mass is always the same. This time is called the *half-life*. The half-life is the amount of time taken for half the atoms in a mass of radioactive atoms to undergo nuclear decay.

The half-life varies for different radioactive elements. Here are some examples for a few of the radioactive elements that have been proven most useful for dating geological times: carbon-14, half-life of 5,730 years; potassium-40, half-life of 1.3 billion years; uranium-238, half-life of 4.5 billion years.

The half-life determines the interval of time over which a certain radioisotope can be useful for dating. For example, carbon-14, with a relatively short half-life, is valuable for dating ruins of the Pueblo Indians of ancient America. They used wood (which contains carbon) to build roofs for their cliff dwellings. In contrast, carbon-14 is not useful for dating rocks a billion years old. First of all, even if such ancient rocks do contain carbon (as the carbonate rocks do), so many half-lives have passed that the amount of carbon-14 left would be not measurable; it would essentially be zero.

To perform the dating of a rock, we would need to know the original mass of a radioisotope that was in the rock at the time of the rock's formation and the current, reduced mass of the radioisotope in the rock. By comparing the masses, we can then compute how many half-lives have passed to lower the original amount of radioisotope to the current amount. For example, if the original amount of carbon-14 in some ancient charcoal is $M$ and the current amount is $\frac{1}{8} M$, we know that three half-lives have passed (count them: $M \rightarrow M/2 \rightarrow M/4 \rightarrow M/8$). Because we know that the half-life of carbon-14 is 5,730 years, we then know that the sample is 17,190 years old (3 × 5,730 years).

This strategy for calculation works well in the case of carbon-14, because carbon-containing materials (such as wood) started off with about the same ratios of carbon-14 as when they grew during their lives (because the carbon-14 comes from the atmosphere). But in the case of the very important radioisotope potassium-40, which is used for dating rocks, we don't know how much potassium-40 was in the original rock. What can scientists do?

What is done in the case of potassium-40 is to measure not only the current amount of potassium-40 in a rock, but also the amount of argon-40. Why? Argon-40 is a daughter product of potassium-40 radioactive decay. In other words, when potassium-40 undergoes radioactive decay, argon-40 is created. (What is the daughter product of carbon-14? You'll be asked that in one of the practice questions.)

Here's an important fact about igneous rocks. Magma contains no argon-40, because the argon-40 is driven off by heat. Thus, when any ancient rock that contains a mixture of potassium-40 and argon-40 is heated into magma, it loses its argon-40, but it keeps its potassium-40. When the magma solidifies to become a new igneous rock, the atomic clock of potassium-40 is restarted.

Thus, when igneous rock forms, it contains a certain amount of potassium-40 but zero argon-40. Here we must introduce one slight complication to the story of the radioactive decay of potassium-40. Potassium-40 decays into not one but two daughter products. This happens randomly for any given atom, but with perfect regularity for a mass of potassium-40 as a whole. Twelve percent of the decay goes into argon-40 and 88% of the decay goes into calcium-40, but this fact doesn't affect our analysis, because these percentages of daughter products are constant. It doesn't matter what minerals the potassium is in. Neither do the temperatures or pressures.

So let's return to a newly formed igneous rock with an unknown amount of potassium-40 and no (zero) argon-40. Millions or billions of years later, a modern geologist takes a sample of that rock and measures the amounts of both potassium-40 and argon-40. The rock today contains argon-40 because some of the potassium-40 over time has changed into argon-40. So we know that the rock formed with zero argon-40, and we know today's amounts of potassium-40 and argon-40. These numbers are all that are needed to calculate the age of the rock.

We won't do the calculation here, except to lay out the logic. Measuring the amount of argon-40 in a piece of igneous rock allows us to calculate how much potassium-40 underwent radioactive decay since the solidification of the rock (using the fact that 12% of the decayed potassium-40 goes to argon). Then, measuring how much potassium-40 is currently in the rock, we can compute how much original potassium-40 was in the rock by adding to the current amount the amount that must have been lost through radioactive decay, computed from the argon-40 measurement.

Then, because we know the original and current amounts of potassium-40, as in our example with carbon-14, we can compute how many half-lives have passed since the igneous rock was formed. Because the half-life of potassium-40 is 1.3 billion years, it is certainly possible that some rocks will have gone through several half-lives of potassium-40 since the time they were born as igneous rocks. But it's even more common, of course, to find igneous rocks not as old as one half-life of potassium-40. That's okay. Scientists can easily measure fractions of a half-life. Indeed, potassium-40 and argon-40 are so useful as a pair of measurements (called potassium–argon dating) for the precise dating of rocks that the measurements can even be used for volcanic rocks as young as 50,000 years old. At the other end of the time scale, potassium-argon dating can measure rocks that go back to the oldest rocks we have on Earth. We can use the various radioisotopes to perform atomic dating to find out when the first rocks on Earth were formed, and it turns out that they are 3.9 billion years old.

When astronauts brought back rocks from the moon, starting in 1969 and for the few years of the Apollo Program, those rocks were dated in laboratories on Earth. The oldest moon rocks (all igneous) are about 4.1 billion years old. Why would the moon rocks be older than rocks on Earth? As we've seen, the moon formed when a rogue body, about the size of Mars, smashed into the earth very early in Earth's history, so you would think their oldest rocks would be about the same age. On Earth, the forces of plate tectonics have continuously reshaped the surface. So we can assume that rocks older than 3.9 billion years did exist at one time on Earth, but none remain on the continents.

The atomic dating can also be used for meteorites that land on Earth from space. Meteorites clock in at about 4.6 billion years old. This well-verified date of the meteorites is taken to be the time when the earth and all the other planets of the solar system condensed out of a huge gas nebula in space, which also formed the sun. So the earth as a planet is 4.6 billion years old or, rounded to the nearest half-billion, about 4.5 billion years old.

## ▶ Practice

**6.** An atom of a chemical element that is a radioisotope has which one of the following?
   **a.** an unstable nucleus
   **b.** excess electrons
   **c.** an unusual positive charge
   **d.** energy turning into mass

**7.** What is the name of the daughter product of carbon-14?
   **a.** argon
   **b.** carbon-13
   **c.** nitrogen
   **d.** carbon-12

**8.** Assume that a rock, when it was formed, had a certain amount of radioisotope, and that today, it has $\frac{1}{8}$ of that original amount. For how many half-lives of that isotope has the rock "lived"?
   **a.** 3
   **b.** 8
   **c.** 2
   **d.** $\frac{1}{4}$

**9.** Potassium–argon measurements can be used to date what?

    **a.** sedimentary rocks, because there was no potassium when the rock was formed

    **b.** igneous rocks, because there was no potassium when the rock was formed

    **c.** sedimentary rocks, because there was no argon when the rock was formed

    **d.** igneous rocks, because there was no argon when the rock was formed

**10.** Determining dates by using radioisotopes has given the oldest ages which one of the following?

    **a.** the moon

    **b.** meteorites

    **c.** Earth

    **d.** the sun

## ▶ The Geological Time Scale

Planet Earth condensed from a gas nebula and was brought together by gravity about 4.6 billion years ago. The entire time from that fiery origin to today has been carefully divided by geologists into various named intervals of time. This is something like the way our calendar divides the year into months, weeks, days, hours, and so forth.

To create the geologic time scale, geologists have relied to a large extent on the presence of different kinds of organisms, preserved as fossils, who have inhabited the earth at different times. For example, thanks to the movie *Jurassic Park*, most people know that one of the times that dinosaurs lived is called the Jurassic. As we go back in time, the fossil record becomes more and more incomplete. Indeed, for much of Earth's history, the only fossils are tiny, single-celled, mineralized organisms that don't look very distinct because they are only round, microscopic spheres or elongated rods in rock. So the divisions of geologic time are not as finely resolved back in the early Earth as the divisions are within, say, the last 100 million years.

The biggest scale of the divisions (like dividing the year into months) are called *eons*. The earliest eon was the Hadean (time of "hell"). There were still many bombardments from space coming to Earth. It lasted to about 3.9 billion years ago.

The next eon was the Archean, from 3.9 to 2.5 billion years ago. Life originated early in the Archean, but it was all singled-celled.

After the Archean came the Proterozoic, about 2,500 to 680 million years ago. (We've switched to millions of years ago, because the dating becomes better.) This eon saw a great rise in atmospheric oxygen about 2,000 million years ago. Near the end of the Proterozoic, multicelled life evolved (organisms with many cells to their bodies, such as simple worms).

Skipping the Vendian, we come to the eon called Paleozoic (545–250 million years ago). It started with an explosion of new kinds of life forms. By the end of the Paleozoic, plants had evolved to tall trees on land, and the dominant life forms on land were giant amphibians and early reptiles.

Next came the eon we are currently in, called the Phanerozoic. It is divided into eras, which are subdivided into periods. For example, the Mesozoic era (248–65 million years ago) is itself subdivided into three main periods called Triassic, Jurassic, and Cretaceous. A mass extinction at 65 million years ago ended the dinosaurs and the Mesozoic era.

The final era (the subdivision of the Phanerozoic called the Cenozoic) is the age of mammals, beginning 65 million years ago and lasting until today. The most recent—two million years or so—is the epoch (a subdivision of a period) called the Pleistocene, a time of the growth and then retreat of giant ice sheets, in cycles of about 100,000 years each. At the final deglaciation,

| EON | ERA | PERIOD | EPOCH | MILLIONS OF YEARS |
|---|---|---|---|---|
| Phanerozoic | Cenozoic | Quaternary | Holocene | 0.01–today |
| | | | Pleistocene | 2.0–0.01 |
| | | Tertiary | Pliocene | 5.1–2.0 |
| | | | Miocene | 24.6–5.1 |
| | | | Oligocene | 38.0–24.6 |
| | | | Eocene | 54.9–38.0 |
| | | | Paleocene | 65.0–54.9 |
| | Mesozoic | Cretaceous | | 144–65.0 |
| | | Jurassic | | 213–144 |
| | | Triassic | | 248–213 |
| | Paleozoic | Permian | | 286–248 |
| | | Carbon-iferous | Pennsylvanian | 320–286 |
| | | | Mississippian | 360–320 |
| | | Devonian | | 408–360 |
| | | Silurian | | 438–408 |
| | | Ordovician | | 505–438 |
| | | Cambrian | | 545–505 |
| Vendian | NO SUBDIVISIONS IN COMMON USE. | | | 680–545 |
| Proterozoic | | | | 2500–680 |
| Archean | | | | 3900–2500 |
| Hadean | | | | 4600–3900 |
| | | | | Start _ End Time   Time |

Figure 8.2   The geologic time scale

about 10,000 years ago, geologists end the Pleistocene and start a new epoch, called the Holocene.

During these billions of years, plate tectonics have shaped Earth's surface. Continents have combined and split repeatedly, oceans have widened and disappeared, mountain ranges have risen and then eroded to hills, and rocks formed under water in sediments have been lifted into plateaus and mountains.

To see the geologic time scale in more detail, study Figure 8.2. Then move right on to the practice questions. You'll need to use the figure to help you with some of the answers.

## ▶ Practice

**11.** Assume a stratigrapher is studying a large formation of Mesozoic rocks. She thinks she can discern three main layers, corresponding to the three periods of the Mesozoic. She is sure that the principle of superposition holds. What is the order of rock layers that she finds, from the uppermost, to the middle layer, to the lowermost?

   **a.** Jurassic, Triassic, Cretaceous

   **b.** Cretaceous, Jurassic, Triassic

   **c.** Triassic, Jurassic, Cretaceous

   **d.** Triassic, Cretaceous, Jurassic

**12.** A geologist is studying a type of unconformity called a disconformity. Which two layers might possibly be the one being studied? Assume the first in the pair is on top, the second is below the first. Also assume that the principle of superposition holds.

   **a.** Devonian/Silurian

   **b.** Tertiary/Cretaceous

   **c.** Ordovician/Silurian

   **d.** Jurassic/Permian

**13.** The Archean is an example of the geological division of time called which of the following?

   **a.** an eon

   **b.** an era

   **c.** a period

   **d.** an epoch

**14.** How many millions of years was the duration of the Paleozoic?

   **a.** 40

   **b.** 297

   **c.** 11.1

   **d.** 545

**15.** Which was the longest interval of time?

   **a.** Cenozoic

   **b.** Jurassic

   **c.** Phanerozoic

   **d.** Miocene

# What Is Air?

## LESSON SUMMARY

From ancient times, people knew that air was crucial to life. But they did not know that air, which seems to be a single substance, is actually a mixture of many different gases. We will examine the contents of air later in this lesson. But first, we start with the atmosphere's general properties of temperature and pressure and examine how these properties change with altitude.

## ▶ Pressure, Temperature, and Altitude

We all know that *air pressure* is less at the top of a mountain than at sea level. But what exactly is air pressure? Quite simply, air pressure is the total weight of the air above any spot. For example, one of the common numbers for air pressure is 14.7 pounds per square inch, at sea level. Imagine yourself at a sunny beach looking at a square inch area of sand (approximately at sea level). Extend that column of one square inch all the way up, miles and miles to the upper reaches where the atmosphere fades into outer space. All the air in that thin column weighs about 14.7 pounds.

Meteorologists—scientists who study the weather—have found it convenient to define another unit for air pressure called the *bar*. One bar is the downward force exerted by 1 kilogram of mass upon 1 square centimeter of area at sea level. It turns out that the mass in a column of air of one square centimeter in cross-section area, extending from sea level all the way to the outer reaches of the atmosphere, is just about one kilogram. In fact, the mass of air in that column is 1.013 kilograms. So this standard air pressure is 1.013 bar.

Meteorologists measure small differences in air pressure that occur when various air masses move across the land. That's why the air pressure at sea level changes slightly with the weather. To speak in terms that are simple to understand, meteorologists therefore like to use the unit of the millibar, or one-thousandth of a bar. Another way of expressing the standard air pressure of 1,013 bar is 1,013 millibar, or 1,013 mbar.

Yet other ways of expressing air pressure exist, for example by putting the mass of air in our column into equivalent masses of other substances. Air pressure at sea level, for example, is equal to a column of mercury about 760 mm or 29.9 inches high. Water is less dense than mercury, so the equivalent height of a column of water that is equal to air pressure at sea level is higher, about 33 feet. Still another way to measure air pressure is to use the metric unit of *pressure*, noted in *pascals* (Pa). The standard sea level air pressure is 101,325 Pa. Note that 1 mbar equals 100 Pa.

Measurements of air pressure are made using a *barometer*. In the earliest days when it was understood that air had measurable pressure, barometers were literally made in columns of mercury. And when early scientists, such as the Frenchman Blaise Pascal (for whom the metric unit of pressure was named), took columns of mercury up the slopes of mountains, they discovered that air pressure decreased with altitude.

The reason for the decrease in air pressure with increase in altitude is simple. You climb a mountain and less air is above you. As you climb a mountain, all the air you see below you is no longer above you pressing down on you. When you get to space, no air at all is pressing down on you and the air pressure is zero.

The drop in pressure with increase in altitude is, however, not linear. That means that as you go up, the drop in air pressure is not equal to equal increments of altitude. Consider the following facts about our column of air (either 1 square inch or 1 square centimeter in cross-section, it doesn't matter). About 50% of the total mass of the atmosphere in that column is within the lowermost 5 to 6 kilometers. You have to include the next 25 kilometers to get nearly the equal amount of mass. So it's not just the air pressure that decreases with increase in altitude; the density of the air decreases with altitude as well. In mathematical terms, we can say that air pressure drops exponentially with increasing altitude.

The ocean's water presents a contrasting situation. Ocean pressure increases with depth linearly. This is because the water is virtually incompressible. As the water down deep is squeezed by the weight of the water above, it has more pressure on it but almost no change in density. So water pressure is linear with depth. The water pressure at two miles down is twice that found at one mile down.

As you might now suspect, the reason for the exponential behavior of air pressure is because air is compressible. Its density changes with pressure. So not only is the air pressure greater at sea level than, say, at the top of Mount Everest, but so is its density. The air at sea level is squeezed and made more dense by its local, higher air pressure.

Another important property for us to consider about the atmosphere is *temperature*. Like air pressure, temperature, for much of the mass of the atmosphere, decreases with altitude. The reason, however, is completely unrelated. And, as we shall see, important regions of the atmosphere exist in which the pattern reverses, that is, in which temperature increases with altitude.

What causes the earth's surface to be so much hotter than the biting cold of outer space? Recall that outer space is about 3° above absolute zero—the temperature at which all molecular motion ceases. Though some energy comes up from the interior of the hot, inner Earth, that energy is very small. Over long times, the earth's inner heat does drive plate tectonics, but on a day-to-day basis, the inner energy that comes to

Earth's surface is small. By far, the main source of energy that warms the earth to the temperature we enjoy is the sun.

Consider the fact that we see the sun clearly through the atmosphere (but please don't look at it directly). That means the air is mostly transparent to the rays of energy from the sun that our eyes respond to (which happen to be the same kinds of rays that contain most of the energy from the sun). The atmosphere scatters some of the sun's energy, which is why the sky is blue. And clouds reflect sunlight back to space. But where the sky is clear, a lot of the sun's energy goes through the atmosphere and is absorbed at the surface of the earth—by the ground or the surface of the ocean.

So the atmosphere at Earth's surface is heated by the sun. The following two facts mean that the average pattern will be cooling of the atmosphere with altitude: (1) that most of the heating from the sun takes place at the surface, and (2) that outer space is cold. Indeed, we have all felt this. When you climb a mountain on a hot day, you might start off in a T-shirt but need a heavy jacket at the top of the mountain. And look where snow occurs on mountains: at the tops. It's cold up there.

The exact relationship between temperature and altitude is called the *lapse rate*. There are two kinds of lapse rates. To develop the theory to explain the lapse rate, meteorologists use a specialized term: *adiabatic*. This term simply refers to the fact that the meteorologists assume that no additional heating from the sides come in to the parcel of air that is being considered (this will be clear in a moment). Two kinds of lapse rates have been defined: dry and moist. We will consider the *dry adiabatic lapse rate* first.

As a parcel of warm air from the ground rises, what happens? Because the pressure is lower as it rises, the parcel expands. This happens all the time—when air currents rise to form clouds, for example. Calcula-

tions show that for the part of the atmosphere we live in (the *lower troposphere*), the dry adiabatic lapse rate is about 1° C per 100 meters (or 1° F per 183 feet). That means that for every hundred meters you climb, the temperature, on average, will drop about 1° C.

Water vapor in the atmosphere, however, creates dynamics that make this number lower (that is, the drop in temperature is less). This is a more realistic situation for places where substantial water vapor is in the atmosphere, for instance, above tropical rain forests or above the ocean. (The dry adiabatic lapse rate works in other places, such as in deserts.) When water vapor plays a role in creating the lapse rate, the lapse rate is called the *moist adiabatic lapse rate*.

The basic idea behind the moist adiabatic lapse rate is the fact that as the air cools when it rises, water vapor condenses out of it. When the condensed vapor accumulates into droplets, we see clouds. Furthermore, when the water vapor condenses, it releases heat. This is simply the opposite process of water evaporating, which requires heat. So evaporating water into water vapor takes energy, and condensing water vapor into water releases heat. That heat goes into the air that is rising, warming it slightly. This is why the moist adiabatic lapse rate is less than the dry adiabatic lapse rate. The heat released by the condensed water vapor somewhat counters the cooling created by the air expanding as it rises.

What is the number for the moist adiabatic lapse rate? It depends on latitude and air temperature. But the average is about 0.6° C per 100 meters of altitude.

This discussion of the reason for why temperature cools with altitude and the two different kinds of lapse rates holds true for the most important zone of the atmosphere, the lowermost layer called the *troposphere*. We live in the troposphere, and most of the mass of the atmosphere is in the troposphere. All our most familiar weather takes place in the troposphere, because the troposphere is where those rising and falling currents of air make clouds, where water vapor condenses into rain and snow, and where the variable winds we feel every day blow. On average, the troposphere goes from the earth's surface to about 15 kilometers in altitude. This altitude at which the troposphere ends is called the *tropopause*, and it varies with latitude and seasons.

The next layer of the atmosphere is called the *stratosphere*. The stratosphere begins at the tropopause and extends approximately 50 kilometers up beyond that. Commercial jets fly in the lower stratosphere (or upper troposphere, but anyway above the clouds), to escape the variable weather conditions of the lower troposphere, as well as to reduce friction and conserve fuel. Temperature in the stratosphere does not follow the same rules that apply to the troposphere. In the stratosphere, temperature increases (not decreases) with altitude. How can that be?

For temperature to increase with altitude in the stratosphere, there has to be a source of energy. And there is. The stratosphere contains a certain type of molecule called *ozone* ($O_3$, three atoms of oxygen in a molecule of ozone). Ozone has the property of absorbing ultraviolet light from the sun. Though as we said before, much of the sun's energy is contained in light rays that go through the atmosphere to the ground or ocean's surface, a small amount of energy is contained in the ultraviolet rays. It is this energy that is absorbed by the ozone in the stratosphere. This absorption warms the stratosphere and causes temperature to increase with altitude. The altitude at which the stratosphere ends is called the *stratopause*.

Additional layers of the atmosphere can be found above the stratosphere. But remember that the air here is very thin. In fact, even though levels of the stratosphere are technically warm, you would freeze if you tried to live there unprotected, because your body would radiate much more heat away from your skin than you would gain from the small amounts of warm air molecules hitting against your skin.

Above the stratosphere comes the *mesosphere*. In the mesosphere, which extends from the stratospause up to about 80 kilometers, temperatures again drop with increasing altitude. The mesosphere ends with the *mesopause*, and the *thermosphere* begins.

Some of the gases in the uppermost, very thin region called the thermosphere absorb some of the sun's energy, and, in addition, protons and electrons given off by the sun are absorbed in the thermosphere and serve as a source of energy. Thus, temperature again rises in the themosphere with altitude. Within the thermosphere is a sublayer called the *ionosphere*, which has electrically charged particles that sometimes light up the skies in the high latitudes with colorful lights called the *auroras*. At an altitude of about 500 kilometers, the atmosphere fades gradually into outer space (see Figure 9.1).

## ▶ Practice

1. Which of the following is NOT one of the units of air pressure?
   a. pascals
   b. pounds
   c. millibars
   d. pounds per square inch

2. When climbing a mountain, which of the following is a true statement about the atmosphere?
   a. Pressure decreases and density decreases.
   b. Pressure increases and density decreases.
   c. Pressure decreases and density remains constant.
   d. Pressure increases and density increases.

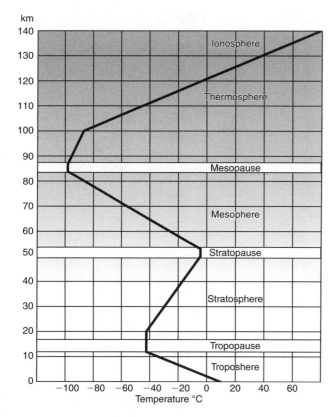

**Figure 9.1** The temperature structure of the atmosphere creates layers.

**3.** If you climbed a mountain to an altitude of 2,000 meters, how much would you expect the air to cool during your hike? Assume you are in a moist region where the moist adiabatic lapse rate applies.

   **a.** 12° C

   **b.** 1.2° C

   **c.** 20° C

   **d.** 2° C

**4.** The layer of the atmosphere that contains ozone and absorbs the sun's ultraviolet rays is called what?

   **a.** thermosphere

   **b.** mesosphere

   **c.** troposphere

   **d.** stratosphere

**5.** For a layer of the atmosphere to ha[...] ture increase with altitude, that lay[...] which one of the following?

   **a.** pressure increase with altitude

   **b.** connection to Earth's surface

   **c.** a means of absorbing energy

   **d.** condensation of water vapor

## ▶ The Air's Gases

The atmosphere is a mixture of many gases. Though the air gets thinner with altitude, for the most part, the percentages of gases relative to each other are fairly constant. A few exceptions exist to this rule; for example, the ozone that we've already seen is mostly in the stratosphere. That's because special chemical reactions take place in the stratosphere that create the ozone. But for the most part, we can study the kinds of gases in the air as percentages and not pay attention to the altitude from which the air came. Table 9.1 is a list of the main gases in Earth's atmosphere.

Note that the top three gases—nitrogen ($N_2$, 78.08%), oxygen ($O_2$, 20.95%), and argon (Ar, 0.93%)—together make up 99.96% of the atmosphere. All the other gases are only 0.04% of the total. Also note a gas that is missing from the table: *water vapor*. Water vapor is not included because it varies so much from place to place, from season to season, and across different temperatures. The table shows what is known as the composition of the standard dry atmosphere. In other words, water vapor is not included. Also not included in the table of the standard dry atmosphere gases are the *aerosols*, which include salt crystals, ice crystals, smoke particles, dusts, sulfates, unburned carbons from fossil fuel combustion, and others. These, too, obviously vary from place and to place, from condition to condition.

Let us consider first the crucial gas water vapor, and then move on to consider the other gases that are greenhouse gases.

Water vapor creates what we call *humidity*. Two terms for humidity are used by meteorologists: *absolute humidity* and *relative humidity*. Absolute humidity is the actual amount of water vapor in the air, say in terms of grams of water per cubic meter. In terms of actual percentages, compared to the percentages of the other gases in the standard dry atmosphere, water vapor typically varies between 0.3% to 4%. In other words, compared to the other gases, water vapor usually is gas number 3 or 4 in rank.

Much of the time, the concern is about relative humidity, which is given as a percentage relative to how much water vapor a parcel of air at that temperature and pressure could hold. At zero relative humidity (which almost never exists), the air contains no water vapor. At 100% relative humidity, the air has its maximum amount of water vapor. At 100% relative humidity, the air is said to be saturated with water vapor. At that point, the amount of water vapor in the air is said to be at the *saturation vapor pressure*.

For our purposes, the factor that determines the saturation vapor pressure (in other words, the amount of water vapor at 100% relative humidity) is temperature. The higher the temperature, the more water vapor the air can hold. That's why clouds appear high up in the sky where the air is cooler. As air rises from the ground and cools, its saturation vapor pressure drops. If that pressure drops below the amount of water vapor actually in the air, all the vapor cannot stay in the air. Some of the water vapor condenses.

When the condensation occurs as small invisible droplets, clouds start to form. Within clouds, the droplets can grow larger and larger and become rain. Inside the cloud are air currents, and when these take the droplets up high, the droplets can freeze into ice crystals, starting the process of becoming snowflakes.

Table 9.1  Gases of the atmosphere

| CHEMICAL FORMULA | NAME | PERCENTAGE |
|---|---|---|
| $N_2$ | nitrogen | 78.08 |
| $O_2$ | oxygen | 20.95 |
| Ar | argon | 0.93 |
| $CO_2$ | carbon dioxide | 0.037 |
| Ne | neon | 0.0018 |
| $CH_4$ | methane | 0.00014 |
| Kr | krypton | 0.00010 |
| $N_2O$ | nitrous oxide | 0.00005 |
| $H_2$ | hydrogen | 0.00005 |
| $O_3$ | ozone | 0.000007 |

*99.96%*

Clouds are important to climate, not only as the sources of precipitation but as reflectors of sunlight. Globally, clouds reflect about 30% of the sunlight back into space.

Water vapor is also what is known as a *greenhouse gas*. The greenhouse gas called carbon dioxide is much in the news these days, and it will continue to be so for the coming decades. But most people don't realize that the most powerful greenhouse gas in the atmosphere is water vapor, accounting for about 80% of Earth's overall greenhouse effect.

What is a greenhouse gas? In simplest terms, a greenhouse gas is a gas that lets the sun's energy come in but blocks the earth's energy from leaving to space. In more technical terms, a greenhouse gas is transparent to shortwave radiation and is absorbing to longwave radiation. Most of the sun's energy is in the short wavelengths of electromagnetic energy, the so-called shortwave radiation to which the greenhouse gases are transparent. Visible light is shortwave radiation. The fact that the greenhouse gases are transparent to shortwave radiation is why the sky looks basically clear to us.

Longwave radiation, on the other hand, is thermal infrared radiation. Thermal infrared is the wavelength of energy given off by the earth. (Earth's temperature is much less than that of the sun, so the radiation energy given off by the earth consists of much longer wavelengths.) Infrared radiation to space is the means by which the earth cools itself (releases energy to space), balancing the energy it receives from the sun. Greenhouse gases absorb infrared radiation. But they don't absorb all of it. You can think of it this way: The more greenhouse gases, the more absorption of Earth's infrared radiation, the warmer the planet.

Greenhouse gases occur in small amounts in the atmosphere. The largest gases in the atmosphere in terms of amounts are not greenhouse gases. Nitrogen ($N_2$, 78.08%), oxygen ($O_2$, 20.95%), and argon (Ar, 0.93%) are not greenhouse gases. What makes a gas a greenhouse gas or not is fairly technical, but we can use a simple rule of thumb: A greenhouse gas has three or more atoms in its molecule.

Thus, we can list the greenhouse gases in Earth's atmosphere, in decreasing percentages: water vapor, carbon dioxide, methane, nitrous oxide, and ozone. Check this list with the chemical formulas in Table 9.1 to verify that they all have three or more atoms in their molecules.

Without some greenhouse gases, the earth's surface would be very much colder, frozen in fact. So the greenhouse gases are important for life as we know it. However, the greenhouse gas called carbon dioxide (as well as others, e.g., methane) is increasing in the atmosphere from human activities (as are some of the other greenhouse gases), and this is cause of concern for the future of Earth's climate and global warming.

## ▶ Practice

**6.** In terms of percentage, the number one gas in the atmosphere is which of the following?
   **a.** argon
   **b.** oxygen
   **c.** water vapor
   **d.** nitrogen

**7.** In terms of both percentage and effect, the biggest greenhouse gas is which of the following?
   **a.** water vapor
   **b.** carbon dioxide
   **c.** methane
   **d.** ozone

**8.** The air at 30° C contains 6.6 grams of water as water vapor per kilogram of dry air, which makes a 25% relative humidity. How many grams of water as water vapor would that same air have at 100% relative humidity?
   **a.** 1.65
   **b.** 26.4
   **c.** 3.3
   **d.** 6.6

**9.** Water vapor is not included in the list of gases in the standard table of the atmosphere because of which of the following?
   **a.** It is difficult to measure.
   **b.** It makes clouds.
   **c.** It varies so much.
   **d.** It is a greenhouse gas.

**10.** Which three gases make up 99.96% of the standard dry atmosphere?
   **a.** nitrogen, krypton, carbon dioxide
   **b.** water vapor, oxygen, nitrogen
   **c.** oxygen, argon, nitrogen
   **d.** carbon dioxide, oxygen, argon

# 10 ▶ The Dynamic Atmosphere

## LESSON SUMMARY

The earth is a round ball in space. It is bathed by vast quantities of rays of sunlight. These two facts create differences in the amount of sun received by various parts of the planet, and these differences, in turn, set up whirls and swirls in the air at the global scale. Mountain ranges, continental shapes, and the contrast between water and land also contribute to the circulation patterns we experience every day as parts of our dynamic atmosphere.

## ▶ The Global Atmospheric Whirls

The most important fact about the sun, other than its stupendous incoming energy, is the geometry of its rays. The rays of energy that come from the sun across space to fall upon Earth travel in nearly perfectly parallel alignment.

The most important geometric fact about the earth is that it is almost a perfect sphere. Imagine holding a soccer ball in the sunlight. The light is brightest at the place on the ball where the sunlight falls perpendicular to the surface of the ball. Then the degree of illumination fades as you look at spots on the ball further and further away from the brightest point.

We have already seen how the seasons are caused by the amount of sun received by different latitudes at various times of the year. We have also seen how various zones of climate are established, from equator to pole, by the differences in the amount of solar energy received by the zones. Now we will look into how the differences in heating influence the dynamics of the atmosphere.

Molecules of hot air move faster than molecules of cold air move. Wherever warm and cold are in contact, the difference drives a transport of energy. We hear and see this transport as wind, which rustles leaves, pushes waves, and sweeps clouds across the sky. The most important large-scale wind pattern on Earth is caused by the tendency of hot air to rise.

The largest region of hot air on the planet is found in the tropics, the region that borders both sides of the equator. In the tropics, warm buoyant air ascends upward into the high troposphere. The rising air cannot descend back to exactly where it came from because right behind it is more rising air. Thus, at the top of its rise, it pushes out to the north and south, horizontally. Eventually, this air descends, at about latitudes 30° north and south. As we will see in the next lesson, this has implications for the location of some of the world's great deserts. For now, we note that the air returns toward the equator in the lower troposphere, creating a cycle.

Review this cycle: rising air at the equatorial topics, movement in the upper troposphere toward both north and south, then descent around 30° north and south, and finally movement in the lower troposphere back toward the equator. This pattern is named the *Hadley cell*, after its discoverer and is the most important large-scale atmospheric pattern.

We next consider why the lowermost, return portion of the Hadley cell—for example, the southward air flow from 30° N back to the equator—occurs not along a line of longitude but deflected toward the west to become what is known as an *easterly wind*. (Winds are named by the direction from which they blow.) This deflection is caused by what is called the *Coriolis effect*. This is sometimes called the Coriolis force, but it is not really a force in the way the word is used in physics.

The Coriolis effect (again, named after its discoverer) comes about because the earth is spinning.

Everything at a given locale on the planet has a velocity of that locale. For example, if you happen to be near the latitude of New York City (about 40° N), you have an eastward velocity from the earth's spin of 740 miles per hour. If you were at the equator, your local eastward velocity imparted by Earth's spin would be 1,050 miles per hour. Why the difference? Both locations— New York City and a point on the equator—make a complete cycle in 24 hours. The point on the equator travels much farther because it goes around Earth's entire circumference. New York City travels a line of latitude where the circle is much smaller than Earth's circumference at the equator.

Now consider the return flow of the Hadley cell, which moves from 30° N back toward the equator. The eastward velocity from Earth's spin that the air has at 30° N is less than the eastward velocity from Earth's spin of the air at the equator. So as the air from the north moves southward toward the equator, as part of the Hadley circulation, it encounters air that is moving faster eastward. It tends to lag behind, deflected in a relative sense, westward. This westward deflection turns it into what is called an easterly wind.

The same logic can be applied to the Southern Hemisphere. Wind moving northward from 30° S toward the equator will be deflected toward the west, because it lags behind the equatorial air that is traveling faster eastward. So the situation is the same on both sides of the equator. In conclusion, the combination of the Hadley cell circulation and the Coriolis effect imparted by the spinning Earth creates the famous easterly winds of the tropics. These easterlies are called the *Trade Winds*, because commercial sailing ships of centuries ago used them as reliable sources of propulsion with a known direction.

In the higher latitudes, more circulation cells are formed by the dynamics of the sun on the round earth and by its interaction with the dominant presence of the Hadley cell. For most of the readers of this book who live in the midlatitudes, say from 30 to 60° N, the most important fact of atmospheric circulation are the dominant westerlies.

The westerlies of the midlatitudes are also created by the Coriolis effect. In the midlatitudes, a northward flow of air happens as part of the lower troposphere portion of another large-scale system of ascending and descending air (see Figure 10.1 below). The air coming from the south has a faster eastward velocity because of Earth's spin than does the air farther to the north that it encounters. This is just the opposite of the situation described earlier with the Hadley cell's return flow. Here, in the midlatitudes, the air with the faster eastward speed gets ahead of the air it encounters further to the north, which has a slower eastward speed from Earth's spin. The northward moving air is deflected to the east, relative to the air it encounters.

Deflection to the east creates a westerly wind, using the standard terminology for naming winds. Thus, in the midlatitudes, the dominant winds are westerly. That is why the weather patterns in Chicago, say, often reach New York City in the next day or two.

Study Figure 10.1, then move on to the practice questions. Be aware that all these wind patterns are formed as part of the tendency of E[...] to even out the differential heati[...] caused by the rays of sunlight fall[...] sphere.

## ▶ Practice

**1.** At the equator, the major motion in the atmosphere is which one of the following?
   **a.** descent
   **b.** eastward
   **c.** westward
   **d.** ascent

**2.** The trade winds are which one of the following?
   **a.** northerlies
   **b.** southerlies
   **c.** easterlies
   **d.** westerlies

**3.** The effect that is responsible for turning the northward flows in the lower troposphere into westerly winds is named after which of the following scientists?
   **a.** Hadley
   **b.** Coriolis
   **c.** Newton
   **d.** Magellan

**4.** Look at Figure 10.1. Compare the midlatitudes of the Southern and Northern Hemispheres. What is true?
   **a.** Easterlies are in both hemispheres.
   **b.** Westerlies are in both hemispheres.
   **c.** Westerlies are in the north, easterlies in the south.
   **d.** Easterlies are in the north, westerlies in the south.

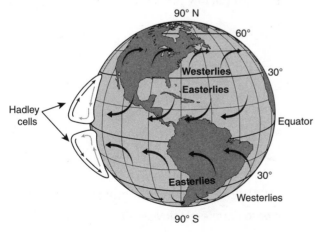

Figure 10.1 The major circulation patterns of Earth's atmosphere

**5.** The sun's rays are spread across more surface area the further from the equator one goes, on the annual average, which creates climate zones because of which one of the following?

    **a.** The earth is a sphere.

    **b.** The rays go through more atmosphere.

    **c.** The high latitudes are further from the sun.

    **d.** The Hadley cells distribute energy.

## ▶ Atmospheric Spins on Smaller Scales

Though the large-scale cycles of the atmosphere determine the average winds for most locations on the earth, we all know that from day to day and season to season, winds come from all directions and can change even in a matter of minutes. Wind patterns occur at various scales, down to the tiny spins that blow dust around a backyard or city street. We won't be concerned here with all the phenomena on all the scales but will describe some of the dominant factors at the next size scale down from the biggest cycles of the Hadley cells, tropical easterlies, and midlatitude westerlies already discussed.

In general, winds blow air from zones of high pressure to zones of low pressure. Low pressure systems occur when air is rising, usually because it is relatively warm and buoyant compared to the surrounding atmosphere. Low pressure systems tend, therefore, to pull in air from those surroundings. High pressure systems, in contrast, occur where the air is sinking, usually because it is colder and thus more dense than the atmosphere all around. (By the way, we are talking here about pressure systems that usually extend over several states of the United States, to give a sense of scale.)

To understand the winds created by this patchwork of systems of high and low pressure, it is neces-

sary to again discuss the Coriolis effect. Let's consider a low pressure system. Without the Coriolis effect, winds would tend to move from the periphery toward the center of a low pressure system along radial lines, like spokes on a wheel. But as we saw in understanding how easterlies are created in the tropics, the fact that air with eastward velocity from the earth's spin encounters air with a different eastward velocity when it moves north or south deflects the air. Study Figure 10.2, then return to the text.

In the Northern Hemisphere, a low pressure system will pull in air from the south and north. The air pulled in from the north will be deflected westward, just like the flow from north to south (in the area from 30° N to the equator) is deflected westward by the Coriolis effect, as we saw in the analysis of the Hadley cell. At the other side of the low pressure system, a wind pulled northward toward the low pressure center from the south will be deflected eastward, because it has a greater eastward velocity from the earth's spin than the more northerly air it encounters. We saw this same analysis in the discussion of why the midlatitudes have westerlies. So, air from the south is deflected eastward. Air from the north is deflected westward. You can see from the diagram that this creates a counterclockwise spin on the air that is coming in from the periphery into the low pressure system.

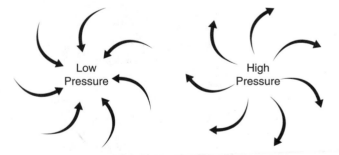

Figure 10.2 Winds around low pressure systems spiral inward counterclockwise. Winds around high pressure systems spiral outward clockwise. This diagram is for the Northern Hemisphere.

The same reasoning can be used to analyze the direction of winds blowing away from a high pressure system (see Figure 10.2). In this case, the winds spiral outward in a clockwise direction. In summary, in the Northern Hemisphere, winds around low pressure zones spin counterclockwise, and winds around high pressure zones spin clockwise.

What about the zones of low and high pressure in the Southern Hemisphere? It's just the opposite. In the Southern Hemisphere, winds around low pressure zones spin clockwise, and winds around high pressure zones spin counterclockwise. Some people even say that water drains down a sink in the opposite direction in the Southern Hemisphere, but factors such as the shape of the basin probably dominate. But even that legend shows the recognition of the opposite effects of the Coriolis effect in the two hemispheres.

Regions of high and low pressure are generally associated with cooler and warmer temperatures, respectively, and *transition zones* between the pressure systems are called *weather fronts*. The systems of pressure and temperature do not sit in place. Indeed, an entire pressure system can move across the landscape of the United States and everywhere else in the world. When the cooler, high pressure system is what is moving, the transition zone is called a *cold front*. When the warmer, low pressure system is what is moving, the transition zone is called a *warm front*. When the transition zone just sits there, we have what is called a *stationary front*. Because fronts are where warm, moist air meets cooler, drier air, a front often has clouds and rain, because the moisture from the warm, moist air mass is condensed from contact with the cooler air mass.

During late summer and early fall, people along the east coast of the United States brace for the possibility of *hurricanes*. A hurricane is a region of extremely low pressure that forms in the hot ocean. (The ocean heats more slowly than the land, so the warmest temperatures of the ocean water occur in August and September, which creates the conditions for hurricanes.) The eye of the hurricane is an extremely low pressure center, in which the warm air is rising. The surrounding air is pulled in to fill the void left by the rising air in the eye. But as we saw in the analysis of the low pressure systems, the air that flows toward the center is spun by the Coriolis force. Hurricanes spin. They are, in essence, a low pressure system with an extremely low pressure center. Can you figure out what direction the winds will spin around a hurricane in the Northern Hemisphere, headed for Florida?

*Tornadoes* are low pressure systems on land, created most often during summer times in the U.S. Midwest. Land during the summer is intensely heated, giving rise to thunderheads and thunderstorms. If the rising air takes on an especially high velocity, a tornado can form. Like winds in a hurricane, winds in a tornado spin. Can you figure out what direction tornadoes spin in the Northern Hemisphere?

Another crucial factor in the atmospheric winds is the border between water and land. The land can go up and down in temperature more easily than can the water of the ocean or large lake. That's because the ocean or lake has a lot of thermal mass, or resistance to heating and cooling. You have probably noticed how, on a hot summer day, the ocean is substantially cooler than the air or the sand, which burns your feet.

The contrast between land and water drives a very important type of atmospheric flow called a *monsoon*. Monsoons are often associated with India or Africa, but they occur in the United States, too, particularly in the American Southwest. In summer, the heating of the Colorado Plateau causes low pressure and rising air, which pulls very moist air inward from the Gulf of Mexico, which lies to the south. Thus, the southwestern states of Arizona and New Mexico have almost half their annual precipitation during the monsoon months of July and August. In India, the summer monsoon winds bring moist air from the Indian Ocean up into India, driven by the rising air from the Tibetan Plateau.

In some places, the wind direction between land and ocean can switch even over the duration of a single day. In the middle of California, for example around San Francisco, daytime heating over the hot central valley can pull air in from the ocean, creating the famed coastal fogs. At night, when the land cools off, the flow can be reversed and the coastal fog disappears.

Mountains affect the winds, too. As the westerlies of the midlatitudes move from the Pacific Ocean onto the United States, they encounter the coastal ranges and the Sierras. The air is forced upward, which cools it, condenses water vapor, and creates clouds and rain. In general, mountains create barriers that cause winds to move up and over or around.

All the atmospheric dynamics described in this lesson contribute to the process of mixing the heat from the tropics into the cold regions of the poles. It's like taking a bath with hot water coming in from the faucet. Most of us don't like all the heat at the faucet end and the cooler bath water at the other end of the tub. So what do we do? We stir the water. This stirring evens out the temperatures at both ends of the bathtub. It's a similar situation in Earth's atmosphere. Here the stirring is done automatically, by the forces that come into play between warm and cold systems, between low and high pressure systems, between land and water.

Scientists have estimated that without the stirring of the atmosphere by the winds, the tropics, rather than their current average temperature of about 80° F, would be 140° F—way too hot for even the most hardy plants and animals. Without the winds, the polar regions, already cold, would be about 100° F colder—bad news for polar bears. Because of Earth's winds, the tropics are cooled and the poles are warmed.

## ► Practice

**6.** In California, during a hot day, winds tend to move in which direction?
   a. from ocean to land
   b. along the coast, northerly
   c. from land to sea
   d. along the coast, southerly

**7.** Why do the spins around a high pressure system go opposite in the Southern Hemisphere, compared to the Northern Hemisphere?
   a. the earth spins from west to east in the southern hemisphere
   b. high pressures form over land, rather than water
   c. reversal of the seasons
   d. the action of the Coriolis effect

**8.** In the Northern Hemisphere, which of the following is true?
   a. Hurricanes spin clockwise, and tornadoes spin clockwise.
   b. Hurricanes spin clockwise, and tornadoes spin counterclockwise.
   c. Hurricanes spin counterclockwise, and tornadoes spin clockwise.
   d. Hurricanes spin counterclockwise, and tornadoes spin counterclockwise.

**9.** The summertime rains in the American Southwest are caused by which one of the following?
   a. rising air over the Tibetan Plateau
   b. low pressure systems coming from the Pacific
   c. monsoon winds
   d. warm, high pressure systems

**10.** The various scales of Earth's winds have the overall effect of which one of the following?

    **a.** cooling the tropics and cooling the poles

    **b.** warming the tropics and cooling the poles

    **c.** cooling the tropics and warming the poles

    **d.** warming the tropics and warming the poles

# LESSON

# 11 ▶ Water Cycles

## LESSON SUMMARY

Life as we know it cannot exist without water. Though other crucial molecules are needed for living things, one might say that water is the most important molecule of all. Where is water found? How does the water cycle work?

## ▶ Forms of Water

The chemical formula of water is well known: $H_2O$. Two atoms of hydrogen are bonded via the sharing of electrons to a single atom of oxygen. The two hydrogen atoms are also slightly attracted to each other, which makes the water molecule slightly bent at an angle. The angle causes the water molecule to be slightly polarized into negatively and positively charged sides, which is why water is so excellent at dissolving a huge number of different substances.

For any substance that cycles around and around among various forms on the earth, it is useful to ask where that substance is found. This, of course, is true for water. The locations of the substance are its compartments, pools, or reservoirs (all words can be used, and they mean the same thing). For water, one reservoir is obviously the salty ocean. Another reservoir is the atmosphere, with its water vapor and water droplets in clouds. Obviously, the ocean has a lot more water than does the atmosphere, but how much more?

We will get to that answer in just a bit (or perhaps that would be a good calculation to do for one of the practice questions). But first, let's briefly describe the *reservoirs of water* and then look at their volumes in Table 11.1.

The *oceans* contain salt water (we will talk more about the ocean's chemistry in an upcoming lesson). The next largest reservoir is water frozen in *glaciers and ice caps*. Glaciers refer to mountain glaciers, such as those found in Alaska and the Himalayas. The ice caps are the great sheets of ice that cover Antarctica and Greenland.

*Groundwater* is another reservoir, which can be divided into *shallow and deep groundwater*. Groundwater is contained and flowing through the pores in rock, moving very slowly (in some cases taking up to thousands of years to percolate across large geographical regions through rock such as sandstone). Most places on Earth have groundwater, if you dig down far enough. It is groundwater that is tapped when people with homes in the country dig wells for their water supply. The groundwater they seek is obviously fresh water, but in many places, the deep ground water is somewhat salty.

*Lakes and rivers* are a reservoir of freshwater. The *soil* itself also contains water, which is necessary for the growth of plants that sink their roots into soil for its supply of water. As noted previously, the *atmosphere* contains water in the form of vapor and small droplets.

Finally, *our own bodies* contain water. In fact, we are mostly water by weight. All life forms contain significant amounts of water as fractions of their bodies. What happens if we add up all the water in all creatures on land and in the seas? It turns out, that of all the reservoirs of water described so far, the water in the sum of all life is the smallest amount.

Now look at Table 11.1 for the numbers.

Table 11.1  The global reservoirs of water

| POOL | VOLUME (THOUSANDS OF CUBIC KM) | PERCENT OF TOTAL (ROUNDED OFF) |
|---|---|---|
| Ocean | 1,400,000 | 97.3 |
| Glaciers and ice caps | 30,000 | 2.1 |
| Groundwater | 9,000 | 0.6 |
| Lakes | 125 | 0.009 |
| Soil moisture | 65 | 0.004 |
| Atmosphere | 13 | 0.0009 |
| Rivers | 2 | 0.0001 |
| All life forms | less than 1 | less than 0.0001 |
| Total | 1,440,000 | 100 |

NOTES: The total of the rounded off percents equals a bit more than 100%. The total volume has also been slightly rounded off.

To consider the global water cycle, we must connect some of the major reservoirs with flows between them, because no reservoir stays constant. Consider lakes, for example. Inflowing rivers supply lakes with water and outlet rivers take water away from lakes. In addition, evaporation takes water away from lakes. A lake, therefore, is a dynamic reservoir. The water in it is not permanent. If you went on visits to a lake in two-year intervals, it is possible (depending on the size of the lake), although it looks the same to you, that all the water in the lake would be different.

Consider your own body as a reservoir of water. You are constantly drinking fluids and excreting water in your wastes. The water in your body, like that of a lake, is continually being renewed. You are a dynamic, not a permanent, reservoir of water.

You drink water from a glass; lakes are supplied with water by rivers. In these particular transfers from one reservoir to another, water stays as water (as a liquid). But some of the changes between reservoirs involve a change in the state of water. Water can occur in three states, like any substance: liquid, solid, and gas. Reservoirs such as the oceans and rivers contain water in its liquid state. The atmosphere contains water in its gas state—water vapor. Finally, glaciers and ice caps contain water as its solid form—ice.

When water changes state, say between ice and liquid or between liquid and gas, energy is either required or is released. Basically, water in its liquid form contains more energy than water in its solid form at the same temperature. In other words, at the freezing point of water, 32° F (0° C), the liquid water contains more energy than does the solid form of water (ice). This extra energy is what makes liquid water move around so easily—its molecules are not locked together like they are in ice.

The energy that is transferred between the states of water is called *latent heat.* Let us consider the latent heat that is transferred when water goes from liquid to ice (the latent heat of freezing) and when water goes from ice to liquid (the latent heat of melting). When liquid freezes, energy must be removed. That's why you put an ice cube tray of liquid water into the freezer of your refrigerator. The latent heat of freezing is 79 calories per gram of water. Let's put that into practical terms. First, remember that a *calorie* is the amount of energy it takes to change the temperature of one gram of liquid water by 1° C. Therefore, the latent heat of freezing is enough energy to lower 79 grams of water by 1° C. The latent heat of melting is also 79 calories per gram of water, which is the energy that must go into a gram of ice to change it into liquid water.

The change of state between liquid water and water vapor requires an even greater latent heat. When liquid water evaporates, an amount of energy equal to 540 calories per gram must be supplied. That's why it takes so much energy on your stove to boil water beyond the boiling point until it is boiled away. In other terms, the energy it takes to boil one gram of water would be able to raise 540 grams of water (more than 1 pound) by 1° C. The latent heat of condensation—going from water vapor to liquid water—is also 540 calories per gram, but in the opposite direction compared to the latent heat of evaporation. The latent heat of condensation is the energy that is released into the air when water vapor condenses into cloud droplets, which as we saw was crucial in the moist adiabatic lapse rate of Lesson 9.

A crucial part of the water cycle takes place when water vapor in the atmosphere forms into water droplets in clouds, which eventually leads to rain, returning liquid water back to the surface of the land or ocean. So how do clouds work?

The first step in changing water vapor into water droplets in the sky takes place when the temperature drops far enough so that the *saturation vapor pressure of the air* (the maximum water that can be held by that air) falls below the amount of water in the air. The water then begins condensing on what are known as *cloud condensation nuclei.* Cloud condensation nuclei are tiny particles that can serve as centers for the beginning of the condensation process, which eventually leads to raindrops.

Substances that can serve as cloud condensation nuclei include the following: salt in the air over the ocean, dust in the air over continents, sulfate aerosols (tiny droplets of sulfuric acid, which can be natural or caused by humans) over both oceans and land, and other substances. The condensation nuclei are invisible to our eyes. They are very small, as are the initial water droplets. The droplets are so small, in fact, that they are kept aloft by the currents inside the clouds. That is why clouds stay in the sky.

As the droplets accumulate more and more water, they increase in diameter and eventually fall as raindrops.

## ▶ Practice

1. About how much more water is in the ocean than in the atmosphere? Use Table 11.1 to do the calculation.
   a. 100,000 times
   b. 1,000,000 times
   c. 10,000 times
   d. 1,000 times

2. What is the second largest reservoir of water on Earth?
   a. groundwater
   b. lakes
   c. glaciers and ice caps
   d. soil moisture

3. Which of the following is true for water?
   a. The latent heat of melting is greater than the latent heat of vaporization.
   b. The latent heat of vaporization is greater than the latent heat of freezing.
   c. The latent heat of melting is greater than the latent heat of freezing.
   d. The latent heat of condensation is greater than the latent heat of vaporization.

4. According to Table 11.1, lakes contain 125,000 cubic kilometers of water. The land of Earth is about 150,000,000 square kilometers. If all the water in all the lakes were to be spread out evenly across the land, about how deep would that water be?
   a. 1 centimeter
   b. 1 meter
   c. 1 millimeter
   d. 10 centimeters

5. Which of the following reservoirs contains the least total amount of water?
   a. lakes
   b. rivers
   c. soil moisture
   d. the sum of life forms

## ▶ The Global Water Cycle

Now we will look at how all these reservoirs of water are connected into a global water cycle. We'll examine some numbers in detail shortly, but let's first get a sense of how the cycle works by following a single molecule of water on a hypothetical but possible path through the water cycle. This water cycle is also called the *hydrological cycle.*

Our water molecule is at the surface of the ocean. Solar energy warms the water and the water molecule obtains a high enough energy to evaporate as water vapor into the atmosphere. In the air, it floats up and up, carried by ascending air, until the temperature drops and the molecule joins others as liquid water around a cloud condensation nucleus—say a microscopic bit of salt—within a cloud. The cloud thickens as the day progresses, and though the molecule might return to the ocean as rain, today the winds blow the pack of clouds over the land.

In the next several days, in fact, the molecule probably does fall back to Earth in a raindrop over land. It hits the ground and runs into the soil, becoming part of soil moisture. Now the droplet has four main potential paths it might take. First, it might sink deeper and deeper, past the soil, into porous rock and become part of groundwater. It might even then be pumped up by a farmer's well and consumed by the farmer in a glass of water for lunch.

Second, the molecule might flow within the soil to enter a stream, which flows into a river and eventually returns to the ocean in what is called *runoff*.

Third, the molecule in the soil moisture might evaporate again, as it did from the ocean's surface, pulled into the atmosphere by the air's dryness and given enough energy by the sun warming the soil. Once in the air, it again will go into a cloud and rain back upon land or even be carried out over the ocean.

The fourth possible path for the molecule is to be pulled into the root of a plant, because the plant needs water to live. The molecule travels up into the stem and then into the leaves, through the plant's network of veins. It could then even be split into an oxygen and two hydrogens, during the process of *photosynthesis*. The oxygen (as $O_2$) would be released by the plant as a waste gas. The hydrogen would go into a carbohydrate of the plant. But in the case of our particular molecule, it serves only as a carrier of nutrient ions from the soil up into the plant. Once in a leaf, the water exits the plant through a tiny pore in the leaf called a *stomate*. This exit is called *transpiration*, the process by which the plant converts liquid to water vapor. That process does take energy, the heat of vaporization, and so acts to cool the leaf. You can notice this cooling when you touch a leaf on a hot day and feel that it is quite a bit cooler than the air.

Once the molecule has been transpired through the leaf to become water vapor again, all the options are open again: to fall as rain back to land or on the ocean. We didn't mention the possibility that the molecule could become part of a lake, or evaporate from a river, or even to fall as snow over Antarctica and be locked up as ice for thousands of years. Many stories are waiting to be explored by the pathways of the water molecule, but you can see how the global hydrological cycle does not simply go round and around, like a Ferris wheel. The hydrological cycle is a complicated network of pathways, linking the reservoirs to each other and necessitating, in many cases, changes of state of the water.

The pathways between the reservoirs are called *fluxes* or *flows*, and earth scientists have figured out the approximate magnitudes for the fluxes of the global water cycle. Let's now look at some numbers several of the major fluxes, in thousands of cubic kilometers per year.

- Evaporation from the ocean: $500 \times \dfrac{10^3 \text{ km}^3}{\text{yr}}$

- Rain on to the ocean: $450 \times \dfrac{10^3 \text{ km}^3}{\text{yr}}$

More water leaves the ocean than returns as rain. What happens to the excess 50 thousand cubic kilometers per year? It is transported by the winds to the land. The ocean is a source of water to the land. Let's now look at this flow (the amount of water carried by wind from ocean to land) and add the known flux of rain to land.

- Wind transport from ocean air to land air: $50 \times$

$$\frac{10^3 \text{ km}^3}{\text{yr}}$$

- Rain on to the land: $120 \times \frac{10^3 \text{ km}^3}{\text{yr}}$

Considering the air over the land, we can see that 120 units rain out, but this land air gets only 50 units from the winds that come from the ocean. Therefore, how much more water does the land need to receive from some other source in order to be able to rain at 120 units per year? Clearly, the land needs $120 - 50 = 70$

more units from somewhere else. Those 70 units come from two sources: (1) evaporation from soils and lakes and (2) transpiration from plants. Those two sources are approximately equal. Therefore, we can write the following numbers.

- Evaporation from land's soil and lake: $35 \times$

$$\frac{10^3 \text{ km}^3}{\text{yr}}$$

- Transpiration from land plants: $35 \times \frac{10^3 \text{ km}^3}{\text{yr}}$

We need one more flux to complete the cycle. (For simplicity, we are leaving out groundwater and ice.) The land receives 120 units from rain and loses 70

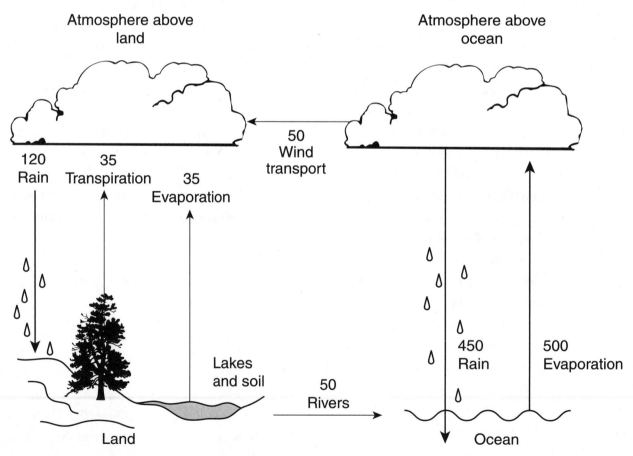

Figure 11.1 The global water cycle, showing some of the most important fluxes. Numbers are in cubic kilometers of water per year.

from evaporation and transpiration. We can now calculate how much the land must lose as runoff in rivers that goes back to the ocean. That number is 120 − 70 = 50. So 50 units must flow in rivers back to the ocean. In fact, those 50 units exactly balance off the amount that is transported by winds from the ocean's air to the land's air to rain over the land. We have now completed the cycle. Note the important point that all the reservoirs are balanced. The air over the land must receive as much water as it loses. The ocean must receive as much water as it loses. All the fluxes can now be put into a figure (see Figure 11.1).

One more concept should be discussed before we close the subject of the global water cycle. This is the concept of *residence time* for a reservoir within the cycle. The residence time is how long the water stays in a particular reservoir, on average. Let's work through an example of residence time, using the atmosphere as the reservoir.

The water in the atmosphere as water vapor leaves the atmosphere as rain and is replaced from the surface of ocean and land by evaporation and transpiration. As you can see from Table 11.1, there are 13 thousand cubic kilometers of water in Earth's atmosphere as water vapor. What are the water fluxes into and out from the atmosphere? From Figure 11.1, it is clear that the total rain from Earth's atmosphere is 120 + 450 = 570 thousand cubic kilometers per year. Verify for yourself that this same amount enters the atmosphere, as the total sum of the evaporation fluxes from both ocean and land plus the transpiration flux from land plants. We can define the residence time as follows:

Residence time = (Mass in reservoir)/(Sum of entering fluxes)

Alternatively,

Residence time = (Mass in reservoir)/(Sum of exiting fluxes)

We can use either definition, because the entering fluxes equal the exiting fluxes, so the calculations will be the same. In the case of the atmosphere's water vapor,

$$\text{Residence time} = (13 \times 10^3 \text{ km}^3)/(570 \times \frac{10^3 \text{ km}^3}{\text{yr}})$$

$$= 0.023 \text{ yr}$$

How long is 0.023 years? Put in terms of days, that's about eight days. That means the water stays as vapor in the air only about eight days, on average, before it rains out and is replaced by new water vapor coming from Earth's surface. This calculation shows the power of the concept of residence time, because it gives us clues about how the cycle works.

## ▶ Practice

**6.** In the global water cycle, which two reservoirs would not be directly connected by a flux?
   **a.** ocean surface and ocean air
   **b.** plants and land air
   **c.** groundwater and ocean air
   **d.** ocean air and land air

**7.** Look at Figure 11.1 and determine the global amount of rain, in thousands of cubic kilometers per year.
   **a.** 450
   **b.** 570
   **c.** 120
   **d.** 70

**8.** Of the following, which flux does not involve a change of state of the water between gas, liquid, or solid?

   **a.** evaporation from ocean

   **b.** transpiration from plants

   **c.** freezing into snow in clouds

   **d.** rivers flowing into the ocean

**9.** Approximately how long does water vapor stay in the atmosphere, on average, before it rains out and is replaced by new water vapor?

   **a.** a week

   **b.** a month

   **c.** a day

   **d.** a year

**10.** Look at Figure 11.1 and determine how much total water enters the ocean each year from all the fluxes that go into the ocean, in terms of thousands of cubic kilometers per year.

   **a.** 500

   **b.** 450

   **c.** 50

   **d.** 400

# 12 ▶ Water on the Land

## LESSON SUMMARY

Rain that falls on land is vital for human life and the lives of all other organisms. This water seeps into the soil, then into groundwater, and some of it eventually flows into rivers. These rivers carry sediments from land to the ocean, thus eroding the continents. Here we look at the main features of water on the land.

## ▶ Rainfall and Rivers

For anyone who has traveled, the different kinds of vegetation and animals that live in a particular region can be striking. The amount of rainfall received in a region plays a large role in determining the kinds of plant and animal life in a particular region. Regions are even named or categorized by the amount of rainfall received and type of vegetation growing.

*Deserts*, for example, are created when a region receives less than 10 inches of rainfall per year. *Rainforests*, in contrast, have more than 80 inches of rain a year, and some very rainy places can have a couple hundred inches of rain per year, more than half an inch per day, on average. The global average rainfall is about 30 inches of rain annually.

What determines how much rain falls in each region? The details are as complex as the landscape itself, but we can discern a couple basic large-scale patterns. To see these patterns, we need to revisit some features of the wind patterns: the *Hadley cells* and *air circulation* over mountains.

Recall that the Hadley cells create warm, rising air currents in the tropical regions. This ascent takes the air up into the troposphere and cools it—perfect conditions for clouds and rain. Indeed, the tropics tend to be very rainy. The high levels of sunlight that create the tropical temperatures also evaporate lots of water from the oceans in the tropics. Winds can bring this moisture-laden air over the continents. But that alone is not enough to make heavy rainfall. This is where the ascending currents of the Hadley cells come into play, for they ensure that the moisture-laden air drops water in those very tropics. Indeed, the great rainforests of the world are located in the tropics: South America, Africa, and Indonesia.

After the air currents of the Hadley cells have lost most of their water vapor to rain, they move north and south in the upper troposphere and then descend (as you recall) around 30° north and south. These descending air currents are dry; their water was lost in the tropics. Descending dry air means little rain, perfect conditions for deserts. And in fact, we find some of the major deserts of the world at about 30° north and south latitudes. Examples include the famous Sahara Desert of Africa. Other examples are the deserts in the Southern Hemisphere, specifically South Africa, most of Australia, and parts of Chile. The Sonoran Desert of Arizona and Mexico is one more example in the Northern Hemisphere.

Another kind of air circulation we discussed was the lifting of wind over mountains. This also has a large impact on rainfall. Consider the westerlies that blow winds from across the Pacific Ocean eastward into Washington, Oregon, and California. These winds carry moisture that they received via evaporation from the Pacific Ocean. They then reach the mountains of those western states, the Sierras and Cascades. The winds lift up, the air cools, the water vapor condenses into clouds, and it rains.

The rain in these mountain systems occurs on their *windward sides,* the sides that first receive the wind, because that's where the uplift takes place. Once the air crosses over the top of the mountain, it is dry. On the other side of the mountain range, the *leeward side,* the air contains little moisture. The eastern side of the mountain ranges of Washington, Oregon, and California are very dry, almost deserts in fact. These dry sides of mountain ranges are called the *rain shadow.*

Rainfall largely determines the flow of rivers. Another determining factor is the total area of drainage of a river, which is known as the *watershed.* The watershed is the area that potentially collects the rain that feeds into a flow of water on whatever scale—creek, brook, stream, or river. The term *watershed* is the same as *drainage area.* Let's look at the ten largest rivers of the world, in terms of their discharges into the ocean, or in other words, their flow rates into the ocean.

You might think: Why isn't the Nile on this list? The Nile, in fact, is the world's longest river. However, its drainage area is not so large because of another factor—that much of the drainage area of the Nile is desert. So you can see the impact that rainfall has on the discharge of rivers.

Let's look at the table in more detail, for patterns. Although the rivers are ranked according to discharge, from the Amazon at number 1 to the Mekong at number 10, the ranking is not the same for drainage area. True, the Amazon and Congo, which are ranked number 1 and 2 for discharge, are also number 1 and 2 for drainage area. But after that, the ranking in terms of drainage area breaks down.

Compare the Mississippi and the Congo, for example. Their drainage areas are almost the same, and yet the Congo's discharge is more than double that of the Mississippi. That is because the Congo is tropical and sits under the ascending rain-creating branch of the tropical Hadley cell. The same reasoning is true when comparing the Lena (primarily in Russia) with the Mekong in Southeast Asia. For the same drainage area, the Mekong has three times the discharge rate as does the Lena.

The flow from the Amazon is truly amazing: 220,000 cubic meters per second. Let's calculate how much water that is per person per day, globally. There are 86,400 seconds in a day. So in a day, the flow of the Amazon is 18.9 billion cubic meters. Today, the world has about 6.4 billion people. Dividing the flow of the Amazon by the number of people on Earth, we can compute that 3 cubic meters per person per day flow out the mouth of the Amazon. At about 250 gallons per cubic meter, that's nearly 750 gallons of water per person per day flowing from the Amazon River.

## ▶ Practice

**1.** The ascending branches of the Hadley cells create which one of the following conditions?
   **a.** dry conditions
   **b.** windy conditions
   **c.** calm conditions
   **d.** wet conditions

**2.** Compared to the Congo River, the Mississippi River has which one of the following?
   **a.** about the same discharge for a much smaller drainage area
   **b.** about the same discharge for a much larger drainage area
   **c.** a much larger discharge for about the same drainage area
   **d.** a much smaller discharge for about the same drainage area

Table 12.1  The top ten rivers of the world

| RIVER SYSTEM | DRAINAGE AREA (1,000 SQUARE KM) | DISCHARGE INTO OCEAN (CUBIC METERS/S) |
|---|---|---|
| 1. Amazon (South America) | 6,915 | 220,000 |
| 2. Congo (Africa) | 3,820 | 46,000 |
| 3. Ganges/Brahmaputra (Asia) | 1,730 | 44,000 |
| 4. Yangtse (Asia) | 1,800 | 32,000 |
| 5. Orinoco (South America) | 1,000 | 29,000 |
| 6. Parana (South America) | 2,970 | 23,000 |
| 7. Yenesei (Asia) | 2,580 | 19,000 |
| 8. Mississippi (North America) | 3,220 | 18,000 |
| 9. Lena (Asia, Russia) | 2,490 | 17,000 |
| 10. Mekong (Southeast Asia) | 810 | 17,000 |

**3.** The term *wind shadow* refers to which one of the following?

    **a.** the dry side of the Hadley cell

    **b.** the dry side of a mountain range

    **c.** the wet side of the Hadley cell

    **d.** the wet side of a mountain range

**4.** Which one of the following is the world's second greatest river in terms of discharge?

    **a.** the Amazon

    **b.** the Orinoco

    **c.** the Nile

    **d.** the Congo

**5.** If the flow rate at the discharge of the Amazon into the ocean is equal to about 750 gallons of water per day for every person on Earth, what is the approximate discharge of the Mississippi, in terms of gallons of water per day for every person on Earth? Use Table 12.1 to make your calculation.

    **a.** 60

    **b.** 270

    **c.** 220

    **d.** 30

## ▶ Features of Water on Land

As described in the previous lesson, water that falls as rain on land can take a number of different pathways. Let's go into more detail now about water's presence on land. Basically, you need to study a number of definitions.

When rain falls, it can immediately run over the land and down into a brook or stream; this is one type of *runoff*. In addition, groundwater can seep out of the ground, say at the sides of a valley, and join brooks, streams, and rivers as runoff. So runoff does not have to come immediately from water that runs over the land to a drainage channel. Brooks, creeks, streams, and rivers all are different scales of drainage channels. Together, these drainage channels, along with ponds and lakes, form what is known as *surface water*, or water at the land's surface.

As we have seen in the previous lesson, a great deal of water is underground, in the soil and in shallow and deep groundwater. The water that falls as rain and does not run off immediately infiltrates the soil. This is called *infiltration*. There are two different places that the infiltration can go. First, it can become part of the soil's water, which is called *capillary water*, because it resides in the fine networks of air passages (capillaries) within the soil. This water adheres to particles in the soil, and is the major source of water for plants. Plants' roots feed on the capillary water of the soil.

The second place that the infiltrated water can go is downward, pulled by gravity toward deeper levels of the soil and eventually into the cracks and passageways in rocks beneath the soil. This is called *gravitational water*, because the water is pulled downward by gravity. Eventually, it will stop when it reaches a layer of rock that has no cracks or porosity. Such a layer is impermeable. However, sometimes the rock is quite porous; in fact, there might be underground layers of gravel or sand that can hold a lot of groundwater. The groundwater also flows, at a limited rate. This is why someone who lives in the country can keep pumping water from their groundwater supply—the groundwater at that spot keeps refilling the well. Of course, one cannot pump too much too quickly, because the well has only a certain recharge rate.

The underground water usually has an uppermost level, which is called the *water table*. A well must reach below the water table, obviously, to obtain water. When there are large, well-developed layers of porous material or rock that contain large amounts of water, the layers are referred to as *aquifers*. The U.S. Midwest has a giant aquifer called the *Ogallala aquifer*, which extends over many states and upon which millions of people depend and will continue to depend until it is depleted.

Groundwater, as mentioned, can emerge from the ground, out of cracks or from the porous layer in which it flows. If it emerges as a definite flow, the spot is called a *spring*. Springs are good to know about when hiking. If the water emerges from the ground as a general area of moisture, the spot is called a *seep*.

Fresh water on land is not salty. Usually, *fresh water* is defined as water that contains less than one-tenth of 1% salt. Contrast that to the ocean's *salt water*, which is about 3% salt. In places where the land meet the ocean, estuaries can form, which are bays or swampy areas that receive fresh water flows from a river that mixes with the ocean water. Thus, in estuaries, the water's salt is in between that of fresh water and that of the ocean. Such estuarine water is *brackish*. More inland, wetlands such as swamps can be completely filled with fresh water. These are *inland wetlands* and are crucial to biodiversity as well as natural water purification.

## ▶ Practice

**6.** Water that adheres to particles in the soil is called which one of the following?
   **a.** transpired water
   **b.** estuarine water
   **c.** capillary water
   **d.** gravitational water

**7.** What is another word for the entire area of land that collects water that is eventually drained by a river?
   **a.** a channel
   **b.** a recharge
   **c.** a watershed
   **d.** an aquifer

**8.** Water whose salt content is in between that of fresh water and that of the ocean is called which one of the following?
   **a.** mixed water
   **b.** saline water
   **c.** brackish water
   **d.** seeped water

**9.** An underground layer of porous rock that conducts water is called which one of the following?
   **a.** an aquifer
   **b.** groundwater
   **c.** seep
   **d.** an estuary

**10.** Chose the best answer. Gravitational water can feed
   **a.** surface water.
   **b.** groundwater.
   **c.** a watershed.
   **d.** runoff.

## ▶ Rivers Erode the Continents

Rivers carry more than water to the ocean. They carry sediment. If you've ever seen the Mississippi in its lower reaches, you see why they call it *the big muddy*. It's full of suspended sediment. The sediment consists of small particles of clay and small amounts of organic materials, but other bits of rock are there as well. This suspended material, carried along by the water because it is so small, is called *suspended solids*. Let's look at the world's top ten rivers again, ranked according to their discharge rate, as before, but now add the numbers for the suspended solids they carry to the ocean each year.

We see some amazing facts in this table. The Ganges/Brahmaputra, number 3 in terms of discharge and equal to only about 25% of the Amazon's flow, has the most suspended solids. Why is that? Though the Amazon drains the eastern side of the Andes mountains, for much of the Amazon's flow, the land is flat and does not add much to the suspended solid load. The Ganges/Brahmaputra drains the Himalayas and drains overall more mountains, which supply that pair of rivers (which meet before they drain together into the Indian Ocean) with lots of sediment. That's why many sedimentologists go to India and Bangladesh to study the tremendous sediment load carried by the Indian rivers.

And look at the tiny load of sediment carried by river number 2, the Congo. Unlike the Amazon, the Congo drains almost no mountains, just highlands in central Africa. The big sediment load of the Mississippi derives partially from the fact that so much of the Mississippi's drainage basin is in agriculture, and often, a lot of erosion comes from land that is cultivated.

What is the total sediment load carried by the world's top ten rivers? If we add up the loads in Table 12.2, we arrive at the number 3,928 million tons of sediment per year. In the practice questions that follow, you will be asked about how much this is per person per year, from these ten rivers.

In addition to the sediment that you can see with your eyes, rivers carry *dissolved material*. For example, the ocean's water is 3% salt, yet you do not see it (though you can taste it). Where is the salt? It exists in the ocean water as dissolved ions, invisible to the eye

Table 12.2 The suspended solids of the top ten rivers of the world, ranked by discharge, as in Table 12.1

| RIVER SYSTEM | FLUX OF SUSPENDED SOLIDS (MILLIONS OF TONS/YR) |
|---|---|
| 1. Amazon (South America) | 900 |
| 2. Congo (Africa) | 43 |
| 3. Ganges/Brahmaputra (Asia) | 1,670 |
| 4. Yangtse (Asia) | 478 |
| 5. Orinoco (South America) | 210 |
| 6. Parana (South America) | 92 |
| 7. Yenesei (Asia) | 13 |
| 8. Mississippi (North America) | 350 |
| 9. Lena (Asia, Russia) | 12 |
| 10. Mekong (Southeast Asia) | 160 |

Total        3,928 million tons/yr

because these ions exist as molecules, not particles, in the water. All rivers carry both solid sediment and dissolved loads.

The difference between solid sediments and dissolved loads carried by rivers reflects a basic distinction that geologists make between two types of weathering processes. *Weathering processes* wear down rocks. Weathering processes slowly destroy mountain ranges. These processes turned what had been an ancient mountain range as mighty as the Himalayas into today's Appalachian Mountains in the eastern United States. As noted, weathering processes come in two types.

The first type of weathering is *physical weathering*. In this process, wind, water, and ice can erode the rock, breaking it down into smaller and smaller particles. You can see some of the results as small grains of minerals in the soil. Sediments suspended in water, for the most part, derive from physical weathering.

The second type of weathering is called *chemical weathering*. In chemical weathering, the rocks and mountains are not broken down; they are dissolved. Before human industry began adding acids to the atmosphere, rain was mildly acidic, from the natural chemicals in the air. Soil water, with these mild acids and other acids added by soil life, dissolves certain rocky materials, turning the minerals into ions of various kinds. For example, chemical weathering creates calcium and phosphorus ions in the water. These ions can be used as nutrients by plants when the plants take up the soil water by their roots. And of course, these ions can flow into the rivers and on to the ocean.

Different elements have different propensities for being dissolved by chemical weathering. Iron, for example, does not dissolve easily. About 99.8% of the iron that is in rivers is in the form of suspended solids. In contrast, calcium dissolves quite readily. Only 40% of the calcium in rivers worldwide is in the form of suspended solids. That means that 60% of the calcium in rivers consists of dissolved ions from chemical weathering.

Globally, the mass of solid sediments carried by rivers is more than the dissolved load. This is because certain abundant elements, such as silicon and aluminum, travel mostly as suspended solids in the rivers.

## ▶ Practice

**11.** The world's top ten rivers, in terms of discharge, carry 3,928 million metric tons of sediment per year. How many kilograms per person is that per year? Assume that the world population is 6.4 billion people. Also, there are 1,000 kilograms per metric ton.
   **a.** 660
   **b.** 6.6
   **c.** 250
   **d.** 25

**12.** Use the text and Table 12.2 to figure out what percent of the suspended solids carried by the world's top ten rivers is carried by the Brahmaputra/Ganges alone. Choose the closest answer.
   **a.** 10%
   **b.** 20%
   **c.** 30%
   **d.** 40%

**13.** Use the text and Table 12.2 to figure out what percent of the suspended solids carried by the world's top ten rivers comes out of South America.
   **a.** 10%
   **b.** 20%
   **c.** 30%
   **d.** 40%

**14.** Which process produces dissolved loads of ions in rivers?

    **a.** estuarine weathering

    **b.** chemical weathering

    **c.** physical weathering

    **d.** watershed weathering

**15.** Which element has a relatively high percent of dissolved load in the world's rivers, compared to the very high percent of the suspended solid forms of the other elements?

    **a.** calcium

    **b.** iron

    **c.** aluminum

    **d.** silicon

# 13 ▶ What's the Ocean?

## LESSON SUMMARY

Some people have noted that planet Earth should really be called planet Water, or perhaps planet Ocean, because the dominant geographical feature is the huge, interconnected single ocean. What is the structure of the ocean? In this lesson, we will look at the geography and chemistry of the seas of planet Ocean. The next lesson will follow up with the ocean's circulation.

## ▶ Geography of the Oceans

Where did the ocean's water come from? No one knows exactly. Because comets in space contain water (they are, in essence, great balls of ice around a rocky core), it is possible that comets contributed to Earth's water soon after the formation of the solar system. At that time, huge numbers of comets would still have been flying around the inner solar system, and as they impacted the earth, they released their water to Earth's surface.

This theory seems to present a problem, because our neighboring planets of Venus and Mars are relatively dry. But Venus probably lost its water through breakdown of the water in its hot temperatures. And the rovers that recently surveyed the chemistry and geology of Mars have provided evidence that Mars once had liquid water on its surface, probably even a shallow ocean. How much water Mars lost to space and how much is locked up frozen as ice beneath the Martian surface is still unknown.

By whatever means Earth got its water, there is plenty of it. All the water on the planet—including rivers, lakes, ice caps, groundwater, and of course the oceans—is collectively called the *hydrosphere*. As we saw in Lesson 11, by far the greatest amount of water in the hydrosphere, more than 97%, resides in the oceans and is salty.

Geographically, the oceans cover about 71% of Earth's surface. But is there one ocean or several? We are all familiar with three oceans: the *Pacific*, the *Atlantic*, and the *Indian* oceans. These are fairly well distinguished by the shapes of the continents. Oceanographers cite two more areas worthy of being called oceans. One is the Arctic Ocean, the area bounded to the south by Russia and Canada, and in the center of which is the North Pole. The *Arctic Ocean* is mostly covered with ice in the winter but large portions of it open up in the summer. Because it is blocked by land around a large part of its perimeter, and it exchanges water with the Atlantic around Greenland and with the Pacific through the narrow Bering Strait, the Arctic Ocean is the most isolated of all the oceans and differs most from the others in its chemistry.

The other region worthy of being called an ocean is hardly bounded at all on one side. It is the *Antarctic Circumpolar Ocean,* also referred to as the Southern Ocean. This is the belt approximately 10° of latitude in width, which rings Antarctica. To its south, it is obviously bounded by the circular continent of Antarctica, which sits over the South Pole and extends to about 70° south latitude. But to its north side, the Antarctic Circumpolar Ocean connects with the southern ends of the Atlantic, Pacific, and Indian oceans.

The reason that the Antarctic Circumpolar Ocean is a well-defined region is because it is also called the *Antarctic Circumpolar Current*. It sweeps around Antarctica, around and around, from west to east, like a giant whirlpool. Its motion stirs in water from the other oceans and gives water back to them as well.

But the question remains: Are there many oceans or one? As we have seen, the oceans are interconnected with each other. The Atlantic, Pacific, and Indian oceans are connected by the Antarctic Circumpolar Ocean, and the Arctic Ocean has its own connections to the Atlantic and Pacific oceans (but not the Indian). In a sense, a single world ocean exists, with different zones that are only partially but not completely isolated from each other. For convenience, though, we will continue to talk about the different regions as oceans. Just keep in mind that they are all connected.

Let us now follow a path starting at a beach, say along the Atlantic coast, perhaps at the famous Jersey shore of New Jersey, and follow the ocean's bottom as it changes in depth. You very quickly get into water over your head and go to a depth of about 100 meters. But then the ocean stays at that depth for perhaps a hundred miles. You are on the *continental shelf.*

The continental shelf is geologically still part of the continent—in this case North America. The shelf rock is continental crust, not ocean crust. Worldwide, the continental shelf is a significant amount of area, about 10% in area of the world's oceans. In places, the shelf is very narrow, for example, off Peru. In other places, the shelf is extensive, for instance, in Indonesia. The Gulf of Alaska, the famous fishing ground for wild salmon, exists over the continental shelf. The continental shelf, in fact, contains most of the world's most productive fishing regions, or fisheries, as well as much of the world's petroleum-producing rock formations.

At some point as you continue heading out toward the center of the ocean, the continental shelf starts to bend downward. You have reached the *shelf break*. This is the upper edge of the continental land mass, and as you continue outward, you start to head down in depth quite rapidly. You are on the *continen-*

*tal slope.* The slope is still part of the continent, but it does head downward to the ocean floor itself.

When you leave these underwater parts of the continents, you reach a depth of about 4 kilometers, a part of the ocean called the *abyss, benthos,* or simply the *deep ocean*. For most of the world's oceans, the deep ocean changes little in depth, varying from about 3 to 5 kilometers in depth, with the average of 4 kilometers. Here you are on ocean crust, all of which emerged at some point in the past from the volcanic ridges, as described in Lesson 5.

Deviations from the average depth of the ocean are, in fact, caused by plate tectonics. As we saw in Lesson 5, the Mariana Trench, in the western Pacific Ocean near the island of Guam, is more than 11 kilometers deep. Here the ocean's crust is subducted into the depths of the lithosphere. The fact that much of the ocean's floor is always moving into subduction zones is what makes the ocean's floor very "young" by geological standards, only one or at most two hundred million years old. The continents, on the other hand, contain rocks that are billions of years old.

The other deviation from the average depth of the ocean occurs at the *oceanic ridges,* or *mid-ocean ridges* (so-called, because they are rarely at the continental boundaries, though they are not always really in the middle, either). As you walk across the bottom of the Atlantic Ocean, 4 kilometers down beneath the ocean's surface, where it's pitch dark because no light reaches those depths, you eventually start walking uphill, as if climbing a gently sloping mountain range. You have started up the Mid-Atlantic ridge, where the phenomenon of seafloor spreading was discovered.

As you climb the Mid-Atlantic ridge, you rise for a kilometer or 2, until at the top, you reach regions where volcanic gases emerge from vents in the ocean's crust. This is where the ocean's crust is born. So at the ridges, the ocean is less deep, typically 2 kilometers, or about half the world ocean average depth of 3 kilometers.

The ridges are important in affecting the average level of the ocean itself, over long, geological time periods. Geologists know that sometimes Earth's tectonic activity increases, and sometimes it decreases, throughout periods that last tens of millions of years and longer. If the tectonic activity increases, the volume of the world's ocean ridges increases because ridges that spread faster create more buoyant shallow oceanic lithosphere. The ridges are higher, which pushes the water higher up onto to the continents. It's like getting into a bathtub—the water level rises. Alternatively, if the overall activity of plate tectonics decreases, the volume of the ridges drops, and the sea level goes down. Changes such as these are the reasons why the ocean was over large parts of what is now Colorado, Wyoming, Texas, and Oklahoma many millions of years ago.

One other deviation from the average depth of the world's ocean occurs at hotspots in the deep ocean. Hawaii is the most famous example. The Hawaiian Islands are volcanic islands that have arisen all the way from the deep ocean bottom to break the ocean's surface and present us with a lovely tropical paradise in the middle of the Pacific Ocean. Most oceanic hotspots (and oceanic islands) are in the Pacific Ocean basin.

Figure 13.1 shows the features that we have described. Look at it, then move on to the practice questions.

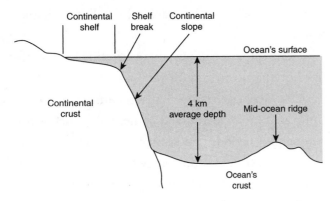

Figure 13.1 The major geographical features of a typical ocean

## ▶ Practice

**1.** Use the conversion factor of 1 kilometer = 0.62 miles to calculate the approximate average depth of the world ocean in miles.
   **a.** 0.06
   **b.** 2.5
   **c.** 1.2
   **d.** 4

**2.** The geographical and geological feature of the ocean that can control sea level over long time periods is called which of the following?
   **a.** ridge
   **b.** continental shelf
   **c.** shelf break
   **d.** ocean abyss

**3.** Which ocean is directly connected to more of the other oceans than any other ocean is?
   **a.** the Pacific Ocean
   **b.** the Atlantic Ocean
   **c.** the Arctic Ocean
   **d.** the Antarctic Circumpolar Ocean

**4.** The shallow zone of the ocean around continents is called which of the following?
   **a.** ridge
   **b.** break
   **c.** slope
   **d.** shelf

**5.** The two geographical parts of the ocean that are actually geological parts of continents are which of the following?
   **a.** shelf and ridge
   **b.** ridge and slope
   **c.** slope and shelf
   **d.** abyss and ridge

## ▶ Chemistry in the Oceans

The ocean is not just water, as any mouthful that you get while swimming at the beach can tell you. There are chemicals in seawater. When you evaporate the water from a cup of seawater, the salt remains. It is typically about 3% by weight of the seawater, quite a significant amount.

Here is the breakdown of the contents of the ocean's salt:

Chloride (chlorine ions) 55%
Sodium ions 30%
Sulfate ions 8%
Magnesium ions 4%
Calcium ions 1%
All the other ions 2%

So just the top five ions equal 98% of the total salt. The top two—chloride and sodium—make 85% of the salt, which is why we typically call salt *sodium chloride*. But if you actually use sea salt, manufactured by evaporating salt water, then the other ions are present as well. Indeed, dozens of other ions are found in the 2% of "all others" in the list above. Some of these lower-ranking ions are crucial to life, which we will see in a moment. But first, you'll need some more information about the ocean's salt.

The ocean does vary a bit from place to place in its salinity. Rather than speaking of *percent salt*, oceanographers use a related term called *parts per thousand*. After all, *percent* is actually *parts per hundred*. So if the ocean's salinity is 3%, that is the same as 30 parts per thousand. The symbol for parts per thousand adds another zero to the denominator of the percent sign. Therefore, 30 parts per thousand is written as 30°/oo. Much of the ocean's salinity is around 34, but it varies from about 33°/oo to as high as 36°/oo. What causes this variation?

Some local variation is caused by the fresh water of rivers that flow into the ocean—for example, the Amazon. But much of the variation in salinity of the open ocean, away from the coast, is caused by different balances of the two processes that add or subtract water from the ocean's surface. These two processes, respectively, are *precipitation* and *evaporation*.

While precipitation (rain and snow) and evaporation occur everywhere across the ocean, they are not always in balance. Where precipitation exceeds evaporation, that area of the ocean will become a little fresher, or less salty. Where evaporation exceeds precipitation, the region will become more salty, or have a higher *salinity*. No area of the ocean is isolated, as we have seen, so no zone gets ever saltier or fresher through time. Zones where evaporation exceeds precipitation will just have a higher salinity than the ocean average.

The Mediterranean Sea is especially salty. Rainfall is low, and the sea doesn't have that many freshwater rivers flowing into it. But the Mediterranean Sea has plenty of evaporation. It has some of the saltiest water in the world, and it flows out into the Atlantic Ocean through the Straits of Gibraltar.

The Arctic Ocean is relatively fresh. It is cold and thus evaporation is low. It does receive snow and rain, but another major factor is that it receives large amounts of fresh water from the rivers in Russia that flow north and empty into the Arctic Ocean. In essence, the Arctic Ocean gets the precipitation that falls on Russia.

The ocean's equatorial belts have a relatively high salinity. Sure, it rains a lot over the tropical oceans because of the Hadley cells. But that rain came from the ocean, from evaporation and then condensation into clouds. The important point is that some of the evaporated water is transported by winds to the continents, feeding rain to the tropical rainforests. Thus, more water is evaporated from the tropical ocean than falls back to the ocean as rain. Both evaporation and precipitation is high in these regions, but evaporation exceeds precipitation, making the tropical ocean belts saltier than the world ocean average.

Now we will look at two of the minor ions of the ocean's chemistry: *phosphate* and *nitrate* (with the chemical formulas: $PO_4^{3-}$ and $NO_3^-$). These are present in tiny amounts in the ocean overall and even less so in the surface ocean, where most of the ocean's life exists. Photosynthesizing algae and bacteria, which together form the phytoplankton, are a major component of the life in the surface ocean.

Phosphate and nitrate are taken up from the ocean's water by the *phytoplankton* during photosynthesis, the process that uses sunlight to convert chemicals from the environment into living bodies. Two of the substances absolutely essential for all living things are *phosphorus* (P) and *nitrogen* (N). These are present in the ocean ions phosphate and nitrate. Thus, the plankton, when living in the sun-drenched upper portion of the ocean, actively take phosphate and nitrate into their bodies.

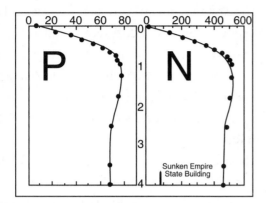

Figure 13.2   Phosphorus and nitrogen as their nutrient ions phosphate and nitrate, as a function of depth in kilometers, averaged over the world ocean. The numbers are in milligrams of each element per cubic meter of seawater.

During this uptake, phosphate and nitrate are removed from the ocean water. The living things actually change the chemistry of the water. In fact, the phytoplankton can be so highly active that the amounts of phosphate and nitrate are reduced to nearly zero across the world ocean, on average. You can see this effect in Figure 13.2, where the amounts of P and N near the ocean's surface are close to zero.

You can also see in Figure 13.2 that the amounts of P and N increase with depth, reaching levels of nearly 80 for P and more than 500 for N at a depth of 1 km, then decreasing a bit but remaining quite abundant all the way to the bottom of the ocean at the average 4 kilometer depth.

The difference in the concentration of phosphorus and nitrate at different depths is caused, as noted, by the consumption of these two nutrient elements by the phytoplankton at the ocean's surface. But another biological factor is at work as well. As the phytoplankton die, their bodies fall downward in the ocean (while alive, the phytoplankton have ways to remain buoyant). Also, other creatures, such as tiny swimming crustaceans, feed on the phytoplankton and excrete wastes. These wastes also float downward into the deep ocean.

The dead cells and various kinds of wastes (from fish, too) carry bacteria on them. The bacteria feed on the falling wastes, and, as they feed, convert the wastes back into phosphate and nitrate, both of which are returned (regenerated) to the seawater by the bacteria. This is the reason that phosphate and nitrate are so abundant in the deep water; they are regenerated back into the water by the bacteria who feed on the falling waste products of the surface life. We see in this example how life in the ocean influences the actual chemistry of our huge expanse of salty water.

## ▶ Practice

**6.** What are the two most abundant ions in the ocean?
  **a.** sulfate and sodium
  **b.** chloride and magnesium
  **c.** magnesium and sulfate
  **d.** chloride and sodium

**7.** One place in the ocean where the water is a bit less saline than the world average is which of the following?
  **a.** the Arctic
  **b.** the Mediterranean
  **c.** the equator
  **d.** deep water

**8.** The symbol for parts per thousand is which of the following?
  **a.** °/o
  **b.** °/oo
  **c.** °/ooo
  **d.** °/oooo

**9.** The difference between abundance of the phosphate ion in the surface water and the deep water is caused by which of the following?

    **a.** regeneration by bacteria down deep and consumption by phytoplankton at the surface

    **b.** consumption by bacteria down deep and regeneration by phytoplankton at the surface

    **c.** regeneration by phytoplankton down deep and consumption by bacteria at the surface

    **d.** consumption by bacteria down deep and regeneration by phytoplankton at the surface

**10.** Phytoplankton are which one of the following?

    **a.** crustaceans

    **b.** bacteria

    **c.** benthic organisms

    **d.** photosynthesizers

# 14 ▶ The Dynamic Ocean

## LESSON SUMMARY

The oceans are not stagnant giant bathtubs of salty water. They are continually in motion. Indeed, the oceans are fluid. Forces upon them make them swirl at the surface and mix into their most abyssal depths. Here we will look at the various mixing processes in the world's oceans.

## ▶ Surface Currents and Gyres

We saw in Lesson 2 how the ocean's tides are caused primarily by the moon and, to a lesser extent, by the sun. As the tides rise and fall, the ocean's water is stirred. But as you know from playing in the surf at the beach, the winds are another potent factor in stirring the sea.

Everywhere on Earth, the winds blow across the ocean's surface, sometimes softly, sometimes with violent atmospheric storms such as in hurricanes. The winds stir the water, like when you blow across a cup of coffee to which you just added cream.

But the winds are not powerful enough to mix the ocean all the way down. The ocean is too simply too deep. How deep can the winds stir the sea into a uniform layer? The depth of intense mixing by the wind is called the *mixed layer*. On average, the mixed layer is about 100 meters in depth. It gets deeper when the winds are stronger and shallower during weaker winds. Scientists, of course, want to know the exact relationship and so they study the mathematics of how the depth of the mixed layer varies with wind speed. Very roughly, doubling the speed of the wind doubles the depth of the mixed layer.

Because the water within the mixed layer moves up and down during its stirring, tiny creatures that live in the mixed layer also go up and down, in and out of more intense light. The mixed layer is roughly the same as the layer where light is available to phytoplankton in the ocean. This surface zone has the technical name of *pelagic zone*. Most of the ocean's living things stay in the pelagic zone; for creatures that do not photosynthesize, feeding on those that do is important, and the photosynthesizers are found in the pelagic zone.

The creation of the mixed layer is one major effect of the winds on the stirring of the seas. For a second effect, we turn to the large-scale wind patterns of the atmosphere, specifically the tropical easterlies and the midlatitude westerlies. The combination of these two kinds of winds (which exist, you will recall, in both hemispheres), make huge whirlpool-like circulations in the ocean called *gyres*. Think of the ocean waters as fluids that are brushed around by the winds, like the way you could make water move with a broom. Just as one might start a floating inner tube spinning by pushing one side with the left hand and pulling the other side with the right, the easterly winds in the tropics and the westerlies in the midlatitudes combine to propel gigantic surface gyres in the ocean basins.

Consider the situation of the Atlantic Ocean in the Northern Hemisphere, which sits between the combined mass of Africa and Europe to the east and North America to the west. On the southern side are the tropical easterlies, which push the south side of the region of the Atlantic from east to west. In the midlatitudes, the winds are westerlies. They push the northern edge of the zone of the Atlantic Ocean from west to the east. Thus, the northern edge is pushed from west to east, the southern edge from east to west. Both pushes reinforce each other to make the ocean start to spin in a clockwise direction. It's just like using your two hands in opposite directions of opposite sides on the inner tube to start the inner tube spinning.

These clockwise gyres exist in both the North Atlantic and North Pacific.

The Southern Hemisphere presents a different situation. Think of the South Atlantic zone. It has easterlies to the north (in the tropics) and westerlies to its south (in the southern midlatitudes). Thus, the South Atlantic is pushed east to west on its northern edge and pushed west to east on its southern edge. When looking at a globe, that means right to left on the upper edge, and left to right on the lower edge. The resulting spin of the ocean gyre is counterclockwise. That is exactly the situation in the South Pacific, South Atlantic, and Indian Ocean (which is mostly in the Southern Hemisphere).

Because the easterly and westerly winds are results of the earth's Coriolis effect, we can say that the ocean gyres are also a result of the earth's Coriolis effect, which of course comes from Earth's spin.

For the most part, the ocean gyres turn rather slowly. You couldn't watch them move before your eyes, for example. They are much slower than the winds, which might take only days to travel across the oceans. The time frames of the ocean gyres are measured in months or even years.

However, in certain regions, parts of the gyres can become concentrated and truly flow as currents. The most famous example familiar to us in the United States is the *Gulf Stream*. But if you lived in Japan, you would more readily recognize the name of the *Kuroshio Current*. And you would know what it is. The Kuroshio Current is an intense giant current of water that flows north, along the eastern coast of Japan. The Kuroshio Current and the Gulf Stream (which flows from the Caribbean, along Florida, then goes further offshore and all the way to the far northern Atlantic) have been called *rivers within the sea*. The Southern Hemisphere has its own rivers within the sea, also, such as the *Brazil Current* off Brazil.

These rivers within the sea, for dynamical reasons, occur in the western portions of the ocean gyres.

Thus, they are sometimes called *western boundary currents.* They do not occur along the southern, northern, or eastern potions of the ocean gyres, only along the west.

Effects of currents such as the Gulf Stream (see Figure 14.1) can be dramatic. The Gulf Stream effectively carries warm tropical water up into more northern, cooler waters. The Gulf Stream does mix somewhat with the cooler waters it encounters, but because it is so powerful and coherent, much of the Gulf Stream's water stays within the stream itself. Sometimes as far as New York City, tropical fish are found, having traveled in the warm Gulf Stream and then spun off into the cooler waters, searching for and never reaching their homes a thousand miles away.

The contact between the Gulf Stream and cooler waters to the north can cause smaller gyres, or *eddies,* called *rings.* Like the gyres, the rings are whirlpools. But unlike the gyres, the cause of the rings is not the winds, but simply the rubbing or friction between the Gulf Stream and the cooler waters it encounters. When the whirlpool-like rings are formed from the cold water, they are called *cold rings.* When the rings are spinoffs of the Gulf Stream itself, the rings are called *warm rings.*

The warm waters of the Gulf Stream have an effect on climate. Just north of Florida, around Cape Hatteras, North Carolina, the Gulf Stream leaves the coast of the United States and travels in water further offshore. The Gulf Stream, in fact, heads over in the direction of England, bringing warmth to the English and Scandinavian climates that those areas would never otherwise have. Some scientists are concerned that because of global warming, the Gulf Stream might weaken or shift course. Thus, it is possible that Northern Europe could grow cooler even while much of the rest of the world grows warmer, if the Gulf Stream were to change dramatically.

## ▶ Practice

1. The ocean's average mixed layer depth is about 100 meters, and the global average wind speed across the ocean is about 10 miles per hour. In a place where the wind speed is about 15 miles per hour, how deep would you expect the mixed layer to be?
   a. 67 meters
   b. 100 meters
   c. 300 meters
   d. 150 meters

2. The ocean gyres are results from which one of the following?
   a. the moon
   b. the earth's spin
   c. the sun's gravity
   d. the seafloor spreading

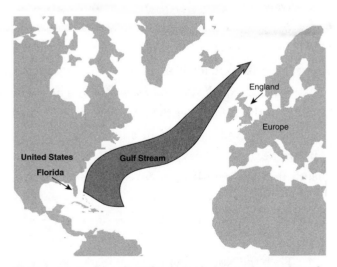

Figure 14.1 The Gulf Stream sweeps along part of the east coast of North America, before bending out to sea and heading north across the Atlantic in the direction of England.

**3.** Which one of the following describes the Atlantic Ocean's gyre, in the Northern Hemisphere?

a. counterclockwise, pushed in part by easterlies to its south

b. counterclockwise, pushed in part by westerlies to its south

c. clockwise, pushed in part by easterlies to its south

d. clockwise, pushed in part by westerlies to its south

**4.** Flows are intensified into actual "rivers within the sea" at which edge of the ocean gyres?

a. northern

b. eastern

c. southern

d. western

**5.** Which one of the following countries' climate is warmed quite a bit by the Gulf Stream?

a. England

b. Canada

c. United States

d. Russia

## ▶ How the Deep Ocean Mixes

The ocean also has a second, very different kind of circulation that has nothing to do with the winds and would exist even in the absence of wind. The technical name for this circulation is the *thermohaline circulation*. The word is a combination of "thermo" for temperature and "haline" for salt, because these factors determine the density of water.

When water gets cold, say in winter at high latitudes, it becomes denser and tends to sink. When sea ice forms, also in winter at high latitudes, the freezing of fresh water into ice leaves the remaining ocean water saltier. At the same temperature, saltier water is heavier water and therefore tends to sink.

In summary, the driving factor behind the thermohaline circulation is the fact that denser water will tend to sink. Both of the processes of cooling water and increasing its salinity cause it to have increased density, and both processes occur at the high latitudes during winter.

These two factors create the densest water at certain high latitude regions, which are called sites for *deep water formation* or *bottom water formation*. One site is in the far North Atlantic, around Greenland and Labrador. The especially salty water in the North Atlantic comes not only from the freezing out of fresher water into sea ice in winter, but also from the fact that water from the relatively salty Mediterranean Sea also manages to contribute (it mixes into the north Atlantic). You see the situation is complex, and oceanographers are always working on refining their understanding of the intricacies of ocean circulation. But certain facts, which we will now review, have become well established.

Water of the far North Atlantic, during winter, becomes very dense and sinks to tremendous depths, almost all the way to the bottom of the ocean (but not quite, for reasons that will become clear in a moment). This is called *North Atlantic Deep Water*. The water travels south, deep under the ocean's surface, pushed by new deep water behind it, and unable to move upward because its heavy density holds it at a certain depth in the ocean. It even crosses the equator at a depth of 3 kilometers under the surface and enters the Southern Hemisphere and passes into the South Atlantic Ocean.

Then the North Atlantic Deep Water gets mixed into the Antarctic Circumpolar Ocean water. Around the continent of Antarctica is the second major place on Earth where deep or bottom water forms. This region is bitter cold in winter, and the waters around Antarctica become the coldest waters in the ocean. The Antarctic Circumpolar Current (recall this region also goes by that name) is so well mixed that virtually the entire water column for many hundreds of meters could be considered a mixed layer; and the vertical mixing is quite vigorous almost all the way to the bottom.

Some of the North Atlantic Deep Water that enters the Antarctic Circumpolar Ocean is spun up to the surface where it cools during winter to become not only the coldest water on Earth, but also the most dense water on Earth. It sinks downward and then is known as *Antarctic Bottom Water*. Because it is the densest water on Earth, it dominates the sinking process and reaches deeper than does the North Atlantic Deep Water. In fact, some of the Antarctic Bottom Water travels north into the Atlantic Ocean underneath the North Atlantic Deep Water.

The Antarctic Bottom Water also travels into the Pacific and Indian Oceans. It goes all the way along the bottom in a wide swath a kilometer or so in vertical extent, reaching as far as the North Pacific.

The northern part of the Indian Ocean is still in the tropics (near southern India), so its surface waters never get cold enough to become deep water. But what about the North Pacific? It also experiences intense winters (think Alaska). Well, the deep and bottom waters of the world are, in a sense, in competition with each other. The densest waters make it to the bottom and become the bottom water. The next densest waters make it not quite as far and become the deep water. The waters of the North Pacific get not quite as dense as those that become either the North Atlantic Deep Water or the Antarctic Bottom Water. It is possible that, at other times in Earth's history, when conditions of climate, rivers, and continental positions were different, the North Pacific did produce deep or bottom water.

Consider the geometry of the ocean. Its average depth is about 4 kilometers, or about 2.5 miles. And the typical width of an ocean is many thousands of miles. The distance from the places that form the North Atlantic Deep Water to the equator is about 4,000 miles or more. Consider now the ratio between the ocean's depth and its length, using $\frac{2.5}{4,000}$. That's a ratio of 0.000625, or $\frac{1}{1,600}$. The ocean is not deep at all, compared to its length! And yet the ocean's layers of density cause it to be so stratified that the deep and bottom waters can travel thousands of kilometers and stay at their depths, confined within those layers of density. Like the solid earth, the ocean is stratified by its density.

A dramatic demonstration of this stratification can be seen by oceanographers who pull up samples of deep water from high-tech buckets that can be lowered down into the ocean deep, then closed to trap the water they encounter. When these insulated buckets are hoisted to the surface and opened up, the water inside is very cold, just a couple of degrees above freezing. This happens even at the equator, where some of the warmest water on Earth is at the surface!

We've now discussed the deep and bottom waters of the world, traveling around way under the ocean. But that situation can't go on. New deep and bottom water has to come from the surface and that requires taking as well as replacing surface water. How do the deep and bottom waters of the world circulate back to the surface? The answer is *little by little*, gradually here and there. The amount of bottom water that reaches the North Pacific, for example, is less than the bottom water that entered the South Pacific from the Antarctic Circumpolar Ocean. As the bottom water travels northward into the Pacific, it sheds some of its mass upward toward the surface. This happens because of mixing processes, similar to the way that the Gulf Stream loses some of its flow as it mixes during its travels.

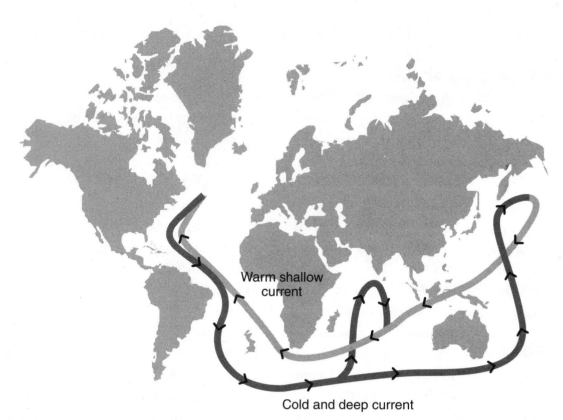

Warm shallow
current

Cold and deep current

Figure 14.2 The thermohaline circulation causes cold, salty, dense water to plunge downward in certain polar regions of the world's ocean, move along the deep layers of the oceans, and circulate slowly back up to surface as it mixes and warms.

So the return flow to the surface of the deep and bottom waters occurs everywhere. This is different from the situations that form the deep and bottom waters, which happen only in special local places in the North Atlantic and around Antarctica. The return flow to the surface is distributed throughout the world's oceans and is given the term *upwelling*.

Recall from Lesson 13 that the levels of nutrient ions phosphate and nitrate are almost zero at the ocean's surface but are high down deep in the ocean. How do the nutrients get back to the surface from which they were removed by photosynthesis? The answer is via the ocean's upwelling. The upwelling of the deep waters, which happens everywhere, carries the phosphate and nitrate nutrients back to the surface to be used again by the phytoplankton.

The thermohaline circulation is very powerful, but the ocean is huge. It takes, on average, about a thousand years for the thermohaline circulation to make a complete cycle around the ocean. The stirring time of the world ocean is thus about 1,000 years. In that time period, the entire ocean, from its surface to its deep abyss, is mixed. That seems like a long time to us, but it's short compared to the time scales of geology. In fact, that time is almost instantaneous.

▶ **Practice**

**6.** The mixing of the deep ocean occurs by what means?

    **a.** wind circulation

    **b.** tectonic circulation

    **c.** Coriolis circulation

    **d.** thermohaline circulation

**7.** The density of the ocean's water is determined by what factors?

    **a.** nutrients and temperature

    **b.** pressure and nutrients

    **c.** temperature and pressure

    **d.** salinity and temperature

**8.** The densest waters on Earth are formed at the surface in the vicinity of what region?

    **a.** Antarctica

    **b.** the North Pacific

    **c.** Greenland

    **d.** the Mediterranean

**9.** What fact is true about the formation of the ocean's deep water and the return flow to the surface?

    **a.** Deep water formation is local, and the return flow is widely distributed.

    **b.** Deep water formation is widely distributed, and the return flow is local.

    **c.** Deep water formation is widely distributed, and the return flow is widely distributed.

    **d.** Deep water formation is widely local, and the return flow is local.

**10.** The timescale for the complete mixing of the world's ocean is about how many years?

    **a.** 100 years

    **b.** 1,000 years

    **c.** 10,000 years

    **d.** 100,000 years

L E S S O N

# 15 ▶ What Is Soil?

## LESSON SUMMARY

We have seen how rain infiltrates the soil and the various pathways that water can take within the soil. But what exactly is soil? We all know it, have held and smelled it, so soil seems familiar. Yet soil is actually quite mysterious, not only because it is such a complex substance, but also because much of the action of the soil takes place on the microscopic and molecular levels. Soil, a unique combination of physical and biological processes, is vital to all life.

## ▶ The Formation and Structure of Soil

Soil is one of the great marriages known to earth science. Two very different actors are linked to create soil. The first is physical; the partner is biological. The first comes from the rock below; the second comes from the life above. Below and above are combined in the middle—soil.

We will consider the physical partner first. In Lesson 12, the process of physical weathering was shown to break down rocks into smaller and smaller particles by the action of wind, water, and ice. Physical weathering turns the bedrock of the continental crust into broken bits and chips these bits smaller and smaller into gravel. Gravel is ground down by the processes of physical weathering still further in size, into sand, silt, and clay.

Definitions of sand, silt, and clay are somewhat arbitrary and made by agreements among soil scientists. Typically, these are the size ranges for the three types:

- **Sand:** 2.0–0.02 mm in diameter
- **Silt:** 0.02–0.002 mm in diameter
- **Clay:** Less than 0.002 mm in diameter

You can see that silt is roughly smaller than sand by a factor of 10, and clay is smaller than silt by a factor of 10 or more.

The physical, mineral components of soil are a mixture of particles of all these different sizes, thus a mixture of sand, silt, and clay. A good mix of all three is called a *loam*, a common soil combination with generally desirable properties. Loam is approximately 40% sand, 40% silt, and 20% clay. When one component is substantially more than these percentages, the soil is called by other names. For example, if the clay component is significantly higher than 20%, at the expense of silt or sand (or both), the soil could be a clay loam. Similarly, soils can be silty loams or sandy loams. If the percent of one of the components is so large that it dominates, the soil can simply be called sand, silt, or clay. The situation gets more complex with additional names, but this gives you the general idea.

In Lesson 12, we also described a process known as *chemical weathering*. This is a physical process, too, but it works on the level of chemical changes, rather than a physical breakdown of particles. Chemical weathering involves the dissolution of minerals to make ions of elements and compounds that exist as dissolved forms in water.

We cannot always perfectly and neatly separate physical and chemical weathering sometimes, even though conceptually, they are distinct. For instance, chemical weathering alters clay particles at the same time they reach their tiny sizes from physical weathering. Nonetheless, it is important to keep in mind the distinction, because chemical weathering adds nutrient ions to the soil's water, which will be important later.

The second partner in the marriage that makes soil is life. Plants live with their roots in the soil. When plants die (or leaves fall in the autumn from the trees that stay alive from year to year), a large amount of material from the photosynthesizers falls down to the top of the soil. This material is called *organic*, because it consists of organic molecules, molecules of complex chains of carbon atoms, with hydrogen and oxygen atoms and a host of other elements required by life. These molecules include carbohydrates such as cellulose and also proteins and lipids—all building blocks of life.

The detritus from plants, as well as dead animals and animal waste that enters the soil, like the minerals, pass through a sequence of diminishing sizes and altered compositions. Devoured by crawling and burrowing scavengers, physically ground and chemically broken by worms, beetles, ants, and other arthropods, the decomposing organic material enters a complex web of life that includes tiny worms called *nematodes*, whose populations per square meter often number in the millions, each of which can gobble thousands of bacteria per minute. Together, they make an organic matrix of different-sized aggregates—sticky, sponge-like, complex, and nourishing.

The result of the nonbiological processes of both kinds of weathering, plus the biological degradation of organic detritus, creates soil. Soil comes in more colors than the human skin. It also comes in layers, which themselves often have different colors. Together, the layers form the soil profile (see Figure 15.1).

The uppermost layer of soil is called the O layer, or O horizon. It consists of the detritus from plants and animals who live above the soil. In a forest, for example, the O horizon is the mat of leaves you can almost lift up with your hands, a tightly woven layer of leaves from several years. Near the base of the O horizon, the materials (think leaves or grass stalks) have decayed into a black mass called *humus*. Humus helps the soil be fertile for future generations of plants.

Below B comes the C horizon, which consists of broken pieces of rock from the bedrock even farther below. The C horizon supplies the minerals for the soil at that site. The bits of rock in the C horizon are on their way, via physical and chemical weathering, to becoming the smaller bits of minerals in the upper levels of the soil. You can see now how soil is a merging of the mineral processes from below with the biological processes above.

Under the C horizon is a layer called the R horizon, for rock. It is the parent bedrock for the site, the ultimate source of the kind of minerals that the soil will contain.

Soil is typically about a meter thick, but this varies tremendously from place to place. As you can see from the descriptions of the layers, the amount of organic matter in the soil decreases with depth.

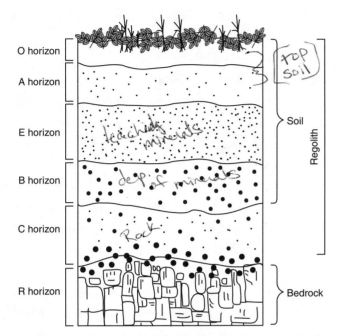

Figure 15.1 A soil profile. The layers (horizons) of a typical soil. Not all soils have all the horizons.

Below the O horizon is the A horizon. This also goes by the well-known name of *topsoil*. It is a rich mixture of the biologically decayed, organic material from the O horizon and the more physical, mineral material from the next horizon below. The topsoil is essential to the productivity of the soil. The minerals of the topsoil supply the new nutrients needed by the plants. The organic components of the topsoil provide a source of recycled nutrients for the plants. Water in the topsoil is called *capillary water* because it is water that is held in the pores and channels of the topsoil's materials. The capillary water can stay there for quite some time.

The next layer down is the E horizon. In the E horizon, many minerals are being leached away from the gravitational water that leaks down from the soil into the groundwater. The E horizon is lighter in color than the A horizon.

Below the E layer is the B horizon. In this layer is a deposition of minerals that were leached away by water from the E horizon.

### ▶ Practice

**1.** The physical components of the soil can be listed in order from largest to smallest. Which is the correct order?
   **a.** sand, clay, silt
   **b.** clay, silt, sand
   **c.** sand, silt, clay
   **d.** silt, sand, clay

**2.** Loam is a desirable mixture of silt, clay, and sand in the following proportions.
   **a.** 40% silt, 20% clay, 40% sand
   **b.** 60% silt, 10% clay, 30% sand
   **c.** 20% silt, 50% clay, 30% sand
   **d.** 80% silt, 10% clay, 10% sand

**3.** Soil can be called a marriage because it is a combination of what two things?
   **a.** physical and biological processes
   **b.** water and air properties
   **c.** animal and plant organisms
   **d.** climate and mineral processes

**4.** Which of the following is true about the O horizon of a soil profile?
   **a.** It is also called topsoil.
   **b.** It contains deposits of leached minerals.
   **c.** It is the bedrock.
   **d.** It has the litter from trees.

**5.** Which of the following is true about the A horizon of a soil profile?
   **a.** It is the bedrock.
   **b.** It is also called topsoil.
   **c.** It has the litter from trees.
   **d.** It contains deposits of leached minerals.

## ▶ Soil as Recycling Compartment for the Land

Because the decomposed products of life make soil so much of what it is, without life, there is no soil. Without life, the forces of weathering that reduce rocks to particles would wash those particles away. Without life and thus soil, every sunny day would be a drought, every rain a flash flood. Without life, particles of soil would quickly wash or blow away, to aggregate in valleys of deep sediment graveyards or tumble into the sea. Much of the continents would be as bare as today's fresh volcanic fields.

We will discuss how the soil's life is essential, not only in creating soil, but in functioning as a recycling process that allows plant life to flourish. But first, we will review some of the properties of soil that make it conducive for living things. In other words, what is a healthy soil?

A healthy soil strikes a balance between water infiltration and water retention (also called *water holding*). If the soil is hard clay, for instance, rain water will not be able to infiltrate it and will run off the surface to be wasted. Water needs to be able to move into the soil to become stored as the reservoir of soil moisture that plants can draw upon during days or weeks when no rain occurs. Thus, infiltration is crucial. The degree of infiltration is normally determined by the amount of sand in soil, which creates large pores for water to move downward.

On the other hand, a soil can be made of too much sand. Beaches, for example, do not make a productive soil. With too much sand, the water simply runs downward as gravitational water, goes into the groundwater system, and is lost to plants. Thus, a healthy soil will retain water as capillary water stored in microscopic spaces and on the mineral grains of the soil (already discussed). Clay and silt are good at retaining water; so is the organic humus.

A healthy soil also needs to allow enough air to circulate within it, as well as between it and the atmosphere. Aeration is obviously high in sandy soils and is inhibited by clay soils. Why is air needed? First of all, the roots of plants are just like us; they need to breathe air to get oxygen for their cells. Without a fresh supply of air from the atmosphere into the soil, plants can die. This is why it can be bad to overwater house plants. It's not the water directly that can kill the plants, but rather the fact that the water is preventing their roots from getting the needed air.

Except for the kinds of bacteria that thrive in the absence of oxygen (called *anaerobic bacteria*), all organisms in the soil must also breathe air for their oxygen. Air moves around in the soil because a healthy soil is porous. The porosity extends right up to the surface, from the A to O horizons, and allows air to move from the atmosphere into the soil, as well as from the soil into the atmosphere.

Also, the roots of plants and organisms in the soil give off carbon dioxide gas as a waste product from their metabolisms, the same metabolisms that use oxygen. The waste carbon dioxide enters the pores of the soil and eventually moves up and out of the soil into the atmosphere. As a result of the breathing of soil organisms, the concentration of carbon dioxide is much higher in the soil than it is in the atmosphere.

A healthy soil also has a large capacity to hold nutrients. To some extent, this property is related to water retention because the nutrients that plants use are in the form of dissolved ions in the water. But a nutrient-holding capacity is also related to the kinds of particles in the soil. Not enough nutrients can be held by the water alone, and the water can sometimes be used up or fall to minimal levels during droughts. Nutrients are also retained on soil particles, and the best kind of particle for nutrient retention is clay.

Organisms are also crucial for a healthy, natural soil. Previously, we saw that countless numbers of tiny nematode worms inhabit soils, as well as other creatures such as ants, beetles, and earthworms. Another crucial type of organism is the fungi, whose microscopic white threads decompose organic materials within the soil. When it is time for some kinds of fungi to reproduce, they make mushrooms.

The soil is an entire ecosystem. Creatures run around (millipedes, centipedes, spring tails) and creep along (slugs, snails). Some of the soil's inhabitants are single-celled protozoans, seen under a microscope. Even smaller, visible only at a microscope's highest power, are the most important inhabitants of all, the bacteria.

Soil would not be soil without its bacteria. Although all the soil creatures participate in the breakdown of plant debris from the O horizon of litter, the bacteria are the ones that perform the greatest part of the final step in decomposition and return the elements in the organic debris into forms available again for the plant's roots to take in for the next round of growth. Bacteria are thus key to the recycling function of soil.

We will next see how the activity of bacteria determines the amount of organic material in the soil. Bacteria, which digest and therefore break down organic matter (say, from fallen leaves), are more active at high temperatures and less active at cooler temperatures. The climate of a region, then, can affect the activity of bacteria and thus the amount of organic matter in the soil. Very cold climates tend to have thick soils with a high content of organic matter. Famous for this are the peats of northern Canada and Siberia, in which the activity of bacteria is extremely slow.

At the other end of the climate spectrum are the tropics. What are tropical soils like? You might think they would be thick, given the abundance of vegetation and growth in the tropics, but no. Tropical soils, despite the rich vegetation, tend to be thin with low amounts of organic matter, because the breakdown (decomposition) is so rapid. Bacteria in the tropics digest at a high rate and keep the organic contents of the tropical soils low. That is why the tropical soils are often not very good for agriculture, after being used just a few years following deforestation.

The main role for bacteria is to recycle elements from the dead vegetation debris of the O horizon into dissolved ions in the soil water, because these ions are then available to plants for uptake and more growth. It is an important point that the processes of physical and chemical weathering are too slow and their products too little to supply the plants with the nutrients the plants need. Plants thus depend upon recycled nutrients.

An example of the importance of recycling can be seen from numbers of that key element for plants, phosphorus. Let us consider phosphorus requirements, summed over all the plants across all the continents. That need is about 40 times higher than the flux of phosphorus supplied to the soil from the breakdown of minerals by weathering. That means that when a plant takes in phosphorus through its roots, 39 parts out of 40 (close to 98%) is, on average, recycled phosphorus. This recycled phosphorus is, for the most part, derived from the actions of the soil bacteria.

A final property of a healthy soil that is related to the human use of soil for agriculture is what is called *workability*. Can the soil be plowed easily? Does it have all the properties of an overall healthy soil that can support intensive cultivation? Can it hold water, be naturally aerated, and retain nutrients?

Traditional agricultural techniques can create a loss of soil by erosion. If the A horizon (the topsoil) is lost, productivity plummets. Plowing also creates some soil loss by exposing loose particles to the eroding effects of wind and water. Plowing can also increase the activity of bacteria and thereby reduce the organic matter of the soil. In fact, on average, cultivated soils have about 25% less organic matter than they did before they were cultivated.

Solutions to the long-term maintenance of healthy soils for human use include better cultivation techniques. One promising technique that is rapidly growing in adoption is no-till agriculture. In no-till, the entire farm soil is not plowed. Instead, only a narrow strip where the seeds will be planted is worked by machinery precisely guided down the same path year after year.

Other advances are coming in irrigation, to attempt to use the minimum amount of water at precisely the time when the water is required. The precision application of fertilizers is also under way.

## ▶ Practice

**6.** The component of soil that is worst at retaining water is which of the following?
   a. silt
   b. sand
   c. humus
   d. clay

**7.** Which of the following represents an advance in agriculture that directly minimizes erosion?
   a. no-till
   b. precision fertilizer
   c. flood irrigation
   d. plowing

**8.** The organic content of tropical soil is which of the following?
   a. low because the large amount of rain washes the material downward
   b. high because of the large amount of plant debris
   c. high because the sun stimulates photosynthesis
   d. low because the hot climate stimulates bacteria activity

**9.** Which of the following kinds of organism is most crucial to the recycling function of soil?
   a. earthworms
   b. nematodes
   c. protozoans
   d. bacteria

**10.** The uptake of phosphorus by plants, on average, uses some phosphorus that was recycled in the soil from the previous generation of plants that gave detritus to the soil. How much of the uptake is recycled phosphorus?

a. 100%

b. 35%

c. 82%

d. 98%

# 16 ▶ Ice and Snow

## LESSON SUMMARY

We drink liquid water, and when the day is sweltering, we rely on ice cubes to cool off our drinks. In winters in the midlatitudes, precipitation falls as snowflakes. Some of us enjoy skiing and snowboarding on the white, solid form of water. Over hundreds of thousands of years, great continental ice sheets have waxed and waned. In this lesson, we look at the science behind ice, from snowflakes to ice sheets.

## ▶ The Magic of Ice

How water turns solid is an interesting story that takes us, once again, into the molecular structure of the water molecule. Recall that the water molecule ($H_2O$) is slightly bent. The two hydrogen atoms that are individually bonded by a bridge of shared electrons with the central, larger oxygen atom do not stick out at 180° from each other in a straight line. Instead, they are slightly bent in toward each other, making a angle of about 109° between them, with the vertex of this angle at the oxygen atom.

Now, the hydrogen atoms in a single water molecule cannot bond with each other, but those in two different water molecules can. The bond between hydrogen atoms goes by the special name of the *hydrogen bond*, because it is unique to hydrogen atoms. In a hydrogen bond, each hydrogen atom, with only one electron, would naturally share its electron with a neighboring hydrogen atom. But in the case we are considering of water, the hydrogen atoms are already committed to sharing their electrons with the oxygen atom. Yet the energetics to share with another hydrogen are still in place. The result is a slight attraction of their hydrogen atoms across neighboring water molecules toward each other.

The hydrogen bond is weak, much weaker than the actual shared electronic bond between the hydrogen and oxygen atoms within the water molecule itself. The weak hydrogen bond makes water, well, watery. Imagine little molecules slightly sticky toward each other, just enough to make water coherent as a liquid. But now imagine that the temperature cools, and the energy (the velocity and vibration) of each molecule gets less and less. The energy gets so weakened with further cooling that the hydrogen bonds start to have more and more influence. At what we call the freezing point of water (0° C, 32° F), the hydrogen bonds start to link the water molecules in a latticework with each other. Ice is born.

The hydrogen bonds are so weak that they can be broken by temperature in the range we live in. The breaking of the hydrogen bonds takes place when ice melts. The formation of the hydrogen bonds occurs when ice forms. As we saw in Lesson 11, the melting and freezing of water involves a transfer of energy, even though the temperature remains the same. For review, this latent heat of freezing or melting (called the *latent heat of fusion*) is 79 calories per gram of water.

At certain places on Earth, it is cold enough to have permanent ice all year round (more on that later), but ice can form at any latitude and longitude—if you go high enough in the atmosphere. Recall that temperatures cool as you go up in the troposphere. They cool so much that there can be snow on mountains in regions that have nice hot summers at sea level. Temperatures in the troposphere can drop so much with altitude that permanent snow and ice are found on top of Mount Kilimanjaro, which is almost right on the equator in Kenya, Africa.

The cooling of temperatures with altitude is governed by the *adiabatic lapse rate*. Recall that two types of lapse rates exist: dry and moist. The dry lapse rate is about 9° C per kilometer, which is applicable in places where water vapor is very low. The moist lapse rate averages about 6° C per kilometer in altitude. If the moist adiabatic lapse rate applies to a given area, would you have to go higher or not as high in the atmosphere to reach the freezing point of water, compared to another area where the dry adiabatic lapse rate holds (assume the same starting temperatures at the ground at sea level)? The answer is higher. Were you correct? Because the temperature decreases at only 6° C per kilometer in the moist adiabatic condition, you would have to go higher up to reach the same cold temperature, compared to a region where the temperature decreases at 9° C per kilometer. Does the lapse rate decrease enough to give us snow on Kilimanjaro? We'll find out in one of the practice questions.

The top of the troposphere is the tropopause, which averages about 10 km high. Using the moist adiabatic lapse rate from sea level, we can see that the tropopause is about 60° C (10 km × 6° C/km = 60° C) cooler than the ground at sea level. Because 60° C is 140° F, any location on Earth will have freezing temperatures at the tropopause, indeed, well before that height is reached.

The troposphere is the zone of the atmosphere where weather takes place. Clouds that go up that high, say, nearly to the tropopause, will be frozen and are called *cirrus*, the wispy very high clouds that look like faint white brushstrokes by the painter called nature. Cirrus clouds consist of tiny ice crystals, so small they stay aloft as clouds.

The fact that the atmosphere gets cold up high is the reason that hail can fall in the hot desert in summer. Air currents go up and down. In fact, the intense heating of the ground during summer can drive air currents upwards, sending water-laden air high enough for the water vapor in the air to freeze. If the currents descend, some of the frozen droplets melt a little. Then if the air rises to the atmosphere's freezing level again, more ice grows on the droplet and it enlarges. Up and down the droplets go, melting a little, freezing some more. Eventually, the droplets, round balls by this time, get too heavy for the winds to keep them aloft and they fall as hailstones. When hailstones are cut open, the layers of freezing events are visible.

Many different kinds of frozen precipitation exist. Sleet, for example, is basically frozen raindrops—messy and nasty. And then, of course, there's snow. The uniqueness of snowflakes provides us with the best metaphor for how every shape in the universe is individual, including each of us as persons. Snowflakes are, of course, hexagonal (see Figure 16.1). As unique as each might be, each has six radiating arms. All crystals made from specific substances have inherent geometries.

Salt (sodium chloride), for example, is cubic. It so happens that the geometry of the hydrogen bonds that lock together when water becomes ice creates a hexagonal pattern. A snowflake forms when water vapor freezes onto a crystal that is already growing (which started around a condensation nucleus). Different temperatures and densities of the water vapor in the atmosphere cause different nuances of crystallization in the growing snowflake. When the flakes become heavy enough, they can no longer be kept aloft

Figure 16.1 Snowflake

and they fall to the ground. See if you can catch one on your tongue.

Snow often accumulates during the winter, sometimes for weeks, sometimes for months. The greatest accumulations are usually in the mountains. Often, it is so cold that the snow doesn't melt until the spring, in what is known as the *spring runoff*. The spring runoff is important for the growth of many plants during the summer, and often, the runoff happens slowly, little by little supplying water over a month or more.

What happens when the ice from winter does not melt entirely during the summer? Then a glacier can form in the mountains. We can see glaciers today in the United States in Glacier National Park in Montana and in Alaska. Kilimanjaro has its glaciers and the Canadian Rockies have many glaciers. Glaciers in the European Alps have names that go back centuries, admired by the tourists and local people.

Glaciers tend to grow near their higher-altitude tops because that's where they are the coldest and where more precipitation occurs. But then the weight of the glacier pushes down on the glacier at lower altitudes and on the glacier's ice that is pressed against the underlying rock. This ice can melt and part of the glacier starts to move. Ice is lost at the lower altitude and under the glacier, but new ice forms farther up the mountain at the higher elevation. Thus, mountain glaciers are dynamic systems; they can grow and shrink.

Glaciers also cause erosion. You can tell when a mountain valley once had a glacier in it because the valley is U-shaped. That's in contrast to a valley that was eroded by water alone. Then the valley is V-shaped.

Another form of ice is *sea ice*. Ice floats because its density is less than liquid water. This is a highly unusual behavior for a molecule or substance. For most substances, their solid forms are denser than their liquid forms. The peculiar behavior of water and ice, again, has to with the hydrogen bond, which causes the water molecules to spread apart when they lock together into the network of ice.

It's a good thing for us that water expands when it freezes, which makes ice float. If ice were denser than liquid water, then the ice in winter during the freezing of a lake would sink. More ice would then form at the surface and that in turn would also sink. Lakes could, in this different world, completely fill up with ice during a winter and the fish would die. Instead, in our world, because ice floats, the lake water is insulated. Yes, the ice grows in thickness but very slowly, because as it gets thicker, it becomes more difficult to cool the water below the ice to the freezing point. Ice on a lake insulates the water.

During winter, tremendous amounts of sea ice on the ocean grow around the continent of Antarctica and upon the Arctic Ocean. These floating ice areas come and go with the seasons, waxing and waning in areas much larger than the United States. As we saw in Lesson 14, the freezing of sea ice makes the water left behind saltier and thus more dense. This process thereby helps drive the thermohaline circulation.

Sea ice also affects climate. The white ice is an excellent reflector of sunlight. In the future, if global warming causes the extent of sea ice to decrease, more of the sun's energy will be absorbed by the darker water (compared to the white ice). This change could enhance the warming from the greenhouse gas carbon dioxide.

## ▶ Practice

1. The technicalities of how liquid water forms into ice are determined by water's ability to create which one of the following?
   a. octagonal networks
   b. surface tension
   c. hydrogen bonds
   d. heat of fusion

2. Assume that around Mount Kilimanjaro in Kenya, the ground temperature is about 30° C (88° F). Also assume a moist adiabatic lapse rate of 6° C/km. At what altitude would you expect to find ice on Mount Kilimanjaro?
   a. 8 km
   b. 5 km
   c. 4 km
   d. 6 km (By the way, Mount Kilimanjaro is high enough.)

3. Layers of melting and freezing can clearly be seen in which type of precipitation?
   a. snow
   b. sleet
   c. icetite
   d. hail

4. Mountain glaciers erode valleys into what shape?
   a. staircase shape
   b. U-shape
   c. V-shape
   d. square shape

**5.** Sea ice around Antarctica and in the Arctic Ocean affects which two processes?

   **a.** latent heat of freezing and adiabatic lapse rate

   **b.** thermohaline circulation and solar absorption

   **c.** adiabatic lapse rate and solar absorption

   **d.** thermohaline circulation and latent heat of freezing

## ▶ Ice Sheets on the Continents

One very important type of ice remains: continental ice sheets. Only two places on Earth have very large continental ice sheets, but in the past, during ice ages, the ice sheets were much more extensive.

Ice sheets are to glaciers what the urban sprawl of Los Angeles is to a single city street. Today, ice sheets cover almost all of Greenland in the Northern Hemisphere and Antarctica in the southern. They are massive almost beyond belief, with ice miles in depth (or height, depending on where you start to measure).

To get a sense of how much ice is in the continental ice sheets of Greenland and Antarctica, recall the number for the amount of water in glaciers and ice caps from Table 11.1 of Lesson 11. (Ice caps are another term for ice sheets because they cap the rock they are on.) That amount is 2.2% of the world's water. Also recall that the ocean has 97.2% of the world's water.

Let's calculate how much sea level would rise if Greenland and Antarctica melted. For simplicity, assume that all the 2.2% of glaciers and ice caps is in Greenland and Antarctica. That's a good assumption. You'll be walked through the calculation here, just up to the answer, and then be asked to compute the answer for one of the practice questions. If Greenland and Antarctica melted, using the assumption just stated, the ocean would rise in sea level by a fraction of

$\frac{2.2}{97.2}$ of its current volume. Disregarding the issue of continental shelves, we will assume that the ocean has a constant depth of 4,000 meters (again, not a bad assumption). So, how much would sea level rise if Greenland and Antarctica melted?

One of the great discoveries of the earth sciences over the last hundred years or so is the recognition that long ago, ice sheets covered massive parts of northern North America, Europe, and Russia. This understanding is still being refined today by hundreds or more specialists around the world who study Earth's past ice ages. Such intensive study is required not only because earth's history is fascinating, but because Earth's past might give us clues to Earth's future.

The earliest evidence for past ice ages is in the form of geological formations left by the great ice sheets (mountain glaciers leave some of these, too, but the results are smaller). Examples of this geological evidence include *moraines*, which are piles of rubble left by the ice sheet (or glacier) as the ice pushes forward across the land. The final, farthest rubble pile left by the advance of an ice sheet (or a glacier) is called the *terminal moraine*. Much of Long Island, New York State, is a giant terminal moraine from a past ice age.

Streams of meltwater that flow from a glacier or in a tunnel under an ice sheet can create a ridge of gravel called an *esker*. When some of the finely ground glacial material is blown by the prevailing winds into an elongated hill (or series of hills), we have what is called a *drumlin*.

Geological features like these, found in the United States, presented the early modern geologists with evidence that giant ice sheets had once covered most of Canada and a good deal of the northern United States. We now know that the ice sheets during the last ice age were very thick. New York City, for example (or Manhattan Island, because New York City did not exist), as recently as 20,000 year ago was covered with an ice sheet a mile thick. How do we know the thickness? The geological evidence can provide some sense of the lateral extent of the ice, but what evidence do we have for its thickness?

Scientists can get numbers for the ice's volume on the continents during the last ice age by using oxygen isotopes. We have already discussed the science behind the radioactive isotope of carbon (C-14) and other radioisotopes (such as potassium-40) that are used for dating the buildings of ancient cliff dwellings and the birth of igneous rocks. In Lesson 8, the stable isotope of carbon (C-13) was briefly noted. Many elements have stable isotopes as well as radioactive ones. Ordinary oxygen is O-16, with eight protons and eight neutrons in its nucleus. Oxygen also has a stable isotope, O-18, with eight protons and ten neutrons in the nucleus.

Water ($H_2O$) contains both O-16 and O-18. The oxygen in water is mostly O-16, but small fractions of the water molecules contain O-18. This "heavy" water is everywhere, in the ocean, in the rain, in your body. When water evaporates from the ocean, the heavy water stays behind with just a little more statistical propensity than the water that contains O-16. That means that water vapor in the sky contains a higher percentage of O-16 water than water in the ocean. That means, in turn, that rain or snow contains a higher percentage of O-16 water than water in the ocean.

When reservoirs of water are all in balance, as they are most of the time, the lighter water in the rain or snow returns to the ocean, so the ocean is not permanently altered. But during the development of an ice age, in which ice sheets on the continents are growing, the water that is locked up as ice, which fell as snow from the sky, is lighter (it has more O-16) than the water in the ocean. During the ice age, so much water was locked up in the ice sheets that the ocean's ratio of O-18 to O-16 was changed. If there was more O-16 locked up in the ice sheets, can you tell whether the ratio of O-18 to O-16 in the ocean increased or decreased?

The ratio of O-18 to O-16 in the ocean increased. The ocean's water became slightly "heavier." That ratio can be measured today, even though the ancient ocean is history. Organisms that make calcium carbonate shells in the ocean use carbonate from the ocean water. The carbonate ($CO_3^{2-}$) is formed by chemical reactions between carbon dioxide and water molecules in the ocean, and therefore, the oxygen isotopes in the carbonate molecules have the same ratio of O-18 to O-16 as does the ocean. The carbonate shells fall to the bottom when the creatures that make them die. For the most part, the shells are preserved in the ocean bottom sediments. Scientists drill into and retrieve these sediments, take them back to their laboratories, and measure the isotope contents of the shells to determine the isotopes of the ancient ocean at various times.

By measuring the ratio of O-18 and O-16 in the shells, which equals that of the ancient ocean in which the shells grew, it is possible to calculate how much ice (with a reduced ratio of O-18 to O-16) would have been on the continents to increase the ocean water's ratio to the value that scientists measure. This technique has shown that so much ice was on land during the middle of the last ice age that sea level was down by about 150 meters! This means that the continents went further out than they are now, out to the edges of the continental shelves in many places.

When did the ice age occur? From studies of geological "calling cards" of the ice sheets, as noted previously, as well as the all-important modern methods of oxygen isotopes (and other techniques), it is known that the ice sheets waxed and waned in a large cycle that lasted about 100,000 years in length. In between the ice ages were warmer times, like the one we live in now. The most recent ice age ended about 10,000 to 12,000 years ago.

Many scientists of climate (climatologists) say we are just about at the start of another ice age and claim that our in-between warm period is coming to an end. Other climatologists say that because we are now increasing the greenhouse gas carbon dioxide, the earth will not be following the same rules that determined its climate in the past. Still other climatologists point to the fact that although most of the warm intervals between ice ages last 10,000 to 12,000 years, sometimes those warm intervals are longer, up to 20,000 years, and that might be the natural case for us now. Only time will tell.

## ▶ Practice

**6.** Finish the calculation in the text. About how much would sea level rise if Greenland and Antarctica melted?
  **a.** 90 meters
  **b.** 10 meters
  **c.** 20 meters
  **d.** 70 meters

**7.** Greenland and Antarctica are examples of what type of ice formation?
  **a.** sea ice
  **b.** ice flows
  **c.** ice sheets
  **d.** dry ice

**8.** Long Island, New York State, is an example of which one of the following?
  **a.** an esker
  **b.** a drumlin
  **c.** a holdar
  **d.** a moraine

**9.** Which one of the following is true about sea level during the last ice age?
  **a.** Sea level was lower and the O-18 to O-16 ratio of the ocean water was lower.
  **b.** Sea level was higher and the O-18 to O-16 ratio of the ocean water was lower.
  **c.** Sea level was lower and the O-18 to O-16 ratio of the ocean water was higher.
  **d.** Sea level was higher and the O-18 to O-16 ratio of the ocean water was higher.

**10.** If sea level was 150 meters below today's level during the maximum of the last ice age, say, 20,000 years ago, then how much of Earth's water was locked up in ice? You'll have to use your calculation from question 6 because that gives you the sea level rise if Greenland and Antarctica melted. Recall that they together have 2.2% of the world's water. To answer the question of how much of the world's water was locked up in ice during the last ice age, include today's 2.2% for Greenland and Antarctica, and add to it the percent necessary to lower sea level by 150 meters. What's the total water locked up in ice during the last ice age?
  **a.** 7.4%
  **b.** 5.9%
  **c.** 3.7%
  **d.** 2.2%

# 17 ▶ The Biosphere Puts It Together

## LESSON SUMMARY

The surface of the earth is a coordinated system that is called the *biosphere*, which includes the reservoirs of life, air, soil, and the ocean. Chemicals in these reservoirs cycle around and around, as rocks are turned into air and life, as ocean becomes soil, and soil becomes ocean. To understand the earth, we need to understand how the reservoirs of the biosphere interact, which is illustrated by the great cycle of carbon.

## ▶ Structure of the Biosphere

The biosphere is the thin, dynamic outermost layer of our planet, which includes air, water, soil, and life. It stretches from the top of the atmosphere to the depths of the ocean. This zone is where most living things not only live, but are connected to each other by the circulations within the physical reservoirs of air, soil, and ocean. It is necessary to talk about life when we talk about the systems of the earth because life makes a huge impact on reservoirs, as we will see. But first, we will examine the time scales of circulation within the physical reservoirs.

We have seen in Lesson 10 how the atmosphere circulates by great risings and fallings of air in the Hadley cells as well as by the tropical easterlies and midlatitude westerlies. Clockwise and counterclockwise winds blow around high- and low-pressure systems, respectively. By measuring certain gases in the Northern and Southern Hemispheres, scientists have determined that the entire atmosphere completely mixes in about one year.

Motions within the ocean are, for the most part, slower than the winds. But we have seen that the ocean, too, is a gigantic mixing machine, with tides and gyres, with the currents such as the Gulf Stream and Kuroshio Current, and with the deep overturning called the *thermohaline circulation*. Oceanographers are very interested in just how fast the ocean circulates. The number turns out to be about 1,000 years. That means any substance you put into the ocean will be mixed throughout the world's waters in about 1,000 years on average. That's quick for such a huge reservoir of water.

Although the soil doesn't have gyres and currents the way the atmosphere and soil do, the soil too does circulate. Winds and water can erode soil and deposit its grains elsewhere. Most important are the organisms, such as worms, that live in the soil and stir it. This process by which creatures mix the soil is called *bioturbation*. As we have seen, litter such as dead leaves from trees enters the soil at the top and degrades in the soil's deeper layers. The time scale for the mixing of soil varies with location, but in general, soil scientists have determined mixing times for soils on the order of 10 to 100 years.

All the reservoirs of the biosphere are connected to each other. This is similar to the way the reservoirs of the water cycle are all connected. Recall from Lesson 11 how ocean water becomes atmospheric water vapor, which becomes rain and then soil water, which can rise up into plant roots to be transpired back into the atmosphere. Indeed, the water cycle is an excellent example of how the four reservoirs of the biosphere—life, ocean, soil, and air—are interconnected. But this interconnection goes well beyond the water cycle. It includes cycles of other elements, such as carbon, nitrogen, and phosphorus.

Consider a system with just two reservoirs. How many back-and-forth connections can there be? Just one, a back and forth between the two reservoirs. Now

consider a system of three reservoirs called A, B, and C. How many connections are there? Exactly three. Here they are: A-B, B-C, C-A. If the biosphere has four reservoirs (life, ocean, soil, and air), how many connections are there? You should come up with the correct answer of six. We must discuss six different types of connections between the four reservoirs of the biosphere: life-air, life-ocean, life-soil, air-soil, air-ocean, and soil-ocean.

## Life-Air

The connection between life and air is primarily what is called *gas exchange*. Every time you breathe, you take in the atmosphere, extract some of its oxygen, and add some carbon dioxide waste from your body's cells; then you exhale the gases back into the atmosphere. This process is called *respiration*. The opposite process, extracting carbon dioxide and adding oxygen, takes places during photosynthesis, performed by green plants such as oak trees and grasses. Other examples of gas exchange occur too, but in general, through gas exchange, life affects the atmosphere and the atmosphere affects life.

## Life-Ocean

Because the ocean is so huge, it is convenient to think of this connection as between life and the ocean, but the same reasoning applies to life and any bodies of water, such as rivers and lakes. Organisms in the ocean exchange chemicals with the water as the organisms take in nutrients and give back wastes. Some of the connection is by gas exchange, because water contains dissolved gases, such as oxygen and carbon dioxide, but other exchanges involve the transfer of ions and actual bits of matter.

For example, creatures such as coral that build shells of calcium carbonate obtain their calcium as ions from the ocean water itself. In this way, the contents of the water become the bodies of organisms. As we saw in Lesson 13 about the nitrogen and phosphorus in the ocean, wastes from creatures sink downward into the ocean and are consumed by bacteria. Thus, a cycling of matter takes place between ocean water and marine organisms.

## Life-Soil

The soil's mineral grains of sand, silt, and clay contain many chemicals required by land creatures to live. In Lesson 7, we saw how some silicates contain calcium and phosphorus, which are both required elements for life. (Chemical elements required by living things are called *essential elements* or, more simply, *nutrients.*) Many creatures actively obtain essential elements from soil minerals by secreting substances to dissolve those minerals. In this process, these creatures perform chemical weathering. In addition, all creatures in the soil, from worms to bacteria, put forth wastes into the soil matrix, and the soil creatures breathe the air in the pores of the soil. So gas exchange occurs between life and the soil, too. Apparently, the exchanges between life and soil are very complex.

## Soil-Air

Rain descends from the atmosphere, bringing with it certain chemicals in the air, and wind can carry off fine particles into the atmosphere, but the primary exchange between the soil and air is gas exchange. Gases move from the atmosphere into the air pockets (pores) of the soil, and they also move in the opposite direction, from the pores of the soil up into the atmosphere. Some of the gases will be used by organisms in the soil, and some gases are generated by organisms in the soil.

## Air-Ocean

As in the case with soil, rain can bring not only water, but other chemicals from air to the ocean, and winds from the continents carry dust particles that are dropped onto the ocean's surface. Like the soil, the primary exchange with the atmosphere is through the movement of gases, back and forth across the surface between ocean and atmosphere. It doesn't appear to our eyes that the ocean is chock full of gases, but it is. The back-and-forth movement affects gases such as nitrogen, carbon dioxide, oxygen, and many more.

## Soil-Ocean

The connection between soil and ocean is a one-way flux, because the only way for substances to go back from ocean to soil is through the reservoir of the atmosphere. But substances do move from soil to the ocean all the time, transported by ground water and, most noticeably, by streams and rivers. As we have seen, rivers carry substances that are in the form of particles and substances that are dissolved ions, such as salts and phosphate ions. Rivers supply the oceans with new materials every day.

When we put together a picture of the four reservoirs and six connections, we have what is known as a *biogeochemical cycle*. Biogeochemical cycles are the cycles of elements essential to life. These cycles are thus biological (bio) and include geological processes (geo) and chemical reactions (chemical).

## ▶ Practice

1. The order of the physical reservoirs, from the one that mixes fastest to the one that mixes slowest, is
   a. atmosphere, soil, ocean.
   b. ocean, soil, atmosphere.
   c. soil, ocean, atmosphere.
   d. atmosphere, ocean, soil.

**2.** The thermohaline circulation is part of the biosphere's physical reservoir that circulates in about
  **a.** 1 year.
  **b.** 100 years.
  **c.** 1,000 years.
  **d.** 10,000 years.

**3.** Organic detritus sinks in the ocean and is consumed by bacteria, which give off wastes. This process is a connection between which two reservoirs?
  **a.** life-atmosphere
  **b.** life-soil
  **c.** atmosphere-ocean
  **d.** life-ocean

**4.** The respiration from the roots of plants drives up the amount of carbon dioxide in the soil. This increase will affect the gas exchange between
  **a.** ocean and life.
  **b.** soil and atmosphere.
  **c.** soil and ocean.
  **d.** ocean and atmosphere.

**5.** The cycle of a nutrient such as nitrogen, around and around through the four reservoirs of the biosphere, is called a
  **a.** chemobiogeological cycle.
  **b.** biogeochemical cycle.
  **c.** geobiochemical cycle.
  **d.** chemobiogeological cycle.

## ▶ The Carbon Cycle

The most important biogeochemical cycle is that of carbon, the essential element in the organic molecules of life. In addition, carbon dioxide is one of the atmosphere's important greenhouse gases, crucial for maintaining Earth's surface above the freezing point of water, and also of concern in the future as a cause of global warming (more about that in Lesson 19). To understand the global carbon cycle, we will first review the amounts and forms of carbon in the four main reservoirs and then look at the fluxes between the reservoirs.

### Life

Carbon in life is present in all organic molecules, the most common of which are proteins, carbohydrates, lipids, and nucleic acids (DNA). Carbohydrates, for example, come in different types, such as sugars, starches, and celluloses (in land plants). How much carbon is there in life? For this, we need to total both land life and marine life. Land life by far dominates the number, totaling at about 700 billion tons of carbon. In contrast, marine life has a miniscule amount of carbon, only about 2 billion tons. The difference comes about because most land life consists of trees, with huge trunks and root systems. Trees are great biological reservoirs of carbon, much of which is in the molecular form called *cellulose*.

### Atmosphere

If you look back at Table 9.1 in Lesson 9, you will see that air contains two major forms of carbon: carbon dioxide ($CO_2$) and methane ($CH_4$). $CO_2$ is 0.037% carbon and $CH_4$ is 0.00014%; thus, $CO_2$ is the dominant form. What is the total tonnage of carbon in the biosphere's atmosphere? The calculation requires knowing the total mass of the atmosphere and the molecular weights of the various gases, but let's go directly to the answer, rounded off: about 700 billion tons of carbon. It is intriguing that the amount of carbon as carbon dioxide gas in the atmosphere is about the same as the amount of carbon in the form of organic molecules in all of life globally.

## Soil

Most of the carbon in the soil occurs in the top two layers, the O and A layers, which are the layers of organic litter and topsoil, respectively (see Lesson 15). Here we count only the carbon in the form of organic matter, because that is the form circulated by life's activities in the soil. Carbon also exists within certain minerals in the soil (such as carbonates), and that varies tremendously from place to place. The carbon in the organic matter of the world's soils is about three times the amount of carbon in the atmosphere, for a total of about 2,100 billion tons of carbon.

The oceans contain by far the largest reservoir of carbon. In addition to invisible amounts of organic carbon (dissolved proteins and carbohydrates from organisms, for example), seawater has carbon in other chemically active forms. One form is simply dissolved carbon dioxide gas, but this reacts with the water molecules to form the two other main types of carbon-containing chemicals in seawater. The first is the *bicarbonate ion* (single negative charge), and the second is the *carbonate ion* (double negative charge). Of all the types of carbon in seawater, the one with the largest amount is the bicarbonate ion. All told, carbon in the ocean totals a whopping 35,000 billion tons.

Now we come to the fluxes of carbon between the reservoirs. Recall from Lesson 11 that water changes state as it moves between some of its reservoirs in the global water cycle, changing, for example, from liquid to gas as it moves from ocean to atmosphere during evaporation. Carbon is much more complicated because carbon changes the atoms it is bonded with into molecules during some (but not all) of its movements between reservoirs.

## Life-Air

The major fluxes between life and air are driven by land organisms. Trees and grasses move about 60 billion tons of carbon per year from its gas state as carbon dioxide in the atmosphere into the various organic molecules inside plants. The process is called *photosynthesis*. In contrast, animals such as flying insects and deer, which consume and digest plants, thereby releasing the carbon from its organic form back into carbon dioxide, create a flux of only about 5 billion tons per year. This release of carbon dioxide by animals takes place during their metabolic process of respiration.

## Life-Ocean

Photosynthesis and respiration also occur in the ocean between the various forms of carbon in seawater and the organic carbon in marine organisms. Estimates peg both processes within the ocean at about 40 billion tons of carbon per year.

## Life-Soil

The flux between life and the ocean seems in balance, with photosynthesis and respiration at about 40 billion tons a year. But the exchange between life and air on land seems out of balance. Land plants remove 60 billion tons of carbon per year, but land organisms (we mentioned deer and flying insects) return only 5 billion tons per year. What happens to the other 55 billion tons per year taken out of the air by photosynthesis on land? The answer is that much of the growth of plants falls to the soil. How much? About 55 billion tons per year. This yearly flux of detritus to the soil provides the food for the soil organisms (not included in the organisms that live above ground, such as flying insects and deer). Organisms such as worms and bacteria in the soil (for a more complete list, review Lesson 15) consume the organic matter in the soil and create carbon dioxide waste during their own processes of respiration, which occur underground. Roots of plants also contribute to this respiration flux of $CO_2$ to the soil.

### Air-Soil

The 55 billion tons of carbon dioxide gas added into the air pockets of the soil each year have to go somewhere. It travels up into the atmosphere in the process of gas exchange between the soil and atmosphere. The net result of this gas exchange is that carbon dioxide moves from the soil into the atmosphere in a flux of 55 billion tons of carbon per year.

### Air-Ocean

As noted earlier, the main flux between the atmosphere and ocean occurs as gas exchange. In the global biogeochemical cycle of carbon, carbon dioxide moves back and forth between the ocean and atmosphere. The flux is about 100 billion tons per year. In the natural system of the biosphere, this back-and-forth flux is in balance. Today, because humans are adding carbon dioxide to the atmosphere during the combustion of coal, oil, and natural gas, a slight net flux (about 2% excess) is going into the ocean, compared to the carbon dioxide that is leaving the ocean into the atmosphere.

### Soil-Ocean

How much carbon goes to the ocean from rivers, carried from the land's soils? The amount is about 0.5 billion tons per year, mostly in the form of dissolved bicarbonate ions. But some organic matter, too, is carried along to the ocean. This half-a-billion tons per year seems smaller than all the fluxes we have considered so far, but its existence will lead us to a very deep understanding, in a moment, of the relationship between the biosphere and Earth's rocks below.

Note that in the numbers given so far for the natural cycle (ignore the human input of carbon dioxide), the ocean as a reservoir is not in balance. Across the ocean's surface, gas exchange with the atmosphere is 100 billion tons per year in both directions. Then we have 0.5 billion tons per year coming in from the soils via the rivers, creating an excess supply to the ocean. If

that were to continue, year after year, the ocean's carbon content would double (from 35,000 to 70,000 billion tons) in 70,000 years (35,000 tons added/0.5 tons per year = 70,000 years). There must be another flux that leaves the ocean that we have not considered.

The additional exiting flux comes about from the organic detritus and carbonate shells of organisms that are buried in the ocean's sediments. Not all the productions of living things are recycled. Some of the productions "leak" out from the ocean and are trapped in the mud of the ocean bottom, to be buried deeper and deeper, someday becoming new rock. This burial flux is 0.5 billion tons per year. With these numbers, the natural ocean is in balance.

Here we come to the profound understanding of the relationship between the biosphere (air, water, soil, and life) and the deep earth below. With the burial of 0.5 billion tons of carbon from the ocean into the sediments each year, the biosphere as a whole is not in balance. The biosphere is losing 0.5 billion tons of carbon each year. At this rate, the biosphere will lose its carbon in how many years? Add up all the carbon in the four reservoirs and divide by the loss rate. You will be asked to provide the answer in a practice question.

For the biosphere not to be depleted of its carbon, new carbon must be entering the biosphere from below, from the geological processes that interact with the biosphere. What processes? Basically, plate tectonics.

Consider volcanoes. They release gases that happen to be high in carbon dioxide. Thus, volcanoes are a source of carbon in the form of carbon dioxide to the atmosphere. Consider, too, the rocks that are brought into the biosphere when the forces of plate tectonics expose fresh rock to the weathering processes of the biosphere during mountain building. Physical and chemical weathering first reduce the rock to particles and then dissolve the elements, thereby bringing those elements into the cycles of the biosphere.

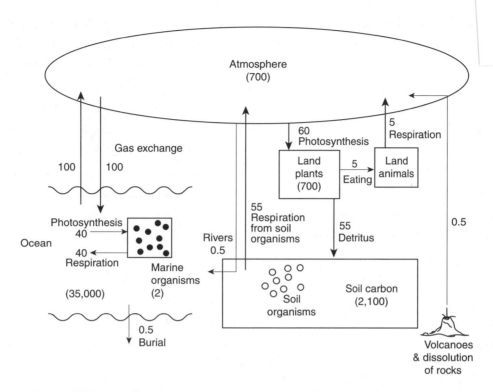

Figure 17.1 **The carbon cycle.** Fluxes (arrows) are in billions of tons of carbon per year. Amounts of carbon in the reservoirs are in parentheses and are billions of tons of carbon.

All told, it is estimated that about 0.5 billion tons of carbon per year enter the biosphere as new carbon from below. This amount balances the loss of carbon from the biosphere that takes place in the sediments of the ocean. Thus, the connection between the surface biosphere—where organisms live—and the deep geological processes of the planet is essential for the maintenance of the biosphere and thus life itself.

Study Figure 17.1, which summarizes the reservoirs and fluxes of the carbon cycle, and then move on to the practice questions.

## ▶ Practice

6. In considering the reservoirs of the biogeochemical carbon cycle, which has the most carbon in it?
   a. ocean
   b. soil
   c. plants
   d. atmosphere

7. Which two reservoirs in the carbon cycle contain about the same amount of carbon?
   a. ocean and soil
   b. atmosphere and soil
   c. life and ocean
   d. life and atmosphere

**8.** In terms of the flux of carbon, gas exchange is closely balanced between which two reservoirs?

  **a.** soil and atmosphere

  **b.** life and ocean

  **c.** atmosphere and ocean

  **d.** soil life and atmosphere

**9.** The total flux of carbon into all organisms during photosynthesis in both ocean and on land (from air) comes to how many tons per year? Refer to the text or to Figure 17.1 to obtain the answer.

  **a.** 55 billion

  **b.** 100 billion

  **c.** 60 billion

  **d.** 40 billion

**10.** If no new carbon were entering the biosphere from the geological processes from below, in how many years would the biosphere lose all its carbon? Consider that the loss from the biosphere is 0.5 billion tons of carbon per year, as burial in the ocean sediments. Add up the total amount of carbon in the biosphere by summing the amounts given in the text for life, atmosphere, soil, and ocean. Then figure out how much time it would take to deplete the total biosphere of carbon at a loss of 0.5 billion tons per year.

  **a.** 70,000 years

  **b.** 77,000 years

  **c.** 1,400 years

  **d.** 2,800 years

## LESSON

# 18 ▶ Earth Science and Evolution

### LESSON SUMMARY

Earth today is the product of 4.5 billion years of changes. In Lesson 17, life was shown to be an important player in connecting the earth's surface reservoirs of atmosphere, ocean, and soil. Here we look at questions that surround the history of the oceans, continents, and, in particular, the atmosphere. Did life play a role in the history of the air? Geology certainly played a role in the history of life, especially so when we consider mass extinctions such as the demise of the dinosaurs 65 million years ago.

## ▶ History of the Continents, Oceans, and Atmosphere

Earth formed about 4.5 billion years ago. At that time, the planet was hot, too hot for liquid water, but at some point, Earth was cool enough to stabilize water, presumably in the form of oceans. Direct evidence for those oceans vanished long ago, but geologists search for indirect evidence in the form of sedimentary rock, which must form under water.

When were the first sedimentary rocks formed? Rocks on Earth are always being destroyed (and newly created) by the processes of plate tectonics. So as we look back at earlier and earlier rocks, we find fewer and fewer of them. However, most geologists would say that adequate evidence exists for liquid water by 4 billion years ago and probably earlier. Thus, Earth has had an ocean for at least 4 billion years.

What about the continents? The earliest continents are thought to have been something like the country of Iceland today. Iceland sits along the volcanic midocean ridge of the Atlantic Ocean. In fact, Iceland can be thought of as part of the mid-Atlantic ridge that simply sticks up above water. Iceland, despite its chilly latitude, is full of volcanic activity and steam vents everywhere in the country. Most of the country's energy is hydrothermal, meaning from hot water, supplied by the volcanic magic of plate tectonics.

Thus, the earliest continents were probably small. Earth's more appropriate name of "ocean" was even more true way back then, but continents, as noted earlier, are made of lighter material and tend to float on the heavier asthenosphere. Continental crust is even lighter than the oceanic crust. Continents, once formed, will stay. They might split and merge, driven by the dynamics of plate tectonics, but the continental crust rarely goes very far back down into the deep earth before melting and floating back to the surface. This means that continents have grown over time, and if the continents grew, the total area of the ocean must have shrunk.

Most continents' growth occurred during the first quarter or so of Earth history, when the interior of the earth was hotter and the dynamics of plate tectonics were more active. Geologists today are still debating the exact history of the continents, but all agree that the total area of all the continents probably began much smaller than the area today.

Probably the best understood of the histories (and most interesting for our purposes) is that of the atmosphere. The chemicals of the atmosphere react with the minerals of the soil and ocean sediments. By deciphering the chemical reactions that must have taken place long ago to create certain chemical signatures in sedimentary rocks, geologists and geochemists have been able to make some fairly definite statements about the history of Earth's atmosphere. How did the atmosphere come to be what it is today?

Evidence shows that the early earth's atmosphere contained virtually no oxygen. If you were to step out of a time machine on to an ancient shoreline, you would choke and die in a few breaths. Miniscule amounts of free oxygen were made by cosmic rays that could split molecules of water vapor in the atmosphere into hydrogen and oxygen, but these amounts were millions of times smaller than today's amount of oxygen. Recall that oxygen gas, $O_2$, is the second most abundant gas in the atmosphere, at about 21%.

Some sedimentary rocks are known to contain layers that are ancient fossil soils. Once real soils, these zones were covered and protected by water and overlying sediments and were eventually squeezed into sedimentary rock. By analyzing the chemicals in these fossil soils, it has been discovered that a great change happened to Earth's atmosphere about 2 billion years ago, roughly at the halfway point in Earth's total history.

Two billion years ago, a dramatic increase in the level of atmospheric oxygen took place. This step did not create today's 21% oxygen level, but it did create perhaps 2% oxygen. This was a major change in the chemistry of the atmosphere and a change for the organisms that lived in the biosphere. Then, somewhere in the timeframe between 1 billion and 600 million years ago, a second rise in oxygen brought the atmosphere's oxygen level to a value close to that of today's oxygen level.

What could have caused these rises in oxygen? Oxygen is made as a waste product of photosynthesis. Plants get rid of the oxygen they make, just as we humans get rid of the waste carbon dioxide our cells make. So Earth's oxygen must come from photosynthesizers. At 2 billion years ago, no plants existed on land. So the oxygen for the rise at that time must have been generated by photosynthesizers in the ocean—by phytoplankton.

But remember: Other creatures in the ocean use up oxygen, just like we do, just like cats and dogs and butterflies and frogs do. In other words, just like all respiring organisms do. In particular, the bacteria in the deep ocean that feed upon and thus recycle the elements in dead organic detritus (see Lesson 13) require oxygen for their recycling. So if the phytoplankton make oxygen but the bacteria consume the oxygen, then presumably there should be no oxygen left to accumulate in the atmosphere.

The only way for oxygen to accumulate in the atmosphere is if more oxygen is produced by photosynthesizers than is consumed by the oxygen users such as bacteria. In addition, certain gases given off by volcanoes (such as sulfur gases) also combine with oxygen in the atmosphere; these chemical reactions are essentially consuming oxygen as well. Therefore, for oxygen to accumulate in the atmosphere, more oxygen had to be generated by photosynthesis than consumed by the sum of oxygen-consuming organisms and natural chemical reactions.

We can conclude from this analysis that the rise in oxygen in Earth's atmosphere did not have to coincide with the beginning of photosynthesis. Indeed, most scientists who study the history of life think that photosynthesis began at least a billion or more years before the first great rise in oxygen. What happened 2 billion years ago is not yet certain. But the rise in oxygen could have been driven by an increase in the amount of photosynthesis and thus burial of organic carbon.

If the amount of photosynthesis (which creates oxygen) and the amount of respiration (which consumes oxygen) are equal, then the organic matter created by photosynthesis is all consumed by organisms that feed on the organic matter and derive their energy by performing respiration. But if some of the organic matter slips through the biosphere's recycling systems, then there is excess oxygen created that is not consumed by organisms feeding on the organic matter. Perhaps at 2 billion year ago, more organic matter started being buried, which meant more free oxygen entered the atmosphere. Whatever the answer, we do know that Earth's atmosphere has undergone a dramatic change in its level of oxygen, and furthermore, that this change involved life. Life has been a geological force on the chemistry of the atmosphere.

Life's involvement with the *carbon cycle* means that life could also exert an influence on another important gas in the atmosphere, carbon dioxide ($CO_2$). Living things, of course, create organic molecules made of carbon. When these molecules slip through the biosphere's recycling systems, as already noted, carbon is lost from the biosphere. In Lesson 17, we saw how 0.5 billion tons per year of carbon is actually lost from the biosphere by burial in the ocean's sediments. This amount is made up by the release of new carbon from volcanoes and the chemical dissolution of rocks.

Most of the burial of the 0.5 billion tons of carbon per year is, however, not in the form of organic matter. It is calcium carbonate, the shells of marine organisms, which eventually become carbonate sedimentary rock. The amount of the calcium carbonate that is buried is related to the atmosphere's level of carbon dioxide and to the activities of organisms in the soil, which can increase the amount of chemical weathering of soil minerals.

When earth scientists put together the story of how these influences determine the level of atmospheric $CO_2$, it appears that the $CO_2$ level has been declining gradually over long geological time periods. (Note: This is just the opposite from the rapid rise in $CO_2$ that is happening today.) Apparently, over billions of years, the greenhouse effect of carbon dioxide has been decreasing. This is interesting for another reason—because at the beginning of the earth, the sun was weaker by 30%. A weaker sun meant less solar energy hitting the earth. Were a cosmic dial-turner able to turn down the sun by 30% today, the biosphere would become a solid ball of ice because the oceans would freeze. So a larger amount of carbon dioxide in the atmosphere several billion years ago is probably the reason that liquid water existed back then.

## ▶ Practice

**1.** The earliest evidence in sedimentary rocks for the presence of liquid water on Earth comes from rocks dated around how many billion years ago?
   **a.** 1 billion years ago
   **b.** 2 billion years ago
   **c.** 3 billion years ago
   **d.** 4 billion years ago

**2.** Which is the best statement about the areas covered by the continents and the oceans over time, starting with the early Earth?
   **a.** Continental area grew, and ocean area grew.
   **b.** Continental area shrank, and ocean area grew.
   **c.** Continental area grew, and ocean area shrank.
   **d.** Continental area shrank, and ocean area shrank.

**3.** The first great rise in atmospheric oxygen in Earth's atmosphere occurred when?
   **a.** 1 billion years ago
   **b.** 2 billion years ago
   **c.** 3 billion years ago
   **d.** 4 billion years ago

**4.** Evidence for the rise in Earth's oxygen is found in which one of the following?
   **a.** fossilized soils
   **b.** fossilized bones
   **c.** fossilized water
   **d.** fossilized air

**5.** On average, and ignoring the influence of humans, what did carbon dioxide levels do during Earth's history?
   **a.** increased
   **b.** stayed the same
   **c.** decreased then increased
   **d.** decreased

## ▶ Evolution and Impacts from Space

Organisms not only affect the earth; the earth affects organisms. As continents collide and separate, as sea level rises and falls, as mountains uplift and erode, habitats for organisms are changed. In this section, we first review how evolution works. Then we will concentrate on one of the major findings in earth science over the last 20 years. This finding exemplifies how geological processes can affect life. The focus will be on the mass extinction of the dinosaurs due to an impact from space.

No one knows exactly how life began, but good evidence for the presence of life 3.5 billion years ago exists in the records offered to us by rock. Then, once life started, it was modified over the eons by the process of evolution.

We can consider *evolution* as a recipe for change. Its steps, which occur in a repeating sequence, are inheritance, variation, and selection.

The first step is *inheritance*. Organisms in each generation share many of the same features of their predecessors, because the genetic code of DNA is copied from parent to offspring.

Next, we consider *variation*. Often, offspring are not exactly like their parents. Variation is key because it serves as the raw material that can be molded by evolution into new types of creatures.

Finally comes the all-important step of *selection* (or *natural selection*). Not all offspring live long enough themselves to put forth the next generation. Statistically, the most fit survive: Those survive that can withstand draught, seek out food most efficiently, or run the swiftest. The filtering process selects certain types of creatures to carry on. In summary, evolution is modification by natural selection.

The process repeats: inheritance, variation, selection. It operates over and over, as generations roll along, and it has been doing so for nearly 4 billion years. The scientist and master writer of evolution, Englishman Richard Dawkins, coined the phrase the *blind watchmaker*. Evolution creates wondrous organisms, even though there is no maker, because the process is "blind"; it doesn't know where it is going. The recipe of inheritance-variation-selection is a creative process that has generated new forms of life, taking life from its earliest simple start as bacteria to today's giant redwood trees and 10 million total species, including us.

Here are a few of the major transitions, with dates, taken by the process of evolution on Earth:

- **3.5 billion years ago**. Single-celled, bacteria-type creatures definitely exist.
- **2 billion years ago**. Evolution of complex cells from simpler, bacteria-type cells began. The complex cells have enclosed nuclei for their DNA and are the kinds of cells that eventually led to fungi, plants, and animals.

- **1 billion years ago**. First evidence for multicelled creatures, such as worms.
- **540 million years ago**. The so-called Cambrian Explosion took place. Over a brief period of about 10 million years, quite suddenly all kinds of marine animals with hard parts (which is why they were preserved) explode into the fossil record.
- **350 million years ago**. Evolution of land plants took place. The fossil record shows that plants evolved from tiny, moss-sized beings into tall trees over a period that was only about 20 million years long.
- **220 million years ago**. First dinosaurs diverged from early reptiles. A key invention was a new kind of hip joint. This allowed many early (and late) dinosaurs to run bipedally.
- **200 million years ago**. The first mammals evolved from previous mammal-like reptiles, which had split off as a branch of reptiles about 260 million years ago.

In the fossil record, the last of the dinosaurs are found in rocks formed at about 65 million years ago. From these dates, you can see that dinosaurs lived for more than 200 million years. This did not mean that all species of dinosaurs were present for that entire time. No. Some species of dinosaurs went extinct and new species evolved. Tyrannosaurus Rex, for example, was a relatively late species in the evolution of dinosaurs and was around when the dinosaurs went extinct at 65 million years ago. Paleontologists have long known that something dramatic must have occurred 65 million years ago. But it took discoveries from geology, about 20 years ago, to determine the cause of the mass extinction. The answer has given new understanding to what factors contributed to the story of life.

Pinhead-size particles enter Earth's atmosphere every night and burn up—these are *shooting stars*. Larger objects can make it through the atmosphere and hit the ground as *meteorites.* Occasionally, the earth is struck by quite large rocks from space. For example, in the United States, a meteor crater can be seen in northern Arizona, evidence of an impact within the time of human beings. A very much larger event about 2 billion years ago created the Sudbury crater in Canada. The longer the time period, the greater the chance for a truly devastating impact to hit the earth.

We see evidence of enormous impacts on the moon and Mars. These planetary bodies show their craters because they have no or little geological change. On Earth, as wind and water shift sediments, as continents merge and split, most ancient craters have been buried or completely erased from the face of Earth.

In the 1980s, an unusually large amount of a rare element called iridium (chemical symbol: Ir) was discovered in a centimeter-thick clay layer in rocks in Italy, dating from the time of the dinosaur extinction. This anomaly of iridium was subsequently found all over the world.

Iridium occurs at such high concentrations only in meteorites. This discovery pointed to a large impactor (a comet or asteroid) as the cause of the iridium and the mass extinction. Such an object would have smashed into the earth at a speed of 20 kilometers per second and is estimated to have been about the size of Manhattan (say 10 kilometers, or 6 miles, in diameter).

A few years later, evidence from gravity patterns revealed a large crater buried under sediments in the Yucatan Peninsula of Mexico. Variations in gravity—tiny changes in Earth's gravitational field—exist because the rocks at Earth's surface can vary enough in density to be measured using sensitive equipment. Oil companies are interested in such gravity patterns because the presence of a reduced gravitational field can be evidence for a low-density reservoir of oil, which would otherwise be invisible beneath the surface. A circular pattern of variation in gravity was discovered in the Yucatan from data taken by a Mexican oil company.

The crater, buried under sediments in the Yucatan, is about 200 kilometers in diameter (about the estimated size of the crater made by a 10 kilometer object). It dates to exactly 65 million years ago, the end of what geologists call the *Cretaceous* (K) period and the beginning of the *Tertiary* (T) period. A wealth of other types of evidence for this K-T impact has been found, including material ejected close to the impact, shocked minerals, as well as chemical evidence for worldwide fires and other environmental disruptions.

At the K-T boundary, 65 million years ago, many other types of life also went extinct, on all scales, all the way down to the plankton. One group of creatures survived that had been alive at the time of the K-T extinction and were directly descended from the dinosaurs. These are birds. And, fortunately for us, mammals survived, too. This probably happened because the mammals back then were only the size of rats and could weather out the catastrophe underground in burrows.

Species are always going extinct. But once in a while, a mass extinction happened; we know this from the fossil record. To explain these extinctions, in some cases, scientists invoke climate change as the culprit. Others suspect that large impacts will be discovered as the general cause.

Though the stories of individual mass extinctions are still being assembled from field data, the discovery of the K-T impact and the mass extinction of the dinosaurs have given us new insight into how precarious life on Earth has been and how evolution has been subjected to random shocks from space. What if the impact had been larger? And what if it had not taken place?

Note from the previous numbers, that mammals lived during the time of the dinosaurs. But before the

K-T mass extinction, the fossil record shows that mammals had remained small for over 100 million years. In the millions of years after the demise of the dinosaurs, mammals evolved into a huge variety of species, some of them as big as hippopotamuses and elephants. In the term of evolutionary biology, the mammals radiated. It is virtually certain that without such an extinction, this radiation would not have occurred. Without the impactor from space 65 million years ago, evolution would have taken a different course. We almost certainly would not be here.

## ▶ Practice

**6.** The fact that the extinction of the dinosaurs was caused by an impact from space was discovered when geologists measured the elements in a clay layer that was formed at the time of the mass extinction. The geologists found what in this clay layer?
   **a.** unusually low amounts of iridium
   **b.** unusually high amounts of iridium
   **c.** unusually low amounts of cesium
   **d.** unusually high amounts of cesium

**7.** Which of the following is NOT true?
   **a.** Dinosaurs evolved after land plants.
   **b.** Land plants came after the Cambrian explosion.
   **c.** Complex cells evolved after land plants.
   **d.** Land plants came before mammals.

**8.** In the recipe for evolution, the step in which only the most fit survive is called which of the following?
   **a.** inheritance
   **b.** distribution
   **c.** selection
   **d.** variation

**9.** Which modern country contains the crater (buried under sediments) formed by the impact that caused the K-T mass extinction?
   **a.** Brazil
   **b.** China
   **c.** Ghana
   **d.** Mexico

**10.** Evolution has been taking place for how long? (Choose the earliest correct date.)
   **a.** 3.5 billion years
   **b.** 13.7 billion years
   **c.** 540 million years
   **d.** 65 million years

# 19 ▶ Humans as a Geological Force

## LESSON SUMMARY

Unlike other species, humans deploy vast arrays of chemical processes outside their biological bodies, via factories, residences, and forms of transportation. Chemical inputs and outputs from these have created a new kind of force within the systems of Earth, altering many aspects of the biosphere's reservoirs. What has changed? Can we reach a balance with nature?

## ▶ Human Impacts on the Atmosphere

Historically, acid deposition was one of the first recognized human impacts on the atmosphere that occurred across a large geographical scale. Although natural rain is slightly acidic, humans have made the rain in many areas of the world even more acidic. In addition, the acids that humans add to the atmosphere come down to Earth's surface in other forms: acid snow and acid attached to minute particles in the air (so-called dry deposition). *Acid rain*, *acid snow*, and *dry deposition* are collectively known as *acid deposition*. To keep things simple, we will sometimes refer simply to acid rain in the following paragraphs.

Acid deposition begins with the combustion of *fossil fuels*, with *coal* being the biggest culprit. Deposits of coal are the remains of ancient plants from hundred of millions of years ago, preserved in a rock-like form that we can burn. Burning coal is possible because the coal contains carbon. Coal also contains sulfur, which is one of the biologically essential elements for all life. When coal is burned in power plants to obtain energy, most of which comes from converting carbon to *carbon dioxide* ($CO_2$), the sulfur is also combined with oxygen to create *sulfur dioxide* ($SO_2$). The $SO_2$ enters the atmosphere as a gas. There, it further combines with water vapor to become *sulfuric acid* ($H_2SO_4$) in cloud droplets. The rain that falls from these clouds is acidic, thus acid rain.

Nitrogen also contributes to acid deposition. In high-temperature combustion of fossil fuels in power plants and automobiles, some of the nitrogen gas ($N_2$) in the air is inadvertently combined with oxygen ($O_2$) in the air to create the pollutants known as *nitrogen oxides*. In the atmosphere, these also react further to create *nitric acid* ($HNO_3$), which combines with raindrops and contributes to acid rain. On average, the contribution of sulfuric acid to the acidity of rain is about twice the contribution of nitric acid.

Acid rain falls mostly in the regions downwind of power plants and large urban areas. In particular, large power plants that use coal with a relatively high sulfur content are the biggest makers of acid rain.

Acid deposition causes numerous kinds of damage. The most important is damage to lakes and forests. Many organisms are sensitive to the level of acidity in their environment. Fish have died in thousands of lakes in Scandinavia, over a thousand lakes in Canada, and in hundreds of lakes in the United States. Certain forests in New England and in Europe have also suffered severe damage. Finally, acid deposition erodes limestone and marble and has caused damage to buildings and priceless outdoor sculptures around the world.

In some geographical regions, the ecology of the lakes is fine, despite the acid deposition. The effects all depend on the local chemistry. Some areas have a natural buffering capacity in their soils and sediments, and so the acids are consumed by these natural chemical buffers. This process ultimately prevents damage by the acid rain.

Laws governing the release of acids from power plants are in place. Between 1980 and 2000, for example, the total emissions of sulfur dioxide from the worst-offending power plants were cut in half. Some of the improvement has come from adding sulfur scrubbers to power plants to "clean" the exhaust gases from those power plants; these scrubbers remove the sulfur. Switching to low-sulfur coal has been another strategy. With regard to the nitrogen emissions from automobiles, better catalytic converters have lowered the nitrogen oxides created by the combustion process.

Another human impact on the atmosphere has come from the release of substances that destroy the earth's ozone layer. Recall from Lesson 9 that ozone ($O_3$) is a gas that occurs naturally in the stratosphere. Ozone absorbs the ultraviolet portion of the sun's energy that strikes the earth and it protects organisms from the potential damage from ultraviolet radiation. Because of its protective properties, the stratospheric ozone has been called a protective shield. Without this protective ozone layer, life would be in big trouble because biologically damaging ultraviolet rays would reach the surface. Ultraviolet radiation is a main cause, for example, of skin cancer.

Ozone is made when ultraviolet radiation strikes oxygen molecules in the stratosphere, initiating a chemical reaction that creates ozone. When ozone absorbs ultraviolet radiation, the ozone is destroyed. A balance is reached between creation and destruction, resulting in a natural amount of ozone that is constantly present and acts as the shield.

Several kinds of human substances that find their way into the air and travel up into the stratosphere increase the destruction rate of ozone. The most worrisome substances are known as *CFCs*, or *chlorofluorocarbons* (containing chlorine, fluorine, and carbon). These industrial chemicals can be used in refrigerators, air conditioners, and some aerosol cans, in the production of industrial plastics, and in the electronics industry for cleaning. When the CFCs are released into the atmosphere, the chlorine is liberated in the stratosphere, where it acts as a catalyst to destroy the ozone at a rate much faster than its natural rate of destruction.

By the late 1970s, it was clear that humans were changing the balance between ozone creation and destruction in the stratosphere. Most dramatically, in 1985, a large hole in the ozone was discovered over Antarctica. Earth scientists were shaken with alarm at this surprise from nature. We now know that special weather conditions over Antarctica intensify the destructive power of the CFCs, during the Southern Hemisphere's spring. The discovery of this hole led to increased efforts to stop the production of CFCs. Additionally, global levels of ozone had been dropping by several percent per decade during the final decades of the twentieth century.

The world did respond. The countries of the world grew concerned at the situation, and in 1987, most signed the *Montreal Protocol*, a global agreement to phase out the production and use of CFCs. An amendment in 1990 stepped up the schedule. By 1996, most of the industrial nations no longer manufactured CFCs. Substitute gases were invented to replace the technological uses of CFCs. The transition was well on the way, and the ozone decline was halted around the year 2000. The ozone level in the stratosphere, however, is still not back to where it once was as a shield. That recovery is expected to take until about 2050, at which time the ozone layer should have returned to its natural level.

An entirely different problem involving human impacts on a crucial gas in the atmosphere is now of concern—the issue of the rising levels of carbon dioxide and the expected warming of the future world.

Recall from Lesson 9 that carbon dioxide ($CO_2$) is a greenhouse gas. A greenhouse gas has the following property: It lets visible radiation (light and short-wave radiation) from the sun pass into the atmosphere and directly through to the ground (we can't see the $CO_2$). But, significantly, a greenhouse gas absorbs infrared radiation. Infrared radiation (or longwave radiation) radiating out to space is the means by which

the earth cools itself, the means to balance the energy received from the sun. Greenhouse gases are like one-way insulation, letting light in but blocking the escape of infrared. The earth's surface will simply warm up to compensate for any extra insulation in the atmosphere.

$CO_2$ is typically measured in units of *parts per million* (ppm), because only small amounts of it exist in the atmosphere. "Million" here refers to a million randomly selected molecules of air (such as $N_2$, $O_2$, and so forth). Today, $CO_2$ is present in somewhat more that 370 ppm (which is equal to 0.037%). Though $CO_2$ is present in such a small amount of the atmosphere, it is of critical importance because it is a greenhouse gas. In contrast, the most abundant gases, nitrogen and oxygen, are not greenhouse gases.

Without $CO_2$, the earth would be very cold, below the freezing point of water, in fact. So present conditions require $CO_2$. But one can also have too much of a good thing. $CO_2$ is emitted as a waste gas from the combustion of fossil fuels (coal, oil, and natural gas, which is mostly methane) and its presence in the atmosphere is rising. Data from bubbles trapped in ice at Antarctica show that for 10,000 years prior to the industrial revolution, $CO_2$ was fairly constant at about 280 ppm. It is now above 370 ppm and rising, from human activities, at the rate of 1.5 to 2 ppm per year.

Basically, fossil fuels contain carbon, originally incorporated by photosynthesis into the bodies of plants on land and algae in the ocean. Some of these bodies escaped the recycling loops of the biosphere. (Recall how net oxygen is made by the burial of organic carbon, as described in Lesson 18.) Quite simply, coal deposits are the remains of ancient land plants, oil comes from ancient algae, and natural gas is derived from either coal or oil, as these substances are "cooked" by the tectonic forces of geology over hundreds of millions of years. When we burn the fossil fuels, we combine their carbon with the oxygen in the

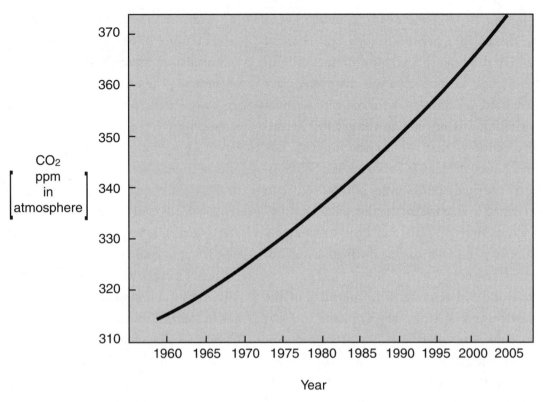

Figure 19.1 The rise in atmospheric carbon dioxide

atmosphere to create energy and the inevitable waste by-product—carbon dioxide (see Figure 19.1).

## ▶ Practice

**1.** Which of the following is the biggest contributor to acid precipitation?
   **a.** calcium
   **b.** nitrogen
   **c.** phosphorus
   **d.** sulfur

**2.** Which gas in the stratosphere absorbs the sun's ultraviolet rays?
   **a.** sulfur dioxide
   **b.** ozone
   **c.** nitrogen oxide
   **d.** carbon monoxide

**3.** The Montreal Protocol was signed by leading industrial nations to limit the emissions of which of the following?
   **a.** ozone
   **b.** carbon dioxide
   **c.** CFCs
   **d.** sulfur dioxide

**4.** Carbon dioxide is today at a level of 370 ppm in the atmosphere. A gas that is 0.1% of the atmosphere would be 1,000 ppm (parts per million). What percent is $CO_2$ in the atmosphere?
   **a.** 0.037%
   **b.** 0.37%
   **c.** 3.7%
   **d.** 37%

**5.** By what percent has carbon dioxide risen in Earth's atmosphere, relative to its preindustrial value?

   **a.** 75%

   **b.** 370%

   **c.** 30%

   **d.** 90%

## ▶ Toward a Sustainable Future

Humans are altering the *biosphere* in ways that will change it for very long periods of time. That's simply what we do. Here we will look at some of the global changes in land use. Then we will focus on several fluxes made by humans that exceed those of nature. Finally, we will note the concept of *sustainability*, which deals with the question of how we will continue to provide life support for what soon will be 7 billion people without further stressing the systems that nature provides.

As of 2005, the human population was about 6.4 billion people. It is growing at approximately 80 million people per year. Population is rising, but, as they say, land is one thing that doesn't increase. The global land area is 140 million square kilometers. The common land unit in the metric system is the *hectare*, which is a square 100 meters on a side. How many square meters in a hectare? You will be asked this in a practice question.

Using the conversion for the number of square meters in a hectare and the fact that one million square meters are in a square kilometer, we can calculate the global land area to be 14 billion hectares. That means there are about 2.2 hectares per person. If you are more familiar with the unit of acres, this figure is about 5.4 acres per person (1 hectare = 2.47 acres).

How much of this do humans currently use? How much could they use? First of all, 31% of the world's land (4.4 billion hectares) is unusable, because it is rock, ice, tundra, or desert. That leaves 9.6 billion hectares for potential use.

The major human land use is for agricultural production, which currently uses 4.7 billion hectares. So agriculture (pastureland and cropland) takes 34% of the world's land (4.7/10.4). Of that, 70% is permanent pasture and 30% is cropland.

Globally, only about 1% to 2% of land (approximately 140–280 million hectares) is considered urbanized. In some local areas, obviously, the urbanized land approaches 100% of land use.

Therefore, summing the unusable land, the agricultural land, and the urbanized land, and then subtracting that from the total land area, we arrive at the figure of 4.8 billion hectares that potentially remain. This is about 33% to 34% of the total land, or about as much as we currently use for all agriculture already. Here is the calculation: 100% − 31% − 34% − (1% or 2%) = 33% to 34%. However, much of the prime land for agriculture has already been used, so what remains is not as high in quality. This is the big picture of global land use.

Obviously, humans have made a big impact on the world's land. There is still more land that could be converted to exclusively human use, and that process is going on yearly. The conversion that is of most concern is the deforestation of tropical rainforests. However, in certain areas of the developed nations, forests are actually regrowing. An example in the United States is in the New England states. These were once nearly all converted into farms. But as the farms became less economical, when farms in the Midwest and California could produce food more cheaply, the farms in New England lost much of their value, and forests were allowed to regrow.

The appropriation of land by humans implies that humans are creating fluxes of matter for their own use. For example, when land is used for agriculture, humans take the organic carbon products of photosynthesis for food. But to produce this food, humans apply fertilizers such as phosphorus and nitrogen to boost the productivity of the agricultural soils. Plowing the soil also allows erosion to proceed at a rate that is faster than what would be the normal rate for nature.

Nature has balanced cycles. Erosion of the continents and the deposition of continental minerals into the ocean are, over the long term, balanced by the uplifting of the continents into mountains from the forces of plate tectonics. The nutrients of phosphorus and nitrogen—required by all life—cycle around and around. These nutrients are incorporated into plants on land and algae in the ocean by the process of photosynthesis. The plants and algae can be eaten, or they die. Eventually, many of the nutrients are recycled back to the soil (on land) or into the deep ocean water, primarily by bacteria. Some of the nutrients leak out and are buried in sediments. These nutrients are replaced over the long term by new nutrients put into the biosphere from the weathering of rocks and the eruption of volcanoes.

How do the fluxes caused by humans compare to the equivalent fluxes in nature? Looking at some numbers instructs us about the power of humans as a new kind of geological force on the planet.

One component or process in the cycle of nitrogen is the conversion of nitrogen gas in the air into forms such as ammonium and nitrate ions. The ammonium and nitrate ions—unlike the air's nitrogen gas—are what plants and algae need for their bodies to grow. The conversion process is called *nitrogen fixation*, and it is accomplished by special kinds of bacteria that are called *nitrogen fixers*.

The natural biological flux of nitrogen fixation, performed by the world's nitrogen-fixing bacteria in the soils and in the ocean, is about 130 million tons per year. (All tons are given in the international unit of metric tons, or 1,000 kilograms, approximately 2,200 pounds or 1.1 U.S. ton.)

Humans also create a flux of nitrogen fixation. Some happens inadvertently, as noted previously, in the creation of nitrogen oxides by fossil fuel combustion. Humans also create conditions for extra nitrogen fixation during rice cultivation. And, importantly, humans take atmospheric nitrogen and use high-temperature and high-pressure industrial processes to manufacture fertilizer for the large-scale agriculture that humans think needs a boost in productivity. All these forms of human nitrogen fixation add up to 140 million tons per year, more than the global flux of nitrogen fixation by the world's nitrogen-fixing bacteria.

Phosphorus is also required by all organisms. And many agricultural soils are deficient in phosphorus. Therefore, applying phosphorus as fertilizer increases the productivity of many soils.

The natural release of phosphorus into the cycles of the biosphere from the chemical weathering of rocks and minerals is about 3 million tons per year. In contrast, humans mine phosphorus and thereby bring this new phosphorus into the cycles of the biosphere. The flux from mining activities, primarily aimed at fertilizer production, is about 12 million tons per year, or 4 times the flux of phosphorus in nature.

One major environmental concern coming from the increases in the fluxes of nitrogen and phosphorus caused by humans is the fact that these nutrients can *runoff* from farmlands after rains and go directly into lakes and coastal regions. Though this might seem like a good thing—to fertilize the lakes and coasts for "free" from farm runoff—it is actually bad. The extra nutrients create a condition called *eutrophication*. During eutrophication, algae go wild with growth. But then the algae die and fall to the bottom, where bacteria consume the bodies of the algae along with oxygen in the water. The water becomes depleted of oxygen, and fish and other creatures such as mussels and oysters die. For instance, there is currently a massive low-oxygen zone in the Gulf of Mexico, around the entry of the Mississippi River into the Gulf. The low-oxygen zone has been created by the runoff of fertilizer from the Midwestern farms.

Finally, we look at *sediment loads* (suspended solids) in the world's rivers. The global sediment load carried by the world's rivers prior to human impact is about 10 billion tons per year (just under two tons per person). With the influence of humans, that number has tripled. In other words, human activity causes about 20 billion tons per year of sediment in the world's rivers that goes into the ocean. Humans are clearly a major geological force!

There is a new science on the horizon that can help us. It is called the science of *sustainability*. The science of sustainability deals with ensuring the sustained connection between humans and Earth. As we have seen, human needs are often fulfilled by compromising the environment. We drain aquifers, convert forests and prairies into farms, use water and land as waste dumps, fish without adequate limits, even change the radiation balance of the atmosphere. How can we harmonize the arrow of human progress with the cyclic, restorative processes of nature? This problem looms before us significantly. Its solution has been taken to constitute the new branch of knowledge called sustainability science.

### ▶ Practice

**6.** Which of the following statements about global land use is not true?
   **a.** Cropland is increasing.
   **b.** Old-growth forest is decreasing.
   **c.** Unusable land area (rock, ice, desert) is greater than urbanized land area.
   **d.** Pastureland is less than cropland.

**7.** How many square meters in one hectare?
   **a.** 100 meters
   **b.** 1,000 meters
   **c.** 10,000 meters
   **d.** 100,000 meters

**8.** An area in the United States where farmland is returning to forest is
   **a.** the Midwest.
   **b.** New England.
   **c.** the Northwest.
   **d.** Texas.

**9.** Eutrophication creates which of the following?
   **a.** low-oxygen levels in water
   **b.** reduced ozone levels in the stratosphere
   **c.** high rates of chemical weathering from minerals
   **d.** forest damage from acidity

**10.** In terms of the percent increase of the human flux over that of untouched nature, which process has the largest impact from humans? Look back at the numbers in the text to help you figure out the correct answer.
   **a.** phosphorus input
   **b.** nitrogen fixation
   **c.** river sediment load
   **d.** carbon dioxide levels

# 20 ▶ Frontiers in Earth Science

## LESSON SUMMARY

For Lessons 1 through 19, earth science was treated as a finished science. You learned facts and processes, from those of our cosmic home to the impact of humans on the planet. Indeed, humans have gained a tremendous amount of understanding about planet Earth, through careful observations, precise experiments, and bold theories, particularly in the last 50 years. But many mysteries remain. Solving some of these mysteries is vital to our future. In this final lesson, we look at some of the frontiers of earth science.

## ▶ How Much Will Earth Warm as Carbon Dioxide Levels Rise?

The atmosphere's $CO_2$ level is about 30% higher than it was prior to the industrial revolution. Most of the increase is from the release of $CO_2$ during the combustion of fossil fuels. Climatologists predict a result of *global warming*. But how much? The best computer simulations predict a warming of 1.5° to 4° C (roughly 3° to 8° F) when the $CO_2$ doubles, perhaps by the end of the century, depending on the use of fossil fuels. That is a great deal of uncertainty, especially given the magnitude of this critical environmental problem.

One of the causes for the uncertainty in the predictions of global warming is the effect of clouds. We know clouds are accumulations of tiny water droplets in the sky. But many of the details of clouds are not yet known. Clouds are simply too complex. You can see their complexity by simply looking up into the sky. Imagine trying to mathematically describe the formation and shape of a cumulus cloud, with filigrees of white trailing off its sides, which changes almost as you look at it. Yet such mathematical description is what is needed for clouds to be accurately put into the computer models of global warming.

In particular, clouds will act to both warm and cool the earth's surface. Clouds cool the surface because they are white and are good reflectors of sunlight. Clouds warm the surface because they contain water vapor, which is the atmosphere's number one greenhouse gas. Which factor will dominate—warming or cooling—will determine much of the future impact of $CO_2$ on Earth's climate.

A related issue in the difficulty of predicting global warming has to do with the general concept of *feedbacks* in the climate system. Feedbacks occur when a change in some property of Earth's surface is either positively amplified or negatively dampened and then the changed property interacts with all the other properties. We have seen how the earth's surface has numerous properties: the amount of sedimentary rock, the types of soils, the water cycle, the Hadley cells, ocean gyres, carbon dioxide in the air, ozone, and even humans. Somehow, these interact to form a complex system that we live within, often without much thought about the interactions.

One example of a feedback is the *ice-albedo feedback*. Albedo is the technical term for *reflectivity*. Sand, for example, has a higher albedo than does a dark green forest. What about the albedo of ice compared to the darker water underneath? Yes, ice has the higher albedo.

Now, when global warming kicks in, large amounts of sea ice are expected to melt. Some climatologists claim this is happening already. Indeed, a majority of mountain glaciers around the world are receding. If the total area of sea ice declines as a result of $CO_2$–induced global warming, the darker water underneath will be exposed. Darker water absorbs more sunlight than did the ice that formerly covered it.

So now the earth would warm even more. This is a positive feedback.

Earth scientists have delineated dozens of potential feedbacks in the climate system. How these various positive and negative feedbacks play out is one of the great unanswered questions in earth science.

## ▶ What Will Happen to the Thermohaline Circulation as the Earth Warms?

This topic is related to the issue of feedbacks just described. But it is broken out as a separate heading because it brings the ocean into the question of global warming. The thermohaline circulation (see Lesson 14) is the plunging of cold, salty water to the depths of the world ocean, primarily from the North Atlantic and around Antarctica. If the thermohaline circulation changes due to global warming, then the warm surface water that is driven toward the poles to replace the surface water that is lost in the downward plunge of the thermohaline circulation will stay nearer to the equator. In one potentially real scenario, the Gulf Stream could diminish, and, paradoxically, northern Europe, which is now warmed by the Gulf Stream, could grow colder even as the rest of the world grows warmer. The dynamics of the thermohaline circulation are not yet well enough known to make a prediction about its future under a changed climate.

## ▶ What Caused the Ice Ages?

It is now more than 160 years since geological evidence first emerged that great ice sheets had once covered almost all of Canada and even parts of the northern United States (and that's just the Western Hemisphere). But scientists do not have a definite, precise theory of the ice ages. It is known that ice ages are partially driven by changes in the sun due to changes in Earth's orbit. There are three major changes in Earth's orbit: The orbit can become more or less elliptical, the tilt of Earth's axis can change from more to less, and the position of the seasons can shift along the narrow and wide portions of Earth's elliptical path. These changes each occur in definite cycles, with periods that vary from 100,000 to about 20,000 years.

But during the coldest part of the last ice age, about 20,000 years ago, the sun received by Earth was close to that of today's distribution. So something else is going on. Ice cores have revealed that $CO_2$ was lower in the air back then, therefore, the greenhouse effect was reduced and the lower amount of $CO_2$ contributed to the cooling. But what caused this lower $CO_2$? Practically speaking, it will be important to understand the ice ages in order to gain a better understanding of Earth's future. After all, if we do not fully understand the past, how can we predict the future?

## ▶ Can We Predict Earthquakes?

The great earthquake in December 2004, took the world by surprise. Not only was the earthquake not predicted, but the possibility of the resulting giant tidal waves in the Indian Ocean had not been anticipated. More than 100,000 people died, mostly in Indonesia. Earthquakes occur from sudden jerks in the friction-locked edges of two continental plates (see Lesson 6). Why can't we predict earthquakes better? Progress has been made, but there is a long way to go. Part of the problem, obviously, is that we have a difficult time seeing what is going on at the edges of the continental plates. But the waves that result from earthquakes provide clues to what is underneath. There is hope for better predictions in the future.

## ▶ Can We Predict Hurricanes?

Similarly, predictions for hurricanes are improving. Now, using temperatures of the surface of the Atlantic Ocean during the Northern Hemisphere's late summer and early autumn, climatologists often can say, in general, whether the hurricane season will be mild or severe. But the details of predicting hurricane formation and pathways are exceedingly difficult. The dynamics of Earth's atmosphere are complex. Think how often during the autumn we sit in front of a television, with a hurricane just a couple days away from the coast of Florida or North Carolina, without absolute predictions about the hurricane's specific path.

## ▶ How Will the Increased Loads on the Biosphere of the Nutrients Phosphorus and Nitrogen Change Ecosystems?

As described in Lesson 19, humans are adding enormous amounts of phosphorus and nitrogen to the biosphere, mainly to fertilize crops. How will these increased amounts alter the chemistry of environments, of the soils, lakes, and coastal ocean? How will the altered chemistry change the types of species in those ecosystems? Finally, can more precision farming techniques keep the benefits of fertilizers but reduce the amounts used? Can organic farming substantially reduce the amount of fertilizer while keeping up the productivity of soils, in a sustainable world?

## ▶ Are There Other Surprises in Store for the Dynamics of Planet Earth?

The discovery of the ozone hole above Antarctica during the Southern Hemisphere springtime was cause for concern to people living near the hole—that is, in Australia and New Zealand. The ozone hole was a surprise. Scientists did not predict it. The hole is a stunning example of the complexity of the earth's surface system. As noted previously in the discussion of feedbacks, the biosphere is complex, with many feedbacks. How many more surprises await us in the future?

## ▶ How Did Life Originate? Did That Require Special Conditions on the Earth 4 Billion Years Ago?

Conditions on the early earth were quite different. It was almost certainly warmer, because of an atmosphere with a high greenhouse effect. Also, the air had no oxygen. Continents were tiny. The ocean's chemistry of that time is unknown. Could life have originated only in very special chemical conditions on this early earth? How did simple organic molecules assemble themselves into complexly coordinated, self-replicating living cells? This is a question that brings together the earth scientists as well as the biologists, because we want to know what the geological conditions were back then.

## ▶ Is There Life Elsewhere?

To return to the cosmic perspective with which we began this book, note that astronomers have now discovered more than 100 planets around stars other than our sun. They find these planets by measuring tiny wobbles in stars, caused by the planets' orbits around their star. Just recently, a couple of new planets have actually been visualized as well.

The planets found so far are all huge, bigger than Jupiter. That's because the huge planets are the ones that cause large enough wobbles in their stars for us to observe. But also astronomical instruments are becoming more and more refined. Is there life elsewhere? If so, it is intelligent? The first question might even be answered positively as we explore our neighboring planet Mars in more detail. The second question will have to await not only better instruments but better ideas of how to search and what to search for. Perhaps you will have some answers.

## ▶ Practice

1. One of the biggest uncertainties to making accurate predictions of how much global warming will occur (in terms of average increase in global temperature) is
   a. the role of clouds.
   b. the effect of biodiversity.
   c. the stirring of hurricanes.
   d. the measurement of $CO_2$ in the air.

2. One of the surprises that came from the last twenty years was the
   a. depletion of soil carbon dioxide.
   b. ozone hole above Antarctica.
   c. stopping of thermohaline circulation.
   d. ending of the final ice age.

**3.** The science of sustainability will have near the top of its agenda a concern for the
   a. discovery of new oil fields.
   b. increased amount of nitrogen in the environment.
   c. temperature of the deep ocean.
   d. origin of life 4 billion years ago.

**4.** If sea ice melts because of global warming, thereby exposing darker water underneath, which absorbs extra sunlight and causes still more warming, we have an example of what is called a
   a. thermohaline.
   b. adiabat.
   c. energy deposition.
   d. feedback.

**5.** The planets that have been discovered outside our own solar system are all
   a. small, like Mercury.
   b. about the size of the earth.
   c. bigger than Jupiter.
   d. almost as large as our sun.

# Posttest

If you have completed all 20 lessons in this book, then you are ready to take the posttest to measure your progress. The posttest has 40 multiple-choice questions covering the topics you studied in this book. While the format of the posttest is similar to that of the pretest, the questions are different.

Take as much time as you need to complete the posttest. When you are finished, check your answers with the answer key at the end of this section. Along with each answer is a number that tells you which lesson(s) of this book teaches you about the earth science skills needed for that question. Once you know your score on the posttest, compare the results with the pretest. If you scored better on the posttest than you did on the pretest, you should look at the questions you missed, if any. Do you know why you missed the question, or do you need to go back to the lesson and review the concept?

If your score on the posttest doesn't show much improvement, take a second look at the questions you missed. Did you miss a question because of an error you made? If you can figure out why you missed the problem, then you understand the concept and just need to concentrate more on accuracy when taking a test. If you missed a question because you did not know how to work the problem, go back to the lesson and spend more time working that type of problem. Take the time to understand basic earth science thoroughly. You need a solid foundation in basic earth science if you plan to use this information or progress to a higher level. Whatever your score on this posttest, keep this book for review and future reference.

## ANSWER SHEET

1. (a) (b) (c) (d)
2. (a) (b) (c) (d)
3. (a) (b) (c) (d)
4. (a) (b) (c) (d)
5. (a) (b) (c) (d)
6. (a) (b) (c) (d)
7. (a) (b) (c) (d)
8. (a) (b) (c) (d)
9. (a) (b) (c) (d)
10. (a) (b) (c) (d)
11. (a) (b) (c) (d)
12. (a) (b) (c) (d)
13. (a) (b) (c) (d)
14. (a) (b) (c) (d)
15. (a) (b) (c) (d)

16. (a) (b) (c) (d)
17. (a) (b) (c) (d)
18. (a) (b) (c) (d)
19. (a) (b) (c) (d)
20. (a) (b) (c) (d)
21. (a) (b) (c) (d)
22. (a) (b) (c) (d)
23. (a) (b) (c) (d)
24. (a) (b) (c) (d)
25. (a) (b) (c) (d)
26. (a) (b) (c) (d)
27. (a) (b) (c) (d)
28. (a) (b) (c) (d)
29. (a) (b) (c) (d)
30. (a) (b) (c) (d)

31. (a) (b) (c) (d)
32. (a) (b) (c) (d)
33. (a) (b) (c) (d)
34. (a) (b) (c) (d)
35. (a) (b) (c) (d)
36. (a) (b) (c) (d)
37. (a) (b) (c) (d)
38. (a) (b) (c) (d)
39. (a) (b) (c) (d)
40. (a) (b) (c) (d)

1. Which element is not made in the nuclear fusion reactions that take place in the cores of stars?
   a. carbon
   b. uranium
   c. oxygen
   d. hydrogen

2. The distance from the moon to Earth is somewhat more than 200,000 miles. How long does it take light to travel from the moon to Earth? Answers are rounded off; choose the best one.
   a. about 1 second
   b. about 10 seconds
   c. about 100 seconds
   d. about 1,000 seconds

3. Which planet is between Earth and Mercury?
   a. Mars
   b. the asteroids
   c. Venus
   d. Triton

4. When the moon is new, which is true?
   a. A solar eclipse could occur.
   b. A lunar eclipse could occur.
   c. An earth eclipse could occur.
   d. A corona eclipse could occur.

5. There are three main factors that cause the mid-latitudes to have seasons. Two are (1) Earth's spin axis remains pointed in the same direction in space, and (2) the sun's energy varies with latitude. What is the third?
   a. orbit of the moon shifts north and south
   b. Earth's spin axis is tilted
   c. distance from Earth to sun changes
   d. Earth's orbit is an ellipse

6. At about 40° north latitude, New York City is in which climate zone?
   a. temperate
   b. deciduous
   c. doldrums
   d. south-arctic

7. The layer of the earth called the asthenosphere is
   a. liquid.
   b. subducted.
   c. "brittle."
   d. "plastic."

8. What statement about the two main types of seismic waves allowed seismologists to discover the fact that Earth has a core?
   a. S waves do not travel in liquids; P waves do not travel in solids.
   b. S waves do not travel in liquids; P waves travel in liquids and solids.
   c. S waves do not travel in solids; P waves do not travel in solids.
   d. S waves do not travel in solids; P waves travel in liquids and solids.

9. Which is the true statement about the oceans?
   a. The Pacific is growing; the Atlantic is shrinking.
   b. The Pacific is growing; the Atlantic is growing.
   c. The Pacific is shrinking; the Atlantic is shrinking.
   d. The Pacific is shrinking; the Atlantic is growing.

**10.** Which is NOT found at Earth's subduction zones?

a. plunging ocean crust

b. the deepest waters

c. emerging ocean crust

d. crust going into the mantle

**11.** The increase in energy of an earthquake between any two integers on the Richter scale is a factor of

a. 2.

b. 10.

c. 20.

d. 30.

**12.** The Himalayas result from

a. a continental collision zone.

b. a plate subduction zone.

c. a volcanic zone.

d. a ridge spreading zone.

**13.** The geometric arrangement of a mineral's atom goes a long way in determining what property of that mineral?

a. luster

b. color

c. streak

d. cleavage

**14.** Quartz is made of which two elements?

a. silicon and calcium

b. oxygen and silicon

c. magnesium and calcium

d. oxygen and magnesium

**15.** The Grand Canyon shows deposits that were established over an interval of about 300 million years. That is about what percent of the age of the earth?

a. 2%

b. 7%

c. 12%

d. 17%

**16.** The radioactive form of carbon that can be used to date archeological sites that contain ancient wood is

a. carbon-14.

b. carbon-13.

c. carbon-12.

d. carbon-11.

**17.** Climbing up a mountain in the desert, the dry adiabatic lapse rate applies. If you go up 10,000 meters, about how much would you expect the air to cool?

a. 5° C

b. 5° F

c. 10° C

d. 10° F

**18.** In terms of percentage, the number 2 gas in the atmosphere is

a. argon.

b. oxygen.

c. water vapor.

d. nitrogen.

**19.** The Coriolis effect causes
   **a.** the Hadley cell to rise at the equator.
   **b.** northward winds to be deflected west in the northern hemisphere.
   **c.** westerlies to move east in the southern hemisphere.
   **d.** southward winds to be deflected west in the northern hemisphere.

**20.** In summer, in certain parts of the world, when hot air rises off the continents and pulls in moist air from the ocean, we can have what is called a(n)
   **a.** monsoon.
   **b.** orographic control.
   **c.** maritime still.
   **d.** cyclone.

**21.** The world's ocean all together contains 1,370,000,000 cubic kilometers of water. The land of Earth is about 150,000,000 square kilometers. If all the water in all the ocean were to be spread out evenly across the land, about how deep would that water be?
   **a.** 9 kilometers
   **b.** 0.1 kilometer
   **c.** 90 kilometers
   **d.** 0.01 kilometer

**22.** Which flux of the following involves a change of state of the water, between gas, liquid, or solid?
   **a.** evaporation from ocean
   **b.** soil water moving into plants
   **c.** shallow groundwater becoming spring water
   **d.** rivers flowing into the ocean

**23.** Which process produces dissolved loads of ions in rivers?
   **a.** estuarine weathering
   **b.** chemical weathering
   **c.** physical weathering
   **d.** watershed weathering

**24.** A watershed is
   **a.** zone of water whose salt content is in between that of fresh water and that of the ocean.
   **b.** an underground layer of porous rock that conducts water.
   **c.** a place where groundwater seeps out to the surface.
   **d.** the area of land that collects water that is eventually drained by a river.

**25.** Which is true about the ocean's ions of phosphorus and nitrogen, as you go from shallow water into the deep ocean water?
   **a.** P increases, N decreases
   **b.** P decreases, N decreases
   **c.** P increases, N increases
   **d.** P decreases, N increases

**26.** The shallow region of the ocean that is around the shorelines of continents is
   **a.** oceanic plain.
   **b.** oceanic sediment floor.
   **c.** continental slope.
   **d.** continental shelf.

**27.** One country whose climate is warmed quite a bit by the Kuroshio Current is
  **a.** Alaska.
  **b.** Japan.
  **c.** England.
  **d.** Australia.

**28.** In the southern hemisphere, the Pacific Ocean's gyre is
  **a.** counterclockwise, pushed in part by easterlies to its south.
  **b.** counterclockwise, pushed in part by westerlies to its south.
  **c.** clockwise, pushed in part by easterlies to its south.
  **d.** clockwise, pushed in part by westerlies to its south.

**29.** Choose the best answer. The two main factors that combine to create the structure of soil are
  **a.** water and air.
  **b.** gravel and humus.
  **c.** life and rock.
  **d.** air and sand.

**30.** The top layer of the soil, which receives the litter from trees, dead grasses, and other plants, is called the
  **a.** O horizon.
  **b.** A stratum.
  **c.** O stratum.
  **d.** A horizon.

**31.** Compare two regions at sea level that have the same local air temperature. Both regions have tall mountains as well. One region is dry, and the temperature as a function of altitude is governed by the dry adiabatic lapse rate. The other region is wet and its temperature as a function of altitude is governed by the moist adiabatic lapse rate. What can you say about the altitude as which ice will occur on the mountains of each region?
  **a.** the same
  **b.** higher up in the moist region
  **c.** higher up in the dry region
  **d.** cannot tell, other factors dominate

**32.** One unusual property of water is
  **a.** heat of vaporization is larger than heat of melting.
  **b.** expands upon freezing.
  **c.** molecular bonds occur at an angle.
  **d.** needs a "seed" to crystallize.

**33.** There are about 700 billion tons of carbon in the form of carbon dioxide in the atmosphere. Terrestrial photosynthesis takes about 60 billion tons of this carbon and incorporates it into the living tissues of plants each year. If there was no return flux of carbon dioxide to the atmosphere from the respiration of animals and soil microbes, in how many years would the atmosphere's carbon dioxide be completely depleted? Round your answer to the nearest whole number.
  **a.** 740
  **b.** 42
  **c.** 12
  **d.** 9

**34.** The biosphere is defined as the system of the four reservoirs of
a. life, ocean, lakes, atmosphere.
b. soil, ocean, atmosphere, life.
c. troposphere, stratosphere, ocean, soil.
d. marine life, land life, soil, atmosphere.

**35.** The dinosaurs went extinct from an impact from space
a. 65 million years ago, which left a chemical imprint of radium.
b. 65 million years ago, which left a chemical imprint of iridium.
c. 540 million years ago, which left a chemical imprint of radium.
d. 540 million years ago, which left a chemical imprint of iridium.

**36.** Evidence for the rise in Earth's oxygen is found in
a. fossilized bones.
b. preserved seawater.
c. preserved air in ice cores.
d. fossilized soils.

**37.** The most important component in human-induced acid deposition is
a. $HNO_3$.
b. $CO_2$.
c. CFCs.
d. $H_2SO_4$.

**38.** Some of the world's land is unusable because it's desert, ice, or rock. Another fraction of the world's land is already used for crops and grazing. About how much, after accounting for these two categories, of the world's land could still be developed for exclusively human use?
a. $\frac{1}{2}$
b. $\frac{1}{3}$
c. $\frac{1}{8}$
d. $\frac{1}{20}$

**39.** A new science that can help us figure out how to live in balance with nature is called
a. econology.
b. sustainability.
c. astrobiology.
d. naturenomics.

**40.** To better predict the effects of the rising levels of carbon dioxide in Earth's atmosphere, scientists will have to forge better understandings of which two processes?
a. acid deposition fallout time and cloud formation
b. thermohaline circulation and duration of eutrophication
c. cloud formation and the thermohaline circulation
d. duration of eutrophication and cloud formation

# ▶ Answers

If you miss any of the answers, you can find help in the lesson shown to the right.

1. **d.** hydrogen [Lesson 1]
2. **a.** about one second [Lesson 1]
3. **c.** Venus [Lesson 2]
4. **a.** A solar eclipse could occur. [Lesson 2]
5. **b.** Earth's spin axis is tilted [Lesson 3]
6. **a.** temperate [Lesson 3]
7. **d.** "plastic" [Lesson 4]
8. **b.** S waves do not travel in liquids; P waves travel in liquids and solids. [Lesson 4]
9. **d.** The Pacific is shrinking; the Atlantic is growing. [Lesson 5]
10. **c.** emerging ocean crust [Lesson 5]
11. **d.** 30 [Lesson 6]
12. **a.** a continental collision zone [Lesson 6]
13. **d.** cleavage [Lesson 7]
14. **b.** oxygen and silicon [Lesson 7]
15. **b.** 7% [Lesson 8]
16. **a.** carbon-14 [Lesson 8]
17. **c.** 10° C [Lesson 9]
18. **b.** oxygen [Lesson 9]
19. **d.** southward winds to be deflected west in the northern hemisphere [Lesson 10]
20. **a.** monsoon [Lesson 10]
21. **a.** 9 kilometers [Lesson 11]
22. **a.** evaporation from ocean [Lesson 11]
23. **b.** chemical weathering [Lesson 12]
24. **d.** the area of land that collects water that is eventually drained by a river [Lesson 12]
25. **c.** P increases, N increases [Lesson 13]
26. **d.** continental shelf [Lesson 13]
27. **b.** Japan [Lesson 14]
28. **d.** clockwise, pushed in part by westerlies to its south [Lesson 14]
29. **c.** life and rock [Lesson 15]
30. **a.** O horizon [Lesson 15]
31. **b.** higher up in the moist region [Lesson 16]
32. **b.** expands upon freezing [Lesson 16]
33. **c.** 12 [Lesson 17]
34. **b.** soil, ocean, atmosphere, life [Lesson 17]
35. **b.** 65 million years ago, which left a chemical imprint of iridium [Lesson 18]
36. **d.** fossilized soils [Lesson 18]
37. **d.** $H_2SO_4$ [Lesson 19]
38. **b.** $\frac{1}{3}$ [Lesson 19]
39. **b.** sustainability [Lesson 19]
40. **c.** cloud formation and the thermohaline circulation [Lesson 20]

# Answer Key

## ▶ Lesson 1

1. **d.** 13.7 billion years ago
2. **a.** N, S, E, P
3. **a.** Matter was left over from matter–antimatter annihilation.
4. **d.** 2.7 K
5. **d.** hydrogen and helium
6. **b.** Red light has a shorter wavelength than ultraviolet light has.
7. **c.** It shifted to red.
8. **c.** the expansion of the universe
9. **b.** the expanding universe
10. **a.** galaxies
11. **a.** as it was 500 years in the past
12. **c.** ring 20
13. **c.** 4,600 times
14. **b.** gravity contracts gas clouds
15. **b.** The speed of light is infinite.
16. **d.** oxygen
17. **a.** supernovas
18. **d.** hydrogen
19. **c.** helium
20. **a.** hydrogen

## ▶ Lesson 2

1. **c.** a month
2. **b.** 8 feet
3. **b.** 4.5 billion years
4. **a.** The sun's core, which is where nuclear fusion reactions take place, is hotter than its surface.
5. **d.** sunspots and prominences
6. **a.** Newton
7. **b.** increases by 4 times
8. **d.** smaller, between $\frac{1}{2}$ to 1
9. **c.** an ellipse
10. **a.** January
11. **d.** Earth, Mars, Venus, Mercury
12. **b.** Uranus
13. **b.** The farther a planet is from the sun, the longer its "year."
14. **b.** Earth compared to Jupiter

**15. d.** Mars

**16. a.** A large body smashed into the early Earth.

**17. a.** new, between the earth and sun

**18. b.** full

**19. c.** 21 to 22 days

**20. d.** 3 hours

## ▶ Lesson 3

**1. a.** 4,000 miles

**2. c.** west longitude and north latitude

**3. d.** about 700

**4. c.** 150° W

**5. d.** England

**6. d.** Earth turns from left to right for you, from left to right for your friend.

**7. b.** Daylight and night would be the same everywhere on Earth all year long.

**8. a.** 23.5°

**9. d.** They have 12 hours daylight and 12 hours night all year long.

**10. c.** true, because it's tilted toward the sun

**11. d.** Earth's spin axis remains pointed in the same direction in space, the sun's energy varies with latitude, and the earth's spin axis is tilted.

**12. c.** March 20 and September 22

**13. a.** midlatitudes to tropics

**14. a.** the sun gets lower and lower

**15. d.** temperate to tropical to temperate

## ▶ Lesson 4

**1. c.** about 7,000 kilometers

**2. a.** the earth's rotation

**3. a.** The inner layer is solid, and the outer layer is liquid.

**4. d.** at a point near the North Pole

**5. b.** Compressing a liquid raises its solidifying temperature.

**6. b.** Density increases, and pressure increases.

**7. b.** continental crust

**8. c.** asthenosphere

**9. a.** lithosphere

**10. c.** 13° C per kilometer

**11. b.** seismic waves

**12. a.** the absence of S waves

**13. d.** P waves

**14. c.** 4 times

**15. d.** P waves

## ▶ Lesson 5

**1. c.** of the Atlantic Ocean

**2. a.** the creation of new seafloor at mid-ocean ridges

**3. b.** Earth's field switches from normal to reversed and back again.

**4. d.** 180 million years ago

**5. c.** The mid-ocean ridge is a bulge made by the two sides of the ocean moving together.

**6. a.** subduction zones

**7. d.** Its subduction zones are stronger than its mid-ocean ridges.

**8. c.** Asthenosphere becomes lithosphere.

**9. c.** subduction zones

**10. d.** 100 kilometers

**11. b.** Earth's surface must remain the same size and thus in balance.

**12. d.** divergent margin

**13. c.** The edge of South America cannot be the edge of a plate.

**14. b.** transform margin

**15. a.** The rafts are like the plates.

# ► Lesson 6

1. c. mid-ocean ridge
2. a. 900 times
3. d. Indonesia
4. c. jerks
5. c. buildings collapse
6. b. a plate moving over a hotspot
7. d. Magma is deeper.
8. c. caldera
9. d. high temperature and low silica
10. b. a pyroclastic flow
11. d. Cascades and Andes
12. b. Some oceanic crust rock is older than the oldest continental rocks.
13. c. They are older.
14. b. Appalachians
15. d. $\frac{2}{200}$

# ► Lesson 7

1. d. oxygen and silicon
2. a. 7
3. a. streak
4. c. crystal
5. c. Protons equal electrons.
6. d. gravel
7. c. It formed by plate tectonics.
8. d. basalt
9. b. sedimentary
10. b. metamorphic

# ► Lesson 8

1. c. stratigraphers
2. b. index fossil
3. a. nonconformity
4. c. Beds are parts of formations; both are types of strata.
5. b. 300 million years
6. a. an unstable nucleus
7. c. nitrogen
8. a. 3
9. d. igneous rocks, because there was no argon when the rock was formed
10. b. meteorites
11. b. Cretaceous, Jurassic, Triassic
12. d. Jurassic/Permian
13. a. an eon
14. b. 297
15. c. Phanerozoic

# ► Lesson 9

1. b. pounds
2. a. Pressure decreases and density decreases.
3. a. 12° C
4. d. stratosphere
5. c. a means of absorbing energy
6. d. nitrogen
7. a. water vapor
8. b. 26.4
9. c. It varies so much.
10. c. oxygen, argon, nitrogen

# ► Lesson 10

1. d. ascent
2. c. easterlies
3. b. Coriolis
4. b. Westerlies are in both hemispheres.
5. a. The earth is a sphere.
6. a. from ocean to land
7. d. the action of the Coriolis effect

**8. d.** Hurricanes spin counterclockwise, and tornadoes spin counterclockwise.

**9. c.** monsoon winds

**10. c.** cooling the tropics and warming the poles

## ▶ Lesson 11

**1. a.** 100,000 times

**2. c.** glaciers and ice caps

**3. b.** The latent heat of vaporization is greater than the latent heat of freezing.

**4. b.** 1 meter

**5. d.** the sum of life forms

**6. c.** groundwater and ocean air

**7. b.** 570

**8. d.** rivers flowing into the ocean

**9. a.** a week

**10. a.** 500

## ▶ Lesson 12

**1. d.** wet conditions

**2. d.** a much smaller discharge for about the same drainage area

**3. b.** the dry side of a mountain range

**4. d.** Congo

**5. a.** 60

**6. c.** capillary water

**7. c.** a watershed

**8. c.** brackish water

**9. a.** an aquifer

**10. b.** groundwater.

**11. a.** 660

**12. d.** 40%

**13. c.** 30%

**14. b.** chemical weathering

**15. a.** calcium

## ▶ Lesson 13

**1. b.** 2.5

**2. a.** ridge

**3. d.** the Antarctic Circumpolar

**4. d.** shelf

**5. c.** slope and shelf

**6. d.** chloride and sodium

**7. a.** Arctic

**8. b.** °/oo

**9. a.** regeneration by bacteria down deep and consumption by phytoplankton at the surface

**10. d.** photosynthesizers

## ▶ Lesson 14

**1. d.** 150 meters

**2. b.** Earth's spin

**3. c.** clockwise, pushed in part by easterlies to its south

**4. d.** western

**5. a.** England

**6. d.** thermohaline circulation

**7. d.** salinity and temperature

**8. a.** Antarctica

**9. a.** Deep water formation is local, and the return flow is widely distributed.

**10. b.** 1,000 years

## ▶ Lesson 15

**1. c.** sand, silt, clay

**2. a.** 40% silt, 20% clay, 40% sand

**3. a.** physical and biological processes

**4. d.** It has the litter from trees.

**5. b.** It is also called topsoil.

**6. b.** sand

**7. a.** no-till

**8. d.** low because the hot climate stimulates bacteria activity

**9. d.** bacteria

**10. d.** 98%

## ▶ Lesson 16

**1. c.** hydrogen bonds

**2. b.** 5 km

**3. d.** hail

**4. b.** U-shape

**5. b.** thermohaline circulation and solar absorption

**6. a.** 90 meters

**7. c.** ice sheets

**8. d.** moraine

**9. c.** Sea level was lower and the O-18 to O-16 ratio of the ocean water was higher.

**10. b.** 5.9%

## ▶ Lesson 17

**1. a.** atmosphere, soil, ocean

**2. c.** 1,000 years

**3. d.** life-ocean

**4. b.** soil and atmosphere

**5. b.** biogeochemical cycle

**6. a.** ocean

**7. d.** life and atmosphere

**8. c.** atmosphere and ocean

**9. b.** 100 billion

**10. b.** 77,000 years

## ▶ Lesson 18

**1. d.** 4 billion years ago

**2. c.** continental area grew and ocean area shrank

**3. b.** 2 billion years ago

**4. a.** fossilized soils

**5. d.** decreased

**6. b.** high amounts of iridium

**7. c.** complex cells evolved after land plants

**8. c.** selection

**9. d.** Mexico

**10. a.** 3.5 billion years

## ▶ Lesson 19

**1. d.** sulfur

**2. b.** ozone

**3. c.** CFCs

**4. a.** 0.037%

**5. c.** 30%

**6. d.** pasture is less than cropland

**7. c.** 10,000 meters

**8. b.** New England

**9. a.** low-oxygen levels in water

**10. a.** phosphorus input

## ▶ Lesson 20

**1. a.** the role of clouds

**2. b.** ozone hole above Antarctica

**3. b.** increased amount of nitrogen in the environment

**4. d.** feedback

**5. c.** bigger than Jupiter

APPENDIX

# A

# How to Prepare for a Test

A standardized test is nothing to fear. Many people clutch and worry about a testing situation, but you're much better off taking that nervous energy and turning it into something positive that will help you do well on your test rather than inhibit your testing ability. The following pages include valuable tips for combating test anxiety, that sinking or blank feeling some people get as they begin a test or encounter a difficult question. Next, you will find valuable tips for using your time wisely and for avoiding errors in a testing situation. Finally, you will find a plan for preparing for the test, a plan for the test day, and a suggestion for an after-test activity.

## ▶ Combating Test Anxiety

Knowing what to expect and being prepared for it is the best defense against test anxiety, that worrisome feeling that keeps you from doing your best. Practice and preparation keeps you from succumbing to that feeling. Nevertheless, even the brightest, most well-prepared test takers may suffer from occasional bouts of test anxiety. But don't worry; you can overcome it.

## Take the Test One Question at a Time

Focus all of your attention on the one question you're answering. Block out any thoughts about questions you've already read or concerns about what's coming next. Concentrate your thinking where it will do the most good—on the question you're answering.

## Develop a Positive Attitude

Keep reminding yourself that you're prepared. You've studied hard, so you're probably better prepared than most others who are taking the test. Remember, it's only a test, and you're going to do your best. That's all anyone can ask of you. If that nagging drill sergeant inside your head starts sending negative messages, combat him (or her) with positive ones of your own.

- "I'm doing just fine."
- "I've prepared for this test."
- "I know exactly what to do."
- "I know I can get the score I'm shooting for."

You get the idea. Remember to drown out negative messages with positive ones of your own.

## If You Lose Your Concentration

Don't worry about it! It's normal. During a long test, it happens to everyone. When your mind is stressed or overexerted, it takes a break whether you want it to or not. It's easy to get your concentration back if you simply acknowledge the fact that you've lost it and take a quick break. You brain needs very little time (seconds really) to rest.

Put your pencil down and close your eyes. Take a few deep breaths and listen to the sound of your breathing. The ten seconds or so that this takes is really all the time your brain needs to relax and get ready to focus again.

Try this technique several times in the days before the test when you feel stressed. The more you

practice, the better it will work for you on the day of the test.

## If You Freeze before or during the Test

Don't worry about a question that stumps you even though you're sure you know the answer. Mark it and go on to the next question. You can come back to the stumper later. Try to put it out of your mind completely until you come back to it. Just let your subconscious chew on the question while your conscious mind focuses on the other items (one at a time, of course). Chances are, the memory block will be gone by the time you return to the question.

If you freeze before you begin the test, here's what to do:

1. Take a little time to look over the test.
2. Read a few of the questions.
3. Decide which ones are the easiest and start there.
4. Before long, you'll be "in the groove."

# ▶ Time Strategies

Use your time wisely to avoid making careless errors.

## Pace Yourself

The most important time strategy is to pace yourself. Before you begin, take just a few seconds to survey the test, making note of the number of questions and of the sections that look easier than the rest. Rough out a time schedule based upon the amount of time available to you. Mark the halfway point on your test and make a note beside that mark of what the time will be when the testing period is half over.

## Keep Moving

Once you begin the test, keep moving. If you work slowly in an attempt to make fewer mistakes, your mind will become bored and begin to wander. You'll end up making far more mistakes if you're not concentrating.

As long as we're talking about mistakes, don't stop for difficult questions. Skip them and move on. You can come back to them later if you have time. A question that takes you five seconds to answer counts as much as one that takes you several minutes, so pick up the easy points first. Besides, answering the easier questions first helps to build your confidence and gets you in the testing groove. Who knows? As you go through the test, you may even stumble across some relevant information to help you answer those tough questions.

## Don't Rush

Keep moving, but don't rush. Think of your mind as a seesaw. On one side is your emotional energy. On the other side is your intellectual energy. When your emotional energy is high, your intellectual capacity is low. Remember how difficult it is to reason with someone when you're angry? On the other hand, when your intellectual energy is high, your emotional energy is low. Rushing raises your emotional energy. Remember the last time you were late for work? All that rushing around caused you to forget important things—like your lunch. Move quickly to keep your mind from wandering, but don't rush and get flustered.

## Check Yourself

Check yourself at the halfway mark. If you're a little ahead, you know you're on track and may even have a little time left to check your work. If you're a little behind, you have several choices. You can pick up the pace a little, but do this only if you can do it comfortably. Remember—don't rush! You can also skip around in the remaining portion of the test to pick up as many easy points as possible. This strategy has one drawback, however. If you are marking a bubble-style answer sheet, and you put the right answers in the wrong bubbles—they're wrong. So pay close attention to the question numbers if you decide to do this.

## ▶ Avoiding Errors

When you take the test, you want to make as few errors as possible in the questions you answer. Here are a few tactics to keep in mind.

### Control Yourself

Remember the comparison between your mind and a seesaw that you read a few paragraphs ago? Keeping your emotional energy low and your intellectual energy high is the best way to avoid mistakes. If you feel stressed or worried, stop for a few seconds. Acknowledge the feeling (Hmmm! I'm feeling a little pressure here!), take a few deep breaths, and send yourself a few positive messages. This relieves your emotional anxiety and boosts your intellectual capacity.

### Directions

In many standardized testing situations, a proctor reads the instructions aloud. Make certain you understand what is expected. If you don't, ask. Listen carefully for instructions about how to answer the questions and make certain you know how much time you have to complete the task. Write the time on your test if you don't already know how long you have to take the test. If you miss this vital information, ask for it. You need it to do well on your test.

### Answers

Place your answers in the right blanks or the corresponding ovals on the answer sheet. Right answers in the wrong place earn no points. It's a good idea to check every five to ten questions to make sure you're in the right spot. That way you won't need much time to correct your answer sheet if you have made an error.

## ▶ Reading Long Passages

Frequently, standardized tests are designed to test your reading comprehension. The reading sections often contain passages of a paragraph or more. Here are a few tactics for approaching these sections.

This may seem strange, but some questions can be answered without ever reading the passage. If the passage is short, a paragraph around four sentences or so, read the questions first. You may be able to answer them by using your common sense. You can check your answers later after you've actually read the passage. Even if you can't answer any of the questions, you know what to look for in the passage. This focuses your reading and makes it easier for you to retain important information. Most questions will deal with isolated details in the passage. If you know what to look for ahead of time, it's easier to find the information.

If a reading passage is long and is followed by more than ten questions, you may end up spending too much time reading the questions first. Even so, take a few seconds to skim the questions and read a few of the shorter ones. As you read, mark up the passage. If you find a sentence that seems to state the main idea of the passage, underline it. As you read through the rest of the passage, number the main points that support the main idea. Several questions will deal with this information. If it's underlined and numbered, you can locate it easily. Other questions will ask for specific details. Circle information that tells who, what, when, or where. The circles will be easy to locate later if you run across a question that asks for specific information. Marking up a passage in this way also heightens your concentration and makes it more likely that you'll

remember the information when you answer the questions following the passage.

## Choosing the Right Answers

Make sure you understand what the question is asking. If you're not sure of what's being asked, you'll never know whether you've chosen the right answer. So figure out what the question is asking. If the answer isn't readily apparent, look for clues in the answer choices. Notice the similarities and differences in the answer choices. Sometimes, this helps to put the question in a new perspective and makes it easier to answer. If you're still not sure of the answer, use the process of elimination. First, eliminate any answer choices that are obviously wrong. Then reason your way through the remaining choices. You may be able to use relevant information from other parts of the test. If you can't eliminate any of the answer choices, you might be better off to skip the question and come back to it later. If you can't eliminate any answer choices to improve your odds when you come back later, then make a guess and move on.

## If You're Penalized for Wrong Answers

You must know whether there's a penalty for wrong answers before you begin the test. If you don't, ask the proctor before the test begins. Whether you make a guess or not depends upon the penalty. Some standardized tests are scored in such a way that every wrong answer reduces your score by one-fourth or one-half of a point. Whatever the penalty, if you can eliminate enough choices to make the odds of answering the question better than the penalty for getting it wrong, make a guess.

Let's imagine you are taking a test in which each answer has four choices and you are penalized one-fourth of a point for each wrong answer. If you have no clue and cannot eliminate any of the answer choices, you're better off leaving the question blank because the odds of answering correctly are one in four. This makes the penalty and the odds equal. However, if you can eliminate one of the choices, the odds are now in your favor. You have a one in three chance of answering the question correctly. Fortunately, few tests are scored using such elaborate means, but if your test is one of them, know the penalties and calculate your odds before you take a guess on a question.

### If You Finish Early

Use any time you have left at the end of the test or test section to check your work. First, make certain you've put the answers in the right places. As you're doing this, make sure you've answered each question only once. Most standardized tests are scored in such a way that questions with more than one answer are marked wrong. If you've erased an answer, make sure you've done a good job. Check for stray marks on your answer sheet that could distort your score.

After you've checked for these obvious errors, take a second look at the more difficult questions. You've probably heard the folk wisdom about never changing an answer. If you have a good reason for thinking a response is wrong, change it.

## ▶ The Days before the Test

To do your very best on an exam, you have to take control of your physical and mental state. Exercise, proper diet, and rest will ensure that your body works with, rather than against, your mind on exam day, as well as during your preparation.

### Physical Activity

Get some exercise in the days preceding the test. You'll send some extra oxygen to your brain and allow your thinking performance to peak on the day you take the test. Moderation is the key here. You don't want to exercise so much that you feel exhausted, but a little physical activity will invigorate your body and brain.

### Balanced Diet

Like your body, your brain needs the proper nutrients to function well. Eat plenty of fruits and vegetables in the days before the test. Foods that are high in lecithin, such as fish and beans, are especially good choices. Lecithin is a mineral your brain needs for peak performance. You may even consider a visit to your local pharmacy to buy a bottle of lecithin tablets several weeks before your test.

### Rest

Get plenty of sleep the nights before you take the test. Don't overdo it though or you'll make yourself as groggy as if you were overtired. Go to bed at a reasonable time, early enough to get the number of hours you need to function effectively. You'll feel relaxed and rested if you've gotten plenty of sleep in the days before you take the test.

### Trial Run

At some point before you take the test, make a trial run to the testing center to see how long it takes. Rushing raises your emotional energy and lowers your intellectual capacity, so you want to allow plenty of time on the test day to get to the testing center. Arriving 10 or 15 minutes early gives you time to relax and get situated.

## Test Day

It's finally here, the day of the big test. Set your alarm early enough to allow plenty of time. Eat a good breakfast. Avoid anything that's really high in sugar, such as donuts. A sugar high turns into a sugar low after an hour or so. Cereal and toast, or anything with complex carbohydrates is a good choice. Eat only moderate amounts. You don't want to take a test feeling stuffed!

Pack a high-energy snack to take with you. You may have a break sometime during the test when you can grab a quick snack. Bananas are great. They have a moderate amount of sugar and plenty of brain nutrients, such as potassium. Most proctors won't allow you to eat a snack while you're testing, but a peppermint shouldn't pose a problem. Peppermints are like smelling salts for your brain. If you lose your concentration or suffer from a momentary mental block, a peppermint can get you back on track. Don't forget the earlier advice about relaxing and taking a few deep breaths.

Leave early enough so you have plenty of time to get to the test center. Allow a few minutes for unexpected traffic. When you arrive, locate the restroom and use it. Few things interfere with concentration as much as a full bladder. Then find your seat and make sure it's comfortable. If it isn't, tell the proctor and ask to change to something you find more suitable.

Now relax and think positively! Before you know it the test will be over, and you'll walk away knowing you've done as well as you can.

## After the Test

Two things are important for after the test:

1. Plan a little celebration.
2. Go to it.

If you have something to look forward to after the test is over, you may find it easier to prepare well for the test and to keep moving during the test. Good luck!

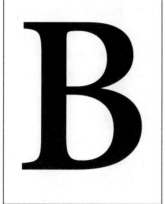 

# Glossary

**adiabatic**   a term used to describe a process in the atmosphere, such as the lifting of a parcel of air, during which no additional heating comes in to the parcel of air from the sides of the parcel

**Arctic Ocean**   the area of ocean bounded to the south by Russia and Canada, in the center of which is the North Pole

**asthenosphere**   layer of the inner earth that begins at about 100 km (60 miles) down from the surface and is completely within the mantle

**atoms**   the most finely divisible parts of matter that possess the characteristics of a particular element, such as copper, gold, carbon, or hydrogen

**bacteria**   microscopic organisms that do not possess a nucleus inside their cells, abundant in the ocean, in the soil, and within the guts of many animals

**biosphere**   the coordinated system of the earth's surface, which includes the reservoirs of life, air, soil, and the ocean

**bioturbation**   the process by which organisms in the soil or in ocean sediments, such as worms, mix the soil or sediment

**the Big Bang**   the sudden beginning of our present universe, which starting expanding about 13.7 billion years ago

**carbon dioxide**   the gas ($CO_2$) given off during respiration, by plants, bacteria, fungi, and animals

**convergent margin**   the edge formed by two geological plates that are moving toward each other

**Coriolis effect**   deflection in the wind caused by the fact that the earth is spinning

**climate**   the average weather conditions

**diameter**   the distance across a circle, of a line passing through the circle's center

**divergent margins**   also known as spreading centers. The edge between two geological plates that are moving apart.

**electron**   one of the building blocks of atoms. Negatively charged, the electrons "whirr" around the nucleus, bound to it by electrical attraction.

**element**　the atoms of a particular element all have the same number of protons in their nuclei, which determines the charge of the nucleus, thus the number of electrons around the nucleus, and thus the chemistry of the element.

**equinox**　days that officially start the seasons of autumn and spring, on or close to September 22 and March 22, respectively. At these times, daylight and nighttime are equal in length everywhere on Earth.

**eutrophication**　a condition in a body of water in which excess nutrients, often from agricultural runoff, cause a dramatically increased growth of algae. The decay of the algae can then cause a severe depletion in the oxygen of the water.

**fault**　large fracture or crack in rock

**hydrogen**　the lightest element, with one proton and one or more neutrons in the nucleus of its atoms

**humus**　the soil's dark layer of decayed material just under the litter at the surface

**igneous rocks**　solid rock that was "born" when hot molten rock solidified

**jovian planets**　the outer planets of the solar system, which are primarily gaseous. They are Jupiter, Saturn, Uranus, Neptune, and Pluto.

**K, or °K**　usually written without the degree sign, the Kelvin scale for temperature has intervals of degrees that are the same as the °C and a reference point of 0 K at absolute zero (about –273° C or about –476° F).

**lithosphere**　the upper layer of the rocky earth, which includes all the surface crust and the uppermost portion of the underlying mantle

**lunar eclipse**　this rare event occurs only at full moon, when the earth's shadow is cast upon the moon.

**mantle**　the layer of the rocky earth between the surface crust and deep core

**mid-ocean ridge**　chain of mountains that are underwater volcanism in an ocean, where two geological plates are spreading apart

**millibar**　a unit of atmospheric pressure (mbar) that is one-thousandth of a bar, which is the downward force exerted by 1 kilogram of mass upon 1 square centimeter of area at sea level. The standard air pressure at sea level is 1.013 bar or 1,013 mbar.

**metamorphic rock**　rock created when either igneous, sedimentary, or other metamorphic rock is subjected to great heat and pressure and transformed (metamorphosed)

**natural selection**　the all-important step in the process of evolution, a filtering process of life and death that selects certain types of creatures with the largest number of mature offspring to carry on their genetic patterns

**neutrons**　the neutral building block in the nucleus of atoms

**nitrogen fixation**　in the cycle of nitrogen, one component in the cycle is the conversion. The ammonium and nitrate ions—unlike the air's nitrogen gas—are what plants and algae need for their growing bodies. The conversion of nitrogen from nitrogen gas in the air into forms such as ammonium and nitrate ions, which are useable by plants, such as algae, is accomplished by special kinds of bacteria that are called nitrogen fixers.

**nuclear fusion**　atomic nuclei from two or more elements are squeezed by hot temperatures and pressures in the center of a star to create a new "fused" nucleus. For atoms from the lightweight hydrogen up to the much heavier iron, energy is released when atoms are fused to make larger atoms.

**photosynthesis**　the process that uses sunlight to convert chemicals from the environment into living bodies

**phytoplankton** tiny photosynthesizing creatures, such as bacteria, certain kinds of which live at the surface of the ocean (also in rivers and lakes)

**plate tectonics** the governing theory of how the earth's continents and oceans change over time

**protons** the positively charged building block of atoms in the nuclei of atoms. Elements can be characterized by their atomic numbers, which is the number of protons in their nuclei.

**Richter scale** a measure of the amount of energy released by an earthquake. Each number grade in the Richter scale, from 1 to 10, measures an earthquake that is 30 times larger in terms of energy than the preceding number.

**sedimentary rock** rock created when other rocks have been physically or chemically broken down and deposited as sediments and then compressed into new rock

**seismic waves** waves generated by both large and small earthquakes that travel through rock

**southern ocean** also called the Antarctic Circumpolar Ocean, the belt approximately 10° of latitude in width, which rings Antarctica

**stratosphere** layer of the atmosphere that begins at the tropopause and extends up to approximately 50 km

**subduction zone** places where the ocean's floor dives downward and disappears back into Earth's deep mantle, remelting in the asthenosphere

**thermohaline circulation** large-scale ocean circulation driven by cold, salty dense water that plunges downward in certain polar regions of the world's ocean

**transform margins** an edge between two geological plates that are sliding past each other

**tropopause** the altitude at which the troposphere ends usually about 15 km above the surface

**troposphere** the lowermost layer of the atmosphere, where most of the weather occurs